Artifacts & Ideas

Bruce G. Trigger

Artifacts & Ideas

Essays in Archaeology

Transaction Publishers
New Brunswick (U.S.A.) and London (U.K.)

Copyright © 2003 by Transaction Publishers, New Brunswick, New Jersey.

All rights reserved under International and Pan-American Copyright Conventions. No part of this book may be reproduced or transmitted in any form or by any means, electronic or mechanical, including photocopy, recording, or any information storage and retrieval system, without prior permission in writing from the publisher. All inquiries should be addressed to Transaction Publishers, Rutgers—The State University, 35 Berrue Circle, Piscataway, New Jersey 08854-8042.

This book is printed on acid-free paper that meets the American National Standard for Permanence of Paper for Printed Library Materials.

Library of Congress Catalog Number: 2002073208
ISBN: 0-7658-0165-5
Printed in the United States of America

        Library of Congress Cataloging-in-Publication Data

Trigger, Bruce G.
    Artifacts and ideas : essays in archaeology / Bruce Trigger.
      p. cm.
    Includes bibliographical references and index.
    ISBN 0-7658-0165-5 (alk. paper)
      1. Archaeology—Philosophy. 2. Archaeology—Methodology. 3. Social archaeology. I. Title.

CC72 .T75 2002
930.1' 01—dc21   2002073208

Contents

Acknowledgements		vii
Preface		ix
1.	Introduction: Understanding the Material Remains of the Past	1
2.	Engels on the Part Played by Labor in the Transition from Ape to Man: An Anticipation of Contemporary Archaeological Theory	31
3.	Archaeology and the Image of the American Indian	45
4.	Alternative Archaeologies: Nationalist, Colonialist, Imperialist	67
5.	Archaeology at the Crossroads: What's New?	87
6.	Hyperrelativism, Responsibility, and the Social Sciences	113
7.	Archaeology and Epistemology: Dialoguing across the Darwinian Chasm	133
8.	The Real, the Perceived, and the Imagined	155
9.	Imagination and Scientific Curiosity	177
10.	The 1990s: North American Archaeology with a Human Face?	195
References		209
Index		237

Acknowledgements

All chapters except the first are revised versions of previous publications. They are included in this volume with the agreement and permission of the original publishers. The papers published here should not be cited as being identical to the original ones. Rights remain with the original publishers.

Chapter 2, "Engels on the Part Played by Labor in the Transition from Ape to Man" first appeared in the *Canadian Review of Sociology and Anthropology*, vol. 4, 1967, pp. 165-176. Reprinted with permission of the Canadian Sociology and Anthropology Association.

Chapter 3, "Archaeology and the Image of the American Indian" first appeared in *American Antiquity*, vol. 45, 1980, pp. 662-676. With permission of the Society for American Archaeology.

Chapter 4, "Alternative Archaeologies: Nationalist, Colonialist, Imperialist" first appeared in *Man*, vol. 19, 1984, pp. 355-370. With permission of the Royal Anthropological Institute and Blackwell Publishers ©.

Chapter 5, "Archaeology at the Crossroads: What's New?" first appeared in the *Annual Review of Anthropology*, vol. 13, 1984, pp. 275-300. With permission of the *Annual Review of Anthropology*, vol. 13, © 1984; by Annual Reviews *www.AnnualReviews.org*.

Chapter 6, "Hyperrelativism, Responsibility, and the Social Sciences" first appeared in the *Canadian Review of Sociology and Anthropology*, vol. 26, 1989, pp. 776-797. With permission of the Canadian Sociology and Anthropology Association.

Chapters 7, 8, 9, based on three lectures that were delivered as the 1997 "Context and Human Society" series sponsored by the Department of Archaeology and the Center for Archaeological Studies at Boston University, were originally published as a single paper titled "Archaeology and Epistemology: Dialoguing across the Darwinian Chasm" in the *American Journal of Archaeology*, vol. 102, 1998, pp. 1-34. Each lecture is reprinted as a separate chapter. With permission of the Archaeological Institute of America.

Chapter 10, "The 1990s: North American Archaeology with a Human Face?" was originally published in *Antiquity*, vol. 64, 1990, pp. 778-787. By permission of Antiquity Publications Ltd.

Preface

Several years ago, Mario Bunge, a distinguished colleague in the Foundations and Philosophy of Science Unit at McGill University and the tireless scourge of much nonsense that currently passes for wisdom in the social sciences, suggested that I should publish a collection of my more recent papers dealing with archaeological interpretation, together with an introductory essay that would relate these papers to each other and to changing modes of interpretation in archaeology. More particularly he wanted me to gather in one place my reactions to changing epistemologies that have influenced archaeology in recent decades.

I wanted such a work to consist of material that was not incorporated in any fundamental way into my later publications and that the papers should address a single, coherent theme. Applying these criteria, I eventually selected nine essays that outline my views about epistemological issues. The earliest of these, published in 1967, is crucial for understanding my position, but all the rest date from the 1980s or 1990s. Each essay has been edited to avoid overlap and remove extraneous material; technical terminology and English usage have been updated; arguments that have become unfamiliar are explained or—if no longer consequential—deleted; passages requiring amplification or clarification have been rewritten; and a standard system of references has been supplied. I have, nevertheless, attempted to preserve the original spirit of each paper. Doing this came naturally to me, as the practitioner of a historical discipline who has long specialized in studying that discipline's intellectual history.

Once I had selected these papers, I realized that they had more thematic unity than I had recognized as I wrote them. Although they are concerned with the theories of knowledge that guide, or can mislead, archaeologists, they are deeply rooted in the ontological realities that constrain the practice of archaeology. As an archaeologist, I am primarily interested in philosophy as it serves the needs and goals of my own discipline. Because of this, the outlook of these papers is quite different from those written by philosophers who use archaeology to explore philosophical issues. The introductory essay (chapter 1) attempts to do what Mario Bunge suggested: it relates the following papers to the development of my own thought and to theoretical developments in archaeology as a discipline during the late twentieth century.

I thank Zarin Machanda for the great amount of help she has given me in preparing these papers for publication. Her word-processing skills have greatly accelerated the work and her superb editorial judgment represents an enduring contribution to the volume. Without her assistance, this book might never have been finished. I also thank Professor Irving Louis Horowitz and Mary Curtis for a timely evaluation of the manuscript, Laurence Mintz for his careful editing, and Stephen Chrisomalis for preparing the index and help with correcting proofs. The expenses of producing the manuscript were defrayed by the stipend attached to my James McGill Professorship. I hope that Mario Bunge will be pleased with the result.

Introduction

Understanding the Material Remains of the Past

Archaeology might have been invented specifically as a case study for the philosophy of science. While some archaeologists narrowly define the ultimate goal of their discipline as being to explain the archaeological record (Clarke 1968; Dunnell 1971; Schiffer 1976), the vast majority regard their discipline as a social science, the goals of which are to trace the evolution of culture, behavior, and human beings themselves, to delineate the history of individual societies prior to written records, and to ascertain how groups of humans lived in prehistoric times. In Europe, archaeologists tend to identify themselves as historians, while in North America, prehistoric archaeology is a branch of anthropology. Studying human behavior and culture is a task common to both archaeologists and anthropologists.

Yet, with respect to the study of behavior and culture, archaeology is a challenged discipline. Unlike all social scientists, except historians, archaeologists are unable to observe human behavior directly and they have no direct access to human thoughts, whether expressed verbally or in writing. Behavior and ideas must be inferred from the material remains of the past and from the impact humans once had on the environment. Many forms of material culture do not survive for archaeologists to study, except in environments marked by extreme cold or aridity, and the artifacts that do survive are often found in contexts of disposal, not where they were used. To infer human behavior or beliefs from such data is a demanding task and an operation that leaves great scope for subjectivity. The paucity of evidential constraint renders archaeology a very revealing example of how data are interpreted by social scientists.

Archaeologists also provide interesting information about how they view what they have accomplished under these challenging circumstances. They are constantly seeking ways to understand the past more completely and effectively. Yet, when it comes to trying to comprehend what they do, or have done in the past, archaeologists, like most other social scientists, tend to prefer self-justifying myths (Kuhn 1962; Trigger 1989a). American archaeologists generally believe that, prior to the 1960s, archaeology was an empirical discipline whose practitioners were content to collect data about the past, classify artifacts, and define chronologies and past cultures. They also agree that, beginning in the 1960s, archaeology was impacted by a positivist epistemology that favored behaviorism and sought to interpret finds as products of ecologically adaptive strategies. In the 1980s, this approach was challenged by an idealist, cultural-relativist epistemology that stressed beliefs and cultural traditions as mediating, and to a large degree determining, human behavior. The two more recent approaches have come to be labeled processual and postprocessual archaeology. They are antithetically associated with two archaeologists: Lewis Binford and Ian Hodder (Willey & Sabloff 1974; 1993).

It is also generally agreed that prior to the 1960s archaeology was either a dismal failure or represented only the primitive, preparadigmatic beginnings of a scientific discipline (Clarke 1973; Sterud 1973). Many archaeologists argue that processual archaeology not only was the first scientific approach to archaeological interpretation, but also is an approach that can never be transcended except to archaeology's extreme detriment (Binford 1972; 1983b; 1989). Postprocessual archaeologists denounce the innovations of the 1960s as a dehumanizing, technocratic blind alley, from which archaeology has been rescued only by their own insistence on beliefs, perceptions, goals, and values as the central foci for explaining human behavior (Hodder 1986; Shanks & Tilley 1987a; 1987b). In recent years, Darwinian or evolutionary archaeology has been striving, with some success, to establish itself as a materialist substitute for processual archaeology (Barton & Clark 1997; Dunnell 1980b; Maschner 1996; O'Brien 1996; O'Brien & Lyman 2000; Teltser 1995). Yet adherents of this school are far from agreed about how selection shapes the archaeological record. Most processual and postprocessual archaeologists, while believing that their approach is the correct one, also agree that their two approaches exhaust the full range of interpretive possibilities.

I have been uncomfortable with these partisan versions of the history of archaeology, because they do not correspond with the development of archaeological theory and practice as I have observed it since the 1950s. Over the years, I publicly recorded my disagreements with successive fashions of doing archaeology. These efforts stimulated my interest in studying the development of archaeological interpretation in its social and intellectual context, which culminated in the publication of *A History of Archaeological Thought* (1989a). My motivation for this research is my belief best expressed by George Santayana's observation that those who cannot remember the past are condemned to repeat it.

The essays reprinted in this volume represent my efforts to formulate an epistemological perspective that would facilitate my study of the past and help others to negotiate the theoretical minefields of anthropological archaeology. While I have been critical, at various times, of views held by both processual and postprocessual archaeologists, I have sought to cultivate what I believe to be of value in both approaches, while exposing and rejecting the dogmatic humbug that accompanies them.

These efforts have convinced me that even a judicious synthesis of these two approaches supplies only a partial explanation of human behavior and the archaeological record. It seems that, for political reasons, and in their desire to achieve their goals quickly, archaeologists of various persuasions have too often embraced epistemologies that did not fully reflect the complexity of what they were studying. The essays that follow represent my attempts, with one exception since 1980, to encourage a more realistic appreciation of the problems archaeology is facing. In the rest of this introductory essay, I will review the circumstances in which each essay was written and relate them to each other as well as to changing modes of interpretation in archaeology.

Archaeology in the 1950s

When I studied archaeology as an undergraduate at the University of Toronto in the late 1950s, the discipline was still in what is now called its culture-historical phase. At its worst, American culture-historical archaeology was as dreadful as processual archaeologists later made it out to be. In the 1930s, archaeologists based mainly at the University of Chicago and the University of Michigan advocated what they called the Midwestern Taxonomic Method (McKern 1939). They argued that the main task of archaeologists was to define artifact types and use these types to distinguish archaeological cultures, which they equated with prehistoric peoples. Cultural change was attributed to diffusion and migration. There was no awareness of significant changes coming about as a result of processes occurring within cultures. Many archaeologists accepted that they were restricted to studying material culture and believed that there was no way to infer prehistoric ideas or behavior from the archaeological record alone. Archaeologists adhering to the Midwestern Taxonomic Method condemned efforts to infer behavior from archaeological data as speculative and unscientific.

I learned about the origins of these ideas only much later, when I studied the history of archaeology. Much of European prehistoric archaeology and of American anthropology, in the institutional framework of which American prehistoric archaeology had developed, was influenced by the work of the late nineteenth-century German anthropogeographer Friedrich Ratzel (1882-91; 1896-98), which in turn was steeped in the traditions of German idealism and romanticism. In an era of growing nationalism and middle-class opposition to socialism, many social scientists sought to counter the Marxist concept of class struggle with the belief that each specific people was united by a common culture that distinguished them from all other peoples. As the spread of industrialization led to increasing international conflicts over access to resources and markets in the late nineteenth century, historians, in their efforts to maintain social peace in their own countries, sought to suppress class conflicts within nation states and to direct aggression outward. Humans were represented as being naturally conservative and resistant to change (Trigger 1989a: 110-167). Yet, where racism was not yet dominant in social science thinking, variations among cultures continued to be celebrated as evidence of human creativity, following a tradition that could be traced back to the German philosopher Johann Herder in the late eighteenth century. Franz Boas introduced these ideas to North America and with them the culture-historical approach to archaeology.

As an undergraduate in the Department of Anthropology at the University of Toronto, I encountered the 1950s version of the Midwestern Taxonomic Method in the person of the department's senior archaeologist, Chicago-trained Norman Emerson. Under his tutelage, I and many other students learned to dig sites, classify pottery, and how archaeological cultures were identified. The great debate convulsing Ontario archaeology in the late 1950s was whether the local Iroquoian Indians had evolved in the Toronto area and later migrated 200 kilometers north to their historic homeland on Georgian Bay or had originally lived in the north and some of them had expanded southward (Emerson 1961; MacNeish 1952; Ridley 1952a; 1952b). It seemed strange to me even as an undergraduate that no one involved in this debate was interested in trying to ascertain why people might have moved in one direction or the other (Trigger 1962; 1963). The anthropologists in the department, whether they were old-fashioned cultural anthropologists, British social anthropologists, or influenced by American neoevolutionary trends, were openly contemptuous of this sort of archaeology, and of archaeology in general, which they regarded as an atheoretical discipline doomed to remain forever the antiquarian study of material culture. The head of the department, Thomas McIlwraith, privately expressed the opinion that an intelligent undergraduate would not wish to become an archaeologist.

Fortunately, much more than this was happening to archaeology in the late 1950s. Already in the 1920s, archaeologists in the Soviet Union had argued the need to understand prehistoric social organization in order to explain technological change. Marxist theory was interpreted as indicating that such change did not occur as a result of people using their natural intelligence to control nature more effectively, as nineteenth-century evolutionary archaeologists had believed; instead it was stimulated or discouraged by socioeconomic conditions. Efforts to infer social conditions led Soviet archaeologists to identify and excavate Palaeolithic houses and entire Neolithic villages for the first time and to seek ways to infer social organization from archaeological evidence. For example, P.N. Tret'yakov, having determined from forensic studies of fingerprints that the ceramic vessels associated with prehistoric hunter-fisher cultures in northern and central Russia had probably been manufactured by women, proceeded to infer that the uniformity of pottery styles within individual sites indicated matrilocal marriage patterns (Trigger 1989a: 207-243).

6   Artifacts and Ideas

The work of Soviet archaeologists was made known in the West by the Finnish archaeologist A.M. Tallgren (1936) and by Gordon Childe (1942). Beginning in the late 1930s, Childe shifted from a culture-historical approach to one focused on changing patterns of social organization (Childe 1946a). At the same time, Grahame Clark (1939), inspired by Tallgren and other Scandinavian archaeologists, began to study prehistoric cultures as adaptive systems, placing a strong emphasis on their subsistence patterns and social organization. In the United States, large-scale excavations carried out in the 1930s under federal government sponsorship to provide work for the unemployed led to a growing awareness of prehistoric community patterns and the possibility of studying how indigenous peoples had lived in these communities in prehistoric times (Fagette 1996; Lyon 1996). The cultural ecologist Julian Steward and the archaeologist F.M. Setzler argued that, because archaeologists could study subsistence practices, population size, and settlement patterns, they controlled the major variables necessary to understand social change (Steward & Setzler 1938). Walter Taylor (1948), while loyal to Boasian cultural idealism, called for more subsistence studies in archaeology and for more efforts to understand the meaning that artifacts had in the cultures that produced them.

While these advances were interrupted by the suspension of archaeological research during the Second World War, they resumed in the late 1940s. Julian Steward persuaded the archaeologist Gordon Willey to carry out the first regional study of changing settlement patterns as part of the Viru Valley project. Willey collected information about the size, distribution, and formal characteristics of prehistoric settlements in this small valley on the north coast of Peru and used these data to study changes in subsistence patterns, demography, social organization, and political structure from the beginnings of agriculture in the area to the Spanish conquest (Willey 1953). Within a few years, archaeologists were studying settlement patterns around the world (R. Adams 1965; Sanders, Parsons & Santley 1979; Willey 1956). Grahame Clark (1954) organized a multidisciplinary excavation of the Mesolithic site of Star Carr in East Yorkshire, interpreting it as a camp that a small group of hunters had revisited over a number of winters to hunt deer. This study set a new standard for the archaeological investigation of hunter-gatherer sites. At Jarmo, in Iraq, Robert Braidwood (1974) carried out the first detailed study of the origins of agriculture, demonstrating that in the Middle East it had been a very gradual process. Richard MacNeish (1978) made similar findings in the Tehuacan Valley of Mexico in the 1960s. In eastern North America, Joseph Caldwell (1958) argued that ecological and demographic changes were able to explain alterations in the archaeological record that had hitherto been attributed to migration and cultural diffusion.

As an undergraduate at the University of Toronto, I became aware of some of these developments. Encouraged by the brilliant ancient economic historian, Fritz Heichelheim, I read many of Childe's works, including his last, and posthumously published, *The Prehistory of European Society* (1958). In this synthesis, he argued that the social and political organization of prehistoric Europe displayed much less variation than did the stylistic aspects of its material culture. Childe hoped that a more significant understanding of the past might be derived if archaeologists adopted a social and political approach to interpreting archaeological data. This proposal resonated powerfully with the functionalist and behaviorist British social anthropology that I was learning about in the anthropology department. I drew most inspiration, however, not from the then mainline social anthropology expounded by my teachers, which was focused on the analysis of static structures. This approach included Edmund Leach's (1954) pseudohistorical *Political Systems of Highland Burma*. My greatest admiration was reserved for the functionalist study of social change as represented by E.E. Evans-Pritchard's (1949; see also 1962) *The Sanusi of Cyrenaica*, which sought to understand cultural integration by observing how social structures changed over time among a single people. I was, however, disappointed that Childe at the end of his book was unable to suggest ways to study prehistoric social and political organization.

I first encountered Willey's (1953) *Prehistoric Settlement Patterns in the Viru Valley, Peru*, when I was required to report on it in a course taught by a young American archaeologist, William J. Mayer-Oakes. One of the aims of this course was to acquaint students with the newest developments in North American archaeology. I realized how it was possible to infer social, economic, and political information from archaeological data and use it to study systemic changes in prehistoric times. St Paul's experience on the Damascus Road was scarcely more dramatic or transforming. I now knew how to do the kind of archaeology I had wished to do and how archaeology could address issues that anthropologists had long believed were the preserve of social and cultural anthropology. My long-term commitment to archaeology was sealed.

As a graduate student at Yale University in the early 1960s, I became involved in archaeological salvage work associated with the UNESCO Campaign to Save the Monuments of Nubia, an area that was threatened by the construction of the High Dam at Aswan. My doctoral thesis, published as *History and Settlement in Lower Nubia*, drew upon archaeological settlement data that had been collected systematically throughout Lower Nubia since 1907 in connection with earlier dam-building projects (Trigger 1965). I attempted to demonstrate that changes in four variables—environment, agricultural technology, and trade and warfare between Egypt and the Sudan—accounted for most of the alterations in the population size and distribution of population during 6,000 years, from the introduction of agriculture to the conversion of Lower Nubia to Islam ca. A.D. 1300. My attempt to identify and rank key variables bringing about changes in settlement patterns in a particular region was different from studies that used settlement data merely as an archaeological source of information about societies or which studied specific problems, such as the relation between the development of irrigation works and that of states (R. Adams 1965).

Processual Archaeology

By the time my thesis was published, a new kid had appeared on the block: New Archaeology, later to be known as processual archaeology. The term "New Archaeology" had been adumbrated in a paper titled "The New American Archaeology," which Joseph Caldwell (1959) published in the journal *Science*. Yet New Archaeology, as a specific set of concepts and as a movement, was the creation of Lewis Binford (1962; 1965; 1972). Binford violently rejected culture-historical archaeology as it was associated with the Midwestern Taxonomic Method and the person of James B. Griffin, who taught at the University of Michigan where Binford studied for his doctorate. From his mentor, evolutionary anthropologist Leslie White (1949), Binford adopted the idea that a culture was a system composed of three interrelated subsystems: the technoeconomic, the social, and the ideational. He further argued that, because artifacts functionally relate to all three subsystems, formal artifact assemblages and their contexts could be made to yield a comprehensive picture of total extinct cultures. Binford also championed the proposition that cultures were humanity's extrasomatic means of adaptation. Changes in all aspects of cultural systems could therefore be explained as adaptive responses to alterations in environment, demography, or competing cultural systems. The technoeconomic subsystem shaped the social and ideational ones.

In practice, Binford's primary focus was on human behavior rather than on culture. He rejected the proposition that either culturally specific ideas or human psychology were appropriate objects of scientific research. Binford also subscribed to the currently popular neoevolutionist belief that human behavior was highly uniform and believed that societies everywhere in the world that were at the same level of development would closely resemble one another (Fried 1967; Sahlins 1968; Service 1962; 1975). As a result of his acceptance of the uniformity of human behavior, Binford became an even more radical uniformitarian than was Leslie White (1945: 346), who believed that, while evolutionary theories account for the general outlines of cultural development, they could not be used to infer the specific features of individual cultures. He also went beyond Steward's (1955) prescription that, while evolutionary anthropologists should seek to account for the common features observed in cultures at similar levels of development, they should ignore their "unique, exotic, and non-recurrent particulars" (p. 209). Binford maintained that beliefs and values, whether cross-culturally regular or idiosyncratic, should be treated as epiphenomenal aspects of human behavior that arose as a consequence of ecological adaptation and therefore had no explanatory value in an ecological context.

Finally, at an epistemological level, Binford embraced a positivist, covering-law model of explanation derived from the philosopher Carl Hempel (1965; Hempel & Oppenheim 1948). All behavioral inferences from archaeological data had to be based on the demonstration of invariant correlations between material culture and human behavior in the modern world. Such findings, in turn, could be used to confirm or reject generalizations about human behavior derived from high-level propositions that Binford advocated should be grounded in cultural ecology. Underlying this approach was a Humean view that held sensory observations to be unproblematic, equated explanation with establishing regularities among observed phenomena, and treated explanation and prediction as equivalent (Binford 1972; Schiffer 1975; Spaulding 1968; Watson, LeBlanc & Redman 1971: 3-19). Binford's belief in the regularity of human behavior led him to assume that cross-cultural research would ensure the rapid establishment of a series of generalizations concerning human behavior. Integral to this assumption was the unstated prediction that, if human behavior were less regular, it would be harder to infer behavior from archaeological data and to explain cultural change.

Binford and his followers presented his ideas as the alternative, rather than an alternative, to culture-historical archaeology. New Archaeology was hailed as a new paradigm, in the sense this term had recently been defined by the philosopher of science Thomas Kuhn. Like Kuhn's revolutionary scientists, New Archaeologists set out to transform their discipline and control it. Preliminary programmatic statements were followed by textbooks expounding New Archaeology (Watson, LeBlanc & Redman 1971) and a struggle to control academic appointments and research funding.

At least part of the popularity of New Archaeology resulted from its offering a clear alternative to a culture-historical archaeology which appeared to many to be moribund. Its popularity was also enhanced by its behaviorist orientation, which aligned it with psychology and other flourishing social sciences. By advocating as its ultimate goal the creation of general laws about human behavior, archaeology was laying claim to having the same technocratic utility as did the other social sciences. This was viewed as useful for deriving continuing financial support from the National Science Foundation and other government agencies that were searching for knowledge that would help them to manage society more effectively (Martin & Plog 1973: 364-368; Watson, LeBlanc & Redman 1971). Experience since the 1930s had demonstrated to archaeologists that government funding permitted them to investigate more interesting questions about life in prehistoric times than did funding by museums and private donors, who were mainly interested in finding magnificent artifacts.

New Archaeology, in advancing its claim to be archaeology's new paradigm, not only repudiated culture-historical archaeology, which it caricatured as resembling in its entirety the archaeology shaped by the Midwestern Taxonomic Method, but also refused to recognize or ally itself with other trends that sought to move beyond traditional archaeological practices. Binford (1968a: 12-13) dismissed settlement archaeology as a mere method that lacked ties to any high-level theory. While settlement archaeologists, such as William Sanders (Sanders, Parsons & Santley 1979), who also advocated an ecological approach, were accepted as adherents of New Archaeology, the rest were dismissed as antiquated culture-historical archaeologists.

For several reasons I was unable to accept New Archaeology, even though I sympathized with the desire of New Archaeologists to move beyond a simplistic culture-historical archaeology. I was aware that prior to 1960 archaeology had not been theoretically uniform and that archaeologists had pioneered many important theoretical developments since the 1930s. Binford's delineation of culture-history corresponded to something real, but what it corresponded to did not constitute the whole of American, let alone world, archaeology. The treatment afforded to many settlement archaeologists was indicative of the exclusion from what aspired to be a new orthodoxy of many archaeologists who were seeking to transform archaeology in their own ways and who easily could have become active participants in a more broadly based movement.

Another problem that I had with New Archaeology and neoevolutionism was the extreme degree to which both postulated that the stage of sociocultural evolution was the principal determinant of differences in human behavior. The advocates of these approaches did not display much interest in subjecting their belief in cross-cultural uniformities to the rigorous testing that was possible by the 1960s (Ford 1967; Moore 1961). Most neoevolutionary schemes had been constructed on the basis of their authors' familiarity with the indigenous societies of Oceania. What I had learned about North American Indians and about African societies convinced me that bands, tribes, and chiefdoms in those regions varied in significant ways from each other and from societies at the same level of development in the Pacific region. It seems curious, in retrospect, that anthropologists who were interested in cross-cultural studies, or who studied societies elsewhere in the world, did not challenge neoevolutionists' claims concerning the uniformity of all societies at the same level of development. Far more archaeologists took the claims of neoevolutionists seriously than did sociocultural anthropologists. Neoevolutionism quickly became a dead issue among most sociocultural anthropologists, being repudiated in whole or in part by some of its most eminent advocates (Fried 1975; Sahlins 1976). Perhaps most sociocultural anthropologists never regarded neoevolutionism as worth attacking.

Finally, I was unable to accept the ecological determinism of New Archaeology. At the University of Toronto a course in human geography had introduced me to environmental possibilism, which argued that, while habitats limit the possibilities for human behavior, they do not determine it. This sensible theory provided me with lifelong immunity against the attractions of any form of environmental determinism.

I also assumed, initially from my exposure to Boasian anthropology, that beliefs and behavioral patterns were largely an inheritance persisting from the past, however much they might be modified to accommodate changing ecological or other conditions. Many aspects of cultural traditions endured over long periods and were distinctive from those associated with other cultures. Cultural traditions appeared to account at least in part for regional differences in societies at the same stage of complexity. They also influenced human behavior in significant ways and therefore could not be dismissed as epiphenomenal (Hall 1985: 33-110; Hallpike 1986: 288-371).

All these considerations made it impossible for me to embrace New Archaeology. While I published papers critiquing various aspects of New Archaeology (Trigger 1970a; 1971; 1973; 1978a), it was very difficult during the 1960s and 1970s to make headway against the well-orchestrated efforts to propagate the new "paradigm." For a time, I focused with my graduate students on studying the Iroquoian archaeology of late prehistoric eastern Canada (Trigger 1981b; 1985a). This research demonstrated that individual communities, rather than archaeological cultures, constituted the most appropriate focus for understanding change in all aspects of Iroquoian life. Because Iroquoian communities practiced swidden agriculture and therefore relocated at frequent intervals, central villages and their satellite hunting, fishing, and collecting camps constituted natural laboratories for the fine-grained study of cultural change.

Becoming a Relativist

In 1967, I published a paper that in retrospect marked the beginning of a new phase in my theoretical contributions to archaeology: "Engels on the Part Played by Labor in the Transition from Ape to Man: An Anticipation of Contemporary Archaeological Thinking" (chapter 2). This paper was rejected by a leading American anthropological journal because, I was later unofficially informed, it was thought that the parallels I drew between interpretations of human evolution originally proposed by Friedrich Engels and those of some prominent modern American physical anthropologists might politically harm the modern anthropologists. Since my argument was based on the assumption that their interpretations had developed independently of Marxist influence, the rejection of my paper was a measure of the enduring scars that McCarthyism had inflicted on academic life in the United States. The paper was published in the newly established *Canadian Review of Sociology and Anthropology* and soon appeared in pirated translations in Portugal and Mexico.

From a palaeontological point of view this paper is dated. It reflects the extreme unilinear version of human biological evolution that prevailed in the 1960s, after physical anthropologists had abandoned the claims of idealistically inclined European palaeontologists who did not wish modern humans to be descended from any known small-brained ancestors, but instead had argued that increasing intelligence had brought about all other anatomical changes. Hence they maintained that smaller-brained *Homo erectus* and larger-brained *Homo sapiens* had coexisted throughout most of the Pleistocene. Since the 1960s, physical anthropologists have interpreted increasingly abundant fossil finds as evidence that a large number of hominid species co-existed in the Lower Pleistocene, although taxonomies are fiercely disputed and clearly the last word has not yet been said about them.

My 1967 paper is historically interesting for at least two reasons. First, it demonstrates that I viewed inductive and deductive approaches as complementary rather than antithetical. This was presented, not as an original idea, but as the accepted view of most archaeologists and scientists. There is no evidence of Binford's effort to prioritize deduction as the only true form of scientific explanation. The second notable feature was the paper's assumption that presuppositions, sometimes of a political nature, influence the interpretation of archaeological data. I had derived this concept, which adumbrated a key tenet of postprocessual archaeology, principally from classical Marxism, through my reading of Childe and other works that I hoped would deepen my understanding of the Marxist background to his thinking. Marxists argued that throughout human history intellectual constructions have been shaped by class interests, although they inconsistently, and disastrously, exempted their own beliefs from this limitation. The Marxist contextualized view of intellectual creativity made sense to me, because it was clear from everyday life that not only rich and not so rich, but also young and old, students and teachers, doctors and patients had their own views of their relations, which reflected their relative power. Moreover, having once been a child did not mean that an adult could understand the needs of a child better than a child could understand those of an adult. Like most males of my generation, I was less aware of the political significance of gender relations than I should have been. That deficiency required an articulate spouse and the feminist movement, as it impacted on archaeology, to significantly rectify.

On the other hand, my memories suggest that I was inclined to believe that scholarly thought was influenced by political commitments even prior to reading about Marxist epistemology. This seems to have been an idea that was in the air. Already in my first year at the University of Toronto, I had brashly observed that histories of Canada invariably reflected the political orientation of their authors. A less politically charged form of subjectivism had been promoted by the Oxford archaeologist-philosopher Robin Collingwood's (1939; 1946) claim that archaeologists recreate the past on the basis of their individual understandings of human behavior. My paper is notable, not as an original contribution to knowledge, but as a record of how at least some archaeologists regarded knowledge subjectively in an era allegedly dominated by empirical research and hostility to theoretical considerations. Archaeology prior to New Archaeology was not the epistemologically atheoretical discipline that it is made out to have been.

I concluded that, while Marxism had facilitated Engels' formulation of a deductive, materialist explanation of human biological evolution, the inability of Soviet archaeologists to work in sub-Saharan Africa or to have close contact with scholars who did, prevented

Engels' ideas from being developed further. I was told that some Maoist intellectuals welcomed my paper as a Marxist attack on the Soviet Union, but this revealed more about their thinking than it did about mine. My only comparison was with the United States, where a growing database encouraged the formulation of a materialist explanation of human evolution in a society in which an idealist explanation, which maintained that bigger brains had led to the creation of technology, had hitherto been preferred. While I argued that preconceived beliefs always played a role in formulating explanations of the past, I concluded that material evidence played an even more conclusive role in elaborating and testing such interpretations. My position, that beliefs and interests influence scientific interpretation but can be overcome by the constraining influences of the archaeological record, made this paper an early example of what would later be called moderate cultural relativism.

Finally, the difficulties I encountered trying to publish this paper in the United States in the late 1960s illustrate the problems that beset public discussion of any political implications of academic interpretations, including the investigation of sociocultural evolution. This helps to explain the failure of American archaeologists to come to terms with the explicitly Marxist concepts found in many of Childe's later publications, including his use of the term "revolution" to designate major economic transitions, despite the respect that they accorded to his earlier culture-historical writings. Fear of political harassment also may explain why Leslie White, a radical socialist who published political tracts under various pseudonyms (Peace 1993), attributed sociocultural change to technological factors and why Julian Steward flourished as an ecological determinist. By attributing cultural changes to forces that existed independently of human will, these evolutionists made it clear that their ideas had nothing to do with Marxist subversion. White's technological determinism and Steward's ecological determinism, despite their materialist ontologies, both conformed with a pattern of explaining human behavior in terms of forces that were not subject to conscious human control that was widespread in Western culture in the mid-twentieth century (Kroker 1984: 12). It is unfortunate that Marxism, which had made important contributions to the understanding of sociocultural evolution in the late nineteenth and early twentieth centuries, was excluded, apparently for political reasons, from explicit debates concerning neoevolution. It is also regrettable that Marxist theory was abandoned almost exclusively to Marxist ideologues. Anti-communist feelings were not confined to the United States, although they were less institutionalized elsewhere. Some senior British archaeologists insisted on treating Childe's Marxism as a "convoluted intellectual joke" rather than something he really believed (Piggott 1958: 311-312). As a consequence, they refused to take his later writings seriously.

My next contribution to the discussion of relativism, "Archaeology and the Image of the American Indian" (chapter 3), grew out of a discussion that followed a lecture I gave in England in the spring of 1977. Someone asked why American Indians were indifferent or even hostile to prehistoric archaeology. I pointed out that indigenous Americans had a right to be mistrustful of archaeology, since archaeologists had shown little interest in them or their concerns and had in the past supported stereotypes that denigrated native people. I cited Robert Silverberg's (1968) *The Mound Builders of Ancient America*, a work that broke new ground in documenting the considerable role that archaeology had played in encouraging the mistreatment of Indians during the nineteenth century. The ensuing discussion convinced me that the time had come to explore further the relation between archaeological interpretation and the context in which archaeology had been practiced in North America. Drawing on Gordon Willey and Jeremy Sabloff's (1974) *A History of American Archaeology*, I examined changing relations between the interpretation of archaeological finds and archaeologists' views about native people. A preliminary version of my findings was well received at the annual meeting of the Society for American Archaeology held in Vancouver in 1979, and the final paper was published in *American Antiquity* in 1980.

That paper examined how political prejudices against Native Americans had influenced the interpretation of archaeological data over the past 200 years. Yet I rejected the suggestion that was already being made by at least one archaeologist that truth is determined only by the context in which it exists (Fitting 1973: 289-290). I demonstrated that, although archaeologists shared the prejudices against indigenous Americans that existed in their society and had used archaeological finds to amplify these prejudices, archaeological discoveries had gradually forced archaeologists to question their beliefs. The idea that the archaeological record had never changed, because Indians were incapable of change, became untenable as more archaeological evidence accumulated. At first, changes in the archaeological record were attributed to migration rather than actual cultural change, but when it became obvious that this did not explain the complexity observed in the archaeological record archaeologists added diffusion to their explanatory tool kit. Nevertheless at first, in accordance with their persisting beliefs in the uncreativity of indigenous people, they generally maintained that these ideas had originated outside North America. As still more data were collected, it became necessary to recognize that innovations had occurred within North American Indian cultures. Thus, slowly and reluctantly, a growing body of archaeological data forced archaeologists to abandon their prejudices against indigenous peoples. Implicit in my argument was the suggestion that archaeological data were more susceptible to misinterpretation in the discipline's early stages than when evidence became more abundant. I also pointed out that New Archaeologists, who had done more than archaeologists associated with any previous approach to establish that Indians were as creative as any other people, had as a result of their commitment to generalization tended to remain as alienated from native people as their predecessors had been.

In the early 1980s, Ian Glover and I explored further the impact that social context exerts on archaeological interpretations by editing two numbers of *World Archaeology* devoted to essays that explored regional traditions in archaeological research (Trigger & Glover 1981a; 1982). As a result of this exercise, I began to consider what factors might shape similarities and differences in the orientation of archaeology from one country to another. My initial findings were presented several times during a working visit to Australia in 1983 and published as "Alternative Archaeologies: Nationalist, Colonialist, Imperialist" (chapter 4) in the British anthropological journal *Man* the following year. I argued that the practice of archaeology is strongly influenced by the position that the countries and regions in which it occurs hold within the modern world system and tentatively identified three general types of archaeology: nationalist, colonialist, and imperialist. In each case, I maintained, archaeological interpretation was influenced by the fundamental interests and fears of dominant classes. I concluded that understanding archaeologists as researchers working in specific social and political contexts was a prerequisite for trying to achieve a more objective understanding of archaeological findings. This paper differed from "Archaeology and the Image of the American Indian" in several ways. Its documentation of the impact of societal influences was more extensive and the Marxist concept of group interest motivating social action was more explicit. Yet I continued to express the hope that more self-awareness concerning these matters would encourage greater objectivity in the interpretation of archaeological data. With the publication of this essay, my course was set for writing *A History of Archaeological Thought* (Trigger 1989a), a book that has been widely read and generously received. Some postprocessual archaeologists have told me that either "Alternative Archaeologies" or "Archaeology and the Image of the American Indian" introduced them to epistemological relativism. As rebels against processual archaeology, however, most of them were more impressed by my documentation of political influences on archaeological interpretation than by my argument that these influences were mitigated by constraints exercised by archaeological findings. More attempts have been made to critique and modify the specific concepts I introduced in this paper than any others I have proposed.

A Sea Change

In 1983, I was invited to review the current state of anthropological archaeology for the *Annual Review of Anthropology*. As I surveyed recent publications, I found that for the first time since the 1960s archaeology appeared to be moving in what I believed was a promising direction. I wrote a positive review of developments titled "Archaeology at the Crossroads: What's New?" (chapter 5). This paper struck a responsive chord with many readers, which drew me back into mainstream debates in archaeology.

Among the trends I noted was a growing realization that the specialized data base of archaeology—the surviving material remains of former cultures —compelled archaeology to be a very different sort of social science from social and cultural anthropology, whose practitioners could observe human behavior directly. This trend was notable in the growing emphasis that Binford (1977a; 1978; 1981a) was placing on middle-range theory, which denoted the universal generalizations needed to infer behavior from material remains. Archaeology was no longer being treated merely as anthropology. I also noted that archaeologists were once again becoming aware of the diversity of human behavior found among societies at the same level of development.

An increasing realization of the extent to which adjacent societies influenced one another also called into question to what extent such societies could be studied independently of one another and treated as separate instances of the operation of cause and effect (Steward 1955: 182). There was renewed awareness of the importance of cultural traditions, the complexity of social change, and the lack of agreement among social scientists about how functionally integrated and clearly bounded either social or cultural systems were (Trigger 1982). Archaeologists were expressing increasing doubts about the viability of ecological determinism and either moving towards a possibilist view of ecology or following Roy Rappaport (1968) in acknowledging the important role played by cultural traditions in adapting societies to their environments (Flannery & Marcus 1976; 1983). These developments called into question the ability of archaeologists to predict sociocultural change or to formulate sets of middle-range generalizations that would facilitate a holistic understanding of prehistoric cultures, especially with respect to particular values and beliefs.

To remedy these deficiencies, archaeologists were once again using historical and ethnographic information concerning societies they were studying, or historically closely related ones, to supplement universal generalizations as a means for interpreting archaeological data. The use of such homologies had been rejected by New Archaeology (Binford 1968a). It was increasingly being realized that any explanation of cultural change must take account of specific cultural traditions as well as how neighboring societies impacted on one another. I drew attention to Marxist philosophy as providing an example of how archaeologists might productively combine an interest in the historically particular and in generalizations about human behavior. Marx, who had observed that humans make their history under circumstances inherited from the past, had never underestimated the importance of cultural traditions in his substantive historical investigations, although he believed that social groupings strove to alter the way things were done for their own materially determined political and economic benefit (Marx [1852] in Marx and Engels 1962, 1: 247). It seemed to me that a successful archaeology must become increasingly historical in orientation, while recognizing generalizations as both a means and an end with respect to historical research. At the same time, ethnohistorians were discovering that most small-scale societies had been irreversibly altered by contact with more complex ones prior to being recorded in any detail by cultural anthropologists (Schrire 1984; Wolf 1982). Hence archaeology alone could determine what small-scale societies had been like prior to such contact. Far from archaeology and sociocultural anthropology paralleling one another, social anthropology was beginning to look like a study of colonialism.

Already in 1982 Ian Hodder had published *Symbols in Action* (1982b), which demonstrated that material culture can symbolically distort and invert as well as reflect social behavior. This discovery, which was as important for archaeology as Willey's earlier demonstration of the potential of settlement pattern studies had been, further called into question the ability of middle-range generalizations to provide reliable guides for inferring all aspects of past social systems. Yet most of the changes I had documented in "Archaeology at the Crossroads" were being initiated by people who thought of themselves as processual archaeologists. Up to this point, the New Archaeology paradigm was being loosened and made more inclusive from within rather than seriously challenged from without. Processual archaeology was retreating from Binford's ideal of it becoming a science like biology, which had been united for over a century by a single, high-level theory. Instead, archaeology was coming to resemble the other social sciences, which were united by a commitment to understand human behavior but riddled with theoretical disagreements from the most general level on down.

Postprocessual Antithesis

In the 1980s, a growing number of archaeologists who were disillusioned with processual archaeology began, under the influence of postmodernism, to adopt positions that would eventually be labeled as postprocessual. In place of a materialist ontology, they adopted an idealist one. Culture replaced behavior as a main focus of interest and ideas were interpreted as explaining why people acted the way they did. There was growing interest in the idiosyncratic rather than in cross-cultural generalizations and sociocultural evolutionism was denounced as a colonialist ideology. Every culture once again was valued as a unique expression of the human spirit (Shanks & Tilley 1987a; 1987b; 1989a; Tilley 1991; for analyses see Patterson 1989; Preucel 1991).

To those who had been around long enough, these ideas appeared to be a revival of Boasian anthropology. Yet some postprocessual archaeologists went far beyond Boasian relativism. The consciousness of every human being was argued (no doubt correctly, but often trivially in relation to specific research problems) to have been shaped by unique experiences, to the extent that no two individuals could be expected to perceive a single performance of a play in precisely the same manner. Extreme relativists emphasized that no two persons or collectivities saw the world in the same fashion and that, because all understandings were underdetermined by evidence, there was no way to prove that one view was more correct than another. This position made all communication problematical but every human being a source of innovation; hence extreme postprocessual archaeologists took pride in empowering individuals as agents bringing about cultural change (Bapty & Yates 1990; Bender 1998; Shanks 1992; Tilley 1991; Ucko 1990). These developments encouraged the adoption of an idealist epistemology of Central European origin which asserted that how individuals perceive and interpret the world is influenced either partly or entirely by what they believe; that sensory data can rarely, if ever, refute strongly held beliefs; that to understand any aspect of an issue an academic must first comprehend the whole (however that was to be done); and that science is only one source of knowledge, not fundamentally different from common sense, religious beliefs, or perhaps even delusions (Barnes 1974; Laudan 1990: 93).

In Britain, postprocessual archaeologists defined themselves in opposition to processual archaeologists and tried to discredit and destroy processual archaeology. In the United States, the impact of postprocessual archaeology has been less intense and there has been a general tendency to view the two approaches as complementary. Processual archaeology is maintained to be suitable for studying subsistence patterns and economic behavior, while postprocessual archaeology is viewed as useful for examining behavior that has been influenced by religious beliefs or culturally specific values. The result has been a naive ecological-cultural archaeology, which lacks explicit theoretical underpinning. Every archaeologist is free to define, or not to define, this approach as he or she wishes. The neoevolutionary anthropologist Marvin Harris (1979: 287-314) has characterized such eclecticism as a repudiation of the scientific method. Yet such a situation offers a challenge to create something more productive, and may be preferable to embracing more explicit high-level theories that do not work. No detailed study has yet been made of the differences between processual and postprocessual archaeologies in Britain and America or why these differences developed.

My relations with postprocessual archaeology have been complex and sometimes acrimonious. My investigations of how social and political factors influenced archaeological interpretations began long before the development of postprocessual archaeology and clearly aligned me with those moderate relativists, including Alison Wylie (1982; 1989; 1992), who, while doubting that any methodology can yield value-free understandings of human behavior, also believe that archaeological evidence exists separately from theory and can constrain to a considerable extent both interpretations and the theories on which such interpretations are based. Nevertheless, I became alarmed when Shanks and Tilley (1987b; 1989a) began to deny that any objectivity was possible in archaeology and to proclaim that the only use that could be made of archaeology was to change society. They wanted to employ archaeology for what most people would agree were benevolent political purposes. Yet, in the final analysis, their position bore a disturbing resemblance to those of fascist and communist ideologues who had also proclaimed that the ultimate *raison d'être* of archaeology must be political.

My response to this trend was given in the John Porter Lecture, which I delivered to the Canadian Sociology and Anthropology Association in 1988 and was published in the society's journal as "Hyperrelativism, Responsibility, and the Social Sciences" (chapter 6). Although the examples I discussed were archaeological, the audience I addressed was mainly composed of social anthropologists and sociologists; hence I sought to make my remarks relevant to what was happening in disciplines other than my own. Extreme relativists expressed indignation at my critical remarks, which came from someone they had anticipated would be a supportive colleague. They also tried to represent themselves as not being as extreme as I had portrayed them. It is true that the joint writings of Michael Shanks and Christopher Tilley (1987a: 114; 1987b: 195) contained mixed messages, but among these were explicit claims that archaeological interpretation was not constrained by archaeological data. Over the past decade, such expressions of extreme relativism have generally disappeared from new works that expound postprocessual theory (Johnson 1999: 174-175; Wylie 1997: 86). So perhaps I was part of a critical reaction that achieved some positive results. On the other hand, some postprocessuals still seek, whenever possible, to undermine confidence in the objective value of any and all archaeological evidence (Hodder 1999: 51-52, 23-24). Others publish studies in which they deny a responsibility to offer arguments in support of their interpretations. Examples are those landscape archaeologists who like to imagine what a Neolithic landscape meant to the people who lived in it. They may seem to be following the methods of Collingwood, but lack his intellectual discipline and determination to systematically expand his own consciousness. Many embrace a Heideggerian interpretative approach to archaeology (Bender 1993; Gosden 1994; Karlsson 1998; Thomas 1996; Tilley 1984; 1993; 1996). If the battle against extreme relativism seems to have been won at the theoretical level, it does not appear to have achieved victory with respect to practice. As for those who claim that I flirted with relativism, then repudiated it, the evidence is clear: my position as a moderate relativist has remained substantially the same since at least 1967. What has changed is how various archaeologists do archaeology.

Chapters 7 to 9 were delivered as a set of lectures collectively titled "Archaeology and Epistemology: Dialoguing across the Darwinian Chasm" in the Context and Human Society series offered by the Department of Archaeology and the Center for Archaeological Studies at Boston University. These lectures were delivered while I was engaged in an extensive survey of similarities and differences among seven early civilizations that was intended to achieve a better understanding of the forces that shaped human behavior and the archaeological record and to transcend the naive theoretical eclecticism that characterized American archaeology in the 1990s (Trigger 1993; 2003). The specific aim of these lectures was to assess the implications of my research for rival positivist, idealist, and realist epistemologies. Achieving this goal involved reconsidering the relations between behavior and culture.

My point of departure was Childe's (1949: 6-8) acceptance of the idealist claim that, because of the ability of human beings to symbolize, the world they adapt to is never the real world but the world as they imagine it to be. Yet Childe (1956a: 58-60), as a materialist, went on to claim that there must be enough congruence between the imagined and real worlds for humans to adapt to the real world and hence for societies to survive biologically. The evident ability of societies to adjust to changing circumstances and endure for more than brief intervals implied that human beings were able to determine, at least to some degree, when nature or other persons were not behaving as expected and to alter their own behavior in response to such perceptions. These observations called into question the usefulness of Marshall Sahlins' (1976) dichotomy between practical and cultural reason. They suggested that all human behavior was more productively treated as culturally mediated.

Explanations of ecological adaptation had to consider how culturally transmitted behavior was modified. Because the human mind had evolved as a means of facilitating human adaptation, the study of cognition remained firmly grounded in a materialist perspective. Idealist claims about the operation of the human mind had likewise to be grounded in a materialist ontology. A realist epistemology oriented towards constructing testable models that explain similarities and differences in human behavior seemed better suited for studying the complexities of human behavior than did positivist efforts to establish covariance. Although I did not go into detail, culture and behavior appear to be interactively linked, as they were in Marx's trail-blazing formulations and more recently in Anthony Giddens' (1984) idea of *structuration* or Pierre Bourdieu's (1977) concept of *habitus*. Archaeology was challenged to better understand the role played by material objects in both realms.

The second lecture considered how behavior and culture might be studied archaeologically. Processual archaeologists, despite their aspirations to do otherwise, have had the greatest success in producing middle-range generalizations that relate to ecological, economic, and technological behavior. This is, as Ernest Gellner (1982) once observed, the realm characterized by natural scarcity and hence by material inflexibility. Yet my research on early civilizations had revealed important cross-cultural uniformities in social and economic inequality that could not be explained as ecologically adaptive in their own right, but seemed more likely to accord with behavioral tendencies that are biologically innate in human beings. Likewise, I discovered important uniformities in general patterns of religious beliefs that were not epiphenomenal reflections of social organization but helped to control behavior in ways that stabilized the political order (Trigger 1993: 94-105). Once again, an ecological explanation seemed inadequate, since the similarities appeared to relate to a species-specific human nature that must have been shaped by natural selection over a long period of time (Butterworth 1999; Gazzaniga 1992; 1998; Low 1999; Mithen 1996). I had been led to conclude that significant cross-cultural uniformities occur in social organization and belief systems as well as in economic patterns, but these represent adaptations to human nature as well as to the natural environment. On the other hand, not only many specific beliefs and symbols, but also complex value systems—which have adaptive significance—display cross-cultural idiosyncrasies. The relations of these phenomena to the archaeological record can be established only hermeneutically, using oral traditions or texts that record meaning in a linguistic format, which is the only way in which meanings can be communicated in a manner that is not vague or polysemous.

The third lecture was a defense of the need to subject all interpretations of archaeological data to critical testing. Such testing is generally easier with respect to human behavior than to beliefs or personal opinions. With beliefs, it is harder to verify meanings that are culturally idiosyncratic than ones that are cross-culturally replicated. Demonstrating the correctness of hermeneutic inferences is as difficult as proving (other than interactively) that a person has accurately determined precisely what someone else is thinking; the hermeneutic operation that humans perform most frequently in their daily lives.

I also rejected the extreme relativist position that different archaeological interpretations cannot be compared. On a purely rational basis it can be determined whether different interpretations of data are complementary or mutually exclusive. If they are complementary, a larger synthesis is possible; if they are mutually exclusive, it is incumbent on archaeologists to try to check explanations against data to see if one or both of them can be refuted. If an explanation cannot be tested, it does not possess scientific status, although it may later acquire such status if ways can be found to test it. I also argued that a realist definition of explanation as accounting for why things happen confers equal legitimacy on both historical and generalizing explanations.

As my research on early civilizations continued, I concluded that human behavior is constrained by at least four major categories of factors: (a) the need to adapt to the external (natural and social) environment; (b) the need to satisfy the requirements of human nature, which necessitates among other things that cultures have sufficient cognitive and psychological patterning that they are meaningful to individuals; (c) functional constraints that limit the forms that social structures can take; and (d) a tendency for particular cultural patterns to persist with only random fluctuations of content until individual human needs or group interests alter all or parts of these patterns (Boyd & Richerson 1985). Archaeologists have long implicitly operated as if they believed that biologically based drives, emotions, and cognition influence human behavior. Zipf's (1949) principle of least effort has played a major role in ecological archaeology. Yet processual archaeologists have generally construed such behavior as the outcome of abstract, universal reasoning guiding human adaptive behavior. The broad, long-term applicability of Zipf's principle for explaining adaptive strategies makes it more likely that tendencies promoting such behavior have become biologically grounded rather than that the principle is merely the result of repeated rational calculations, which to some extent become incorporated into cultural traditions. Cultural anthropologists have generally opposed acknowledging the biological grounding of any aspect of human behavior because universals cannot explain cultural differences and because they fear that biological grounding may promote racism. Yet for archaeologists seeking to understand prehistoric human behavior, any universals that exist are of crucial importance. Biologically grounded human behavioral tendencies must be viewed as products of natural selection operating on hominid cognitive and emotional predispositions over millions of years. It is also clear that the main reason for the unprecedented evolutionary success of human beings to date is their biologically grounded capacity for cultural diversity.

The final essay in this volume, "The 1990s: North American Archaeology with a Human Face" (chapter 10), was the banquet address that I gave at the annual meeting of the Canadian Archaeological Association held in Whitehorse in May 1990. A considerable number of local aboriginal leaders played an active role in this conference and I introduced my talk to them as a discourse on the traditions of my people. I pursued a theme that I had first raised in "Archaeology and the Image of the American Indian": what a mutually productive relationship between archaeologists and indigenous people should be like. Since 1980, I had been involved in various disputes regarding the rights of indigenous peoples to control their heritage, always advocating aboriginal empowerment (Trigger 1988). Because of that, indigenous leaders probably were expecting that my talk would condemn the behavior of archaeologists and offer an apology for past wrongdoings.

I noted that it was easier for aboriginal people to relate to the eclectic ecological-cultural archaeology that was then emerging in North America than it had been for them to relate to processual archaeology. I also argued that archaeology had much to gain from the growing participation of indigenous people in archaeological research. Yet, recalling the past misuse of archaeology to support nationalist and colonialist agendas, I also maintained that archaeology must guard against blindly serving any parochial interests. It could protect itself by seeking a more objective understanding of the past that would help people to think more clearly about issues that related to the common good of all humanity. I would explore these issues in more detail in my book *Sociocultural Evolution: Calculation and Contingency* (Trigger 1998a). Since I gave that talk, the growing abuse of archaeological finds (and alleged finds) to support nationalist causes in Eastern Europe, the former Soviet Union, and India has made archaeologists increasingly aware of the dangers that continue to haunt their discipline, especially when its main objective is seen as being the study of ethnicity and ethnic history (Kohl & Fawcett 1995; Meskell 1998).

Conclusion

One of the main lessons I have learned from my efforts to create an acceptable framework for explaining archaeological finds is the extent to which epistemology parallels life. Human beings are not black boxes but organisms with biologically grounded drives and emotions. The human mind has evolved as an adaptive mechanism but, in the course of doing so, has acquired its own ways of analyzing information. Some of these techniques, such as the ability to conceptualize space, time, and causality, may date from a very early stage of primate development, while the ability to manipulate symbols as modern human beings do is much more recent (Mithen 1996). In place of long-term and not very productive efforts to apply structuralism (Hodder 1990), some archaeologists are now showing interest in the proposition that the logical capacities in the human mind are inextricably linked with a biologically-based tendency to think by means of analogies and metaphors (Lakoff 1987; Lakoff & Johnson 1980; Tilley 1999).

Idealists are right that the world as it is conceived is different from the world as it really is. To understand human behavior, archaeologists and anthropologists must also look to the findings of psychology and neuroscience. Yet these disciplines are in many respects no more advanced than are the social sciences. Therefore archaeology and anthropology have much to offer to the development of these two sciences. How the human mind works and how it influences human behavior are no longer topics for philosophical discussion, they are subjects for scientific research.

Positivism has fallen on hard times. Perceptions are no longer widely regarded as givens but are believed to be shaped by capacities that are innate in the human mind and by concepts that have been acquired through learning. Yet sensory perception has evolved as the means by which organisms can adapt to their environment. Human beings can recognize in at least some instances that what they observe does not correspond with what they expect and adjust their behavior on the basis of such information. Once again, the nature of perception ceases to be a matter for philosophical discussion and becomes an object for scientific study.

Being unable to conceptualize or perceive external reality in a completely objective manner does not make the world as it really is less important for human beings. Failure to adapt to the external world means no warm human bodies and that in turn means no human minds. Ultimately, there is no way to escape from a materialist ontology. At the same time, it is clear that trying to base a scientific study of human behavior on sensory data alone is highly problematical for at least two reasons. Sensory perceptions are influenced by learned or innate concepts already present in the human mind. There is also much in the natural world that we cannot observe. Restricting scientific research to establishing correlations between specific categories of observables seems unduly restricting. Realism, with its focus on trying to understand how things work, seems a reasonable alternative. Biologists were able to postulate major properties of genes by studying their effects long before they were able to observe genes directly. A materialist ontology and a realist epistemology provide the basis for studying human beings as biological entities, who were produced by long-term natural selection and use their cognitive and rational abilities to relate to a world that exists independently of them. Instead of adopting crude ecological adaptation, we are called upon to explain a situation in which human beings have a cognitively mediated relationship with their own bodies and the rest of the social and natural world.

What does this mean to archaeologists in terms of studying the past? Evidence that cross-cultural uniformities characterize not only many aspects of technology, economic behavior, and social organization but also belief systems lends credence to at least some of the epistemological claims of cognitive-processual archaeologists. Yet middle-range theory, in the sense of universal correlations between material culture and specific forms of human behavior, seems to be easiest to establish in realms where physical or biological constraints impose severe limitations on human behavior or where functional limitations restrict economic or social behavior in ways that pattern the archaeological record.

Correlations between general patterns of belief and particular types of political or social organization can be established ethnographically and used to make general statements about what kinds of beliefs might have been associated with a society at a particular level of complexity. Such correlations are, however, more difficult to associate with specific forms of material culture that are likely to turn up in the archaeological record than is the case with middle-range generalizations. What is needed to make these correlations archaeologically relevant is a set of material implications that are likely to be associated with such beliefs or practices. If all early civilizations believed that one of humanity's duties was to nourish the gods, substantial evidence of sacrifice ought to occur in each early civilization, although the specific nature of sacrifice might have varied considerably from one early civilization to another, producing different material correlates. Testing a generalization of this sort archaeologically would involve procedures similar to Hodder's

(1987b) contextual archaeology, which involves studying the relations between different data sets belonging to the same society or culture in order to better understand the behavior that produced them (Fagan 1998: 244-249).

Culturally specific beliefs can only be inferred by hermeneutic comparison, using verbally transmitted information to attribute meaning to the material culture of the same, or historically closely related, cultures. That explains why postprocessual archaeology has made such significant contributions to historical archaeology, which investigates societies where textual and archaeological data are frequently abundant for the same culture (Deetz 1996; Glassie 1975; R. Isaac 1982; M. Johnson 1996; Leone & Potter 1988; McGuire & Paynter 1991; Meskell 1999; Morris 2000). It also suggests why all prehistoric cultures may be studied from a processual viewpoint, while little can ever be known about the culturally idiosyncratic beliefs that were associated with most of these societies. It may be possible for archaeologists to demonstrate that a particular group of Mesolithic hunters behaved in accordance with optimal foraging theory, without being able to learn anything about the specific beliefs by which they conceptualized such behavior. From ethnographic evidence we know that modern Cree hunters in northern Quebec understood their hunting strategies not in terms of calories, as modern ecologists do, but in terms of the quality of the spiritual relations between individual hunters and animal spirits (Tanner 1979).

Ideally, as archaeologists, we would like to understand not only human behavior but also the specific beliefs that were associated with it. In practice, we must accept that in some cases we can study only behavior. While I, like most archaeologists, regard the goal of archaeology as being to study human behavior and culture, I doubt that we will ever find an alchemical formula that will transform archaeological and related information into an understanding of all aspects of human experience. While we strive to expand the explanatory power of archaeology, we must also acknowledge that its grounding in material culture produces a set of limitations and potentials that distinguish archaeology from any other discipline. On the other hand, many of the problems that confront the archaeological explanation, as opposed to the inferring, of human behavior and culture are the same as those that confront the other social sciences, and in particular anthropology. Hence what can be said about archaeological explanation applies in varying degrees to all these disciplines.

2

Engels on the Part Played by Labor in the Transition from Ape to Man: An Anticipation of Contemporary Archaeological Theory

The distinction between the inductive and deductive approaches in anthropology is (as of 1967) now a matter of relatively little concern, except perhaps in courses on the history of anthropological theory. With a respectable history behind the discipline, it is generally agreed that any new hypothesis, whatever its genesis, should make sense in terms of existing bodies of well-established theory and, even more importantly, be capable of withstanding repeated empirical tests (Nagel 1961: 15-28).

Prior to the accumulation of large reserves of data, much of the inquiry in the social and natural sciences was perforce of a deductive nature. The limitations that were encountered by the early theorists were twofold, since they lacked both a background of established theory to build on and the data against which their hypotheses might be tested.

Few of the fields of speculation that flourished in the latter half of the nineteenth century are of greater potential historical and theoretical interest than that concerning human biological evolution. Although Darwin avoided making all but the briefest allusion to human beings in *The Origin of Species*, it was an obvious corollary of his theory of evolution that humans could be regarded no longer as a special creation, but, like all other living things, had to be viewed as the product of evolution through natural selection.

Scarcely any fossil evidence concerning human origins was forthcoming during the nineteenth century. The original Neanderthal find was made in Germany in 1856, but it was not until the early 1890s that Eugene Dubois unearthed remains of *Homo erectus* (*Pithecan-*

thropus erectus) in Java and the first Australopithecine was not discovered until 1924. The study of human origins was further complicated by a lack of basic information (and indeed by a great deal of misinformation) about the behavior of the higher primates, humanity's nearest relatives. Speculations about the forces that had shaped human evolution and the order in which various changes had come about were of necessity based almost entirely on contemporary notions about the nature of human beings and their "role" in the world.

It is perhaps not surprising that the majority of scholars who were dedicated to propagating the theory of evolution retained an essentially conservative, and frequently teleological, view of human beings. Most of them were biologists, not social theorists, and even those who were not especially attached to Christian theology were influenced by the humanist view of human beings that was an essential heritage of the Enlightenment. The most important feature of this view was the Aristotelian postulate that humans were distinguished from other creatures by their reason. Reason was regarded as being so fundamental to humanity that, instead of viewing it as something that had developed in the course of evolution, most evolutionists of the time regarded it as a primary causal factor in human evolution. In doing so, they were in effect setting the essence of humanity outside the basic framework of human evolution (Brace 1964; Brace & Montagu 1965: 122-213).

The chief product of this *idealist* outlook was the assumption that human intellectual capacities had developed almost to their present condition before human beings had begun to acquire culture. In the 1860s, speculations along these lines were in part encouraged by Alfred R. Wallace's (1864) emphasis on the stability of the human species and the importance of increasing mental ability in bringing human physical evolution to an end. While it has been argued that Wallace was led to these conclusions by the failure of paleontologists to discover a small-brained ancestor of human beings and by the large-brained Cro-Magnons and Neanderthals that were being found in Europe, the fact remains that these essentially creationist conclusions seemed ideologically compatible to most scholars of the day and eventually were essential to Wallace's own thinking. Theories of this sort remained very important among French and English-speaking physical anthropologists until the middle of the twentieth century and were espoused by cultural anthropologists as prominent as A. L. Kroeber (1948: 654). One of the variants of this theory provided the conceptual basis for the Piltdown fraud, a hybrid creation consisting of a modern human cranium and an orangutan's jaw, which it was claimed had lived in the Middle Pleistocene (Weiner 1955). The widespread credence given this concoction is evidence that many anthropologists were happy to believe that the development of the human brain had preceded the modernization of the rest of the human anatomy.

Another product of the idealist point of view was the many reconstructions of human evolution which postulated that various human "phyla," that today are classified as *Homo erectus,* co-existed during much of the Pleistocene, with only one surviving to the present day (Vallois 1962). These polyphyletic theories classified most of the lowbrowed, small-brained *non-sapiens* forms of fossil humans as aberrant, dead-end lines of development, at the same time postulating that more human-like, but as yet undiscovered, ancestors of modern human beings had co-existed alongside them. The tenacity with which these theories were maintained in spite of growing evidence that contradicted them is proof of the powerful, implicitly anti-evolutionary biases that continued until recently to characterize the studies of human development in Western Europe and America. These biases seem to have sprung largely unconsciously from views of the nature of human beings that had been inherited from an earlier period.

The theory that systematic tool-making preceded any substantial enlargement of the hominid brain has become dominant only in the last decade (Washburn 1960; Washburn & Howell 1960). Today, it seems well established that the first tool-makers were creatures able to run, if not walk, on two legs and with brains no larger than those of modern apes. Modern human beings are now viewed as a product of changes that occurred in response to natural selection while hominids were pursuing a tool-using way of life. For convenience we may label this a materialist theory of human evolution.

Eighty-one years before Kenneth Oakley (1957) published his paper "Tools Makyth Man," which heralded the beginning of these current views about the nature of human evolution, Friedrich Engels wrote an article (published in 1896) entitled "The Part Played by Labor in the Transition from Ape to Man" (Engels 1962). In it he described, in a terminology that surprisingly parallels the modern one, the process by which "labor created man himself." Engels' conclusions were not based on any palaeontological evidence, but on the deductive application of Marxist theory. One does not have to look far to understand the logic of Engels doing this. The problem of human origins is essentially an historical one, although this was not clear to many Victorians, who insisted on also regarding it as a moral issue. The Marxist dialectic is a method of viewing history and most of the writings of Marx and Engels are about historical problems. Prehistory and human evolution were topics of considerable public interest in the latter half of the nineteenth century, hence it is not surprising that Engels, with his wide range of interests, should have attempted to discuss human origins in the light of Marx's general theories about the dynamics of human history.

Charles Darwin's book *The Descent of Man* appeared five years before Engels drafted "The Transition from Ape to Man," but it was mainly a discussion of sexual selection and in Engels' opinion contributed little to an understanding of the process of human evolution. Engels characterized current views of evolution as trying to explain human actions: "from their thoughts instead of from their needs ... so there arose in the course of time that idealistic outlook on the world which ... has dominated men's minds. It still rules them to such a degree that even the most materialistic natural scientists of the Darwinian school are still unable to form any clear idea of the origin of man, because under this ideological influence they do not recognize the part that has been played therein by labor" (Engels 1962: 87).

Seen in retrospect these strictures appear, for the most part, to be justified. Despite an interest in human origins, nowhere in the literature of the period (except in Engels' paper) does one find a clearly formulated and logically satisfying application of contemporary evolutionary theory to this problem. Darwin, like Marx and Engels, was a materialist, but in his study of human origins he was preoccupied with demonstrating that human beings were an integral part of the animal kingdom, a point that many idealists even in the evolutionary camp (including A. R. Wallace) were unwilling to concede. The result was that Darwin did not recognize as fully as he might have that many of the clues to understanding human evolution were to be found by the study of humanity's special characteristics rather than the investigation of those that humans share with the rest of the animal world. In any case, there was probably not enough factual evidence at hand for Darwin to feel at ease with this problem.

The resemblance between the theory of human evolution proposed by Engels and the materialist one currently in vogue is amazingly close. In spite of this, no contemporary English-speaking physical anthropologist, as far as I know, has acknowledged any awareness of his famous and easily accessible exposition of this theory (Eiseley 1958; Irvine 1955).

Engels bases his argument on the Marxist assumption that labor is the "prime basic condition for all human existence." On a palaeontological level, this assumption could be correlated with the commonly accepted idea that animals are adapted to their environment, but that human beings, through their labor, master it. Engels suggests that, if labor is distinctive of humans, it is only a logical extension of Marx's arguments to regard labor as having created them.

According to Engels, our ancestors took "the decisive step in the transition from ape to man" when they "disaccustom[ed] themselves to the aid of their hands and [adopted] a more and more erect gait" (p. 80). He notes that the ground movement of modern apes preserves numerous stages which exemplify the transition between four-footed and bipedal locomotion, but that for none of them is the latter more than a makeshift.

Engels also notes from the literature that apes use their hands differently from their feet, the former being used among other things to wield clubs and build nests. No simian hand, however, has "fashioned even the crudest of stone knives" (p.81). The decisive development of the hand took place only after the acquisition of upright posture allowed it "to become free" to make tools. Tool-making, in turn, favored natural selection which caused the hand to "attain ever greater flexibility and skill" and this skill was "inherited and increased from generation to generation." Engels concludes that the hand "is not only the organ of labor, it is also the product of labor."

Turning to social development, Engels notes that since modern apes are social, humanity's simian ancestors probably were also. Nevertheless, the development of labor helped to multiply "joint activities" and thus bound groups closer together. This, in turn, led to an increased need for communication and the development of language. Engels treats this problem in a Lamarckian fashion, arguing that "the urge [to speak] created its organ" (p. 83). In support of this theory he claims that dogs and horses, after being exposed for some time to human company, "feel their inability to speak as a defect." Although he failed to recognize that language and tool-making are related aspects of the process of symbolization, he is in line with modern theory when he suggests that tool-making and the development of a capacity for language gradually resulted in the improvement of the human brain and in increasing "clarity of consciousness, power of abstraction and of judgment" (p. 84). This was a development which "far from reaching a conclusion when man finally became distinct from the ape, continued on the whole to make powerful progress [in later times]."

Apes were content to browse over a feeding area predetermined by geographical conditions and the resistance of neighboring bands. The development of a division of labor constitutes the main difference between primate "bands" and "human" societies. Labor begins with the making of tools, of which the oldest appear to have been designed for hunting and fishing. They thus appear to mark a transition from an "exclusively vegetable diet to the concomitant use of meat" (p. 85). This not only resulted in a more complex division of labor but also provided humans with new sources of nourishment to promote their physical development.

Although Engels subscribes to some ideas that have become outmoded, he has hit upon the major concepts that constitute the modern materialist theory of human evolution. These are that the acquisition of upright posture freed human beings' hands for tool-making which, in turn, permitted natural selection to operate in favor of greater manual dexterity and intellectual ability.

Obviously, Engels' theory did not develop in an intellectual vacuum. Many of the ideas he made use of were current at the time. He well may have been influenced, for example, by Wallace's detailed description of the use of missiles by orangutans and other primates and also by Darwin's discussions of the inherited effects of the increased or diminished use of different parts of the body. Much of this material could have been garnered from Darwin's *The Descent of Man*. In spite of this, his theory is sharply distinguished from contemporary ones by the clarity and economy of its formulations. These features were the result not only of Engels' incisive logic but also of the materialistic view of humanity that he had acquired from Marx and his self-conscious departure from the idealist position that was to remain dominant in Western Europe and America for a long time to come.

Engels' theory of human origins is a tour de force of deductive reasoning. In the absence of palaeontological evidence, however, it was compelling only to those who shared Engels' views about the nature of human beings and the forces that shaped human destiny. Engels was not a physical anthropologist and made no attempt to prove or develop his theory; indeed his article remained unfinished and was not published until after his death. In *The Origin of the Family, Private Property and the State* (1884; see Leacock 1972), he made no allusion to this theory whatsoever, in spite of its obvious relevance to a materialist interpretation of human origins. Instead, he focused his discussion of the earliest period of human existence on a reconsideration of the classical problem of group marriage, much along the lines of Lewis Henry Morgan's *Ancient Society* (1877).

Marx had planned to write a book demonstrating the relevance of Morgan's *Ancient Society* to his own views of history; hence the shift from physical to social anthropology in the *Origin* may have been in part the result of Engels' desire to realize, as closely as possible, the original plan of Marx's work. Marx was keenly interested in Morgan's ideas and saw in the American lawyer's "materialist" approach to prehistory an orientation that was highly compatible with his own. It is therefore not difficult to understand how both Marx and Engels came to view Morgan's schemes of social development in prehistoric times as a comprehensive first chapter to Marx's own study of the origins and development of capitalist society. It is perhaps significant for explaining Engels' lack of interest in physical anthropology in the *Origin* that Marx showed very little interest in the questions about the psycho-physical constitution of human beings that were raised by his studies of alienation and his view of humans as agents of history.

Nevertheless, it does seem strange that Engels not only refrained from mentioning his idea that labor had shaped human beings biologically, as well as socially and cognitively, but never bothered to develop his original paper for publication. It would appear that the question of human biological origins intrigued Engels only momentarily, and that, however penetrating his original insights were, his study of the problem was soon given up in view of projects that he regarded as more central to his life's work. This makes his paper an even more extraordinary accomplishment.

"The Transition from Ape to Man" finally was published in 1896 and since that time has been well known and approved of in Communist circles. Engels' theory was thus one of the theories of human evolution already in circulation as major discoveries of fossils began to provide the data needed to test and refine these theories. It should be remembered, however, that for a long time these data were so sparse that theories of evolution, although ostensibly derived from the evidence at hand, remained (and to a degree still remain) deductive instead of inductive.

It is worth comparing the subsequent development of theories of human evolution in the Soviet Union and the West. While I have been unable to examine the Russian literature in detail, at least certain general trends can be observed from summary articles, especially that by G.F. Debetz (1961).

Engels' paper is, of course, well known in the Soviet Union and has been cited frequently in physical anthropological literature. This paper was undoubtedly influential in the rejection by Soviet scholars of all polyphyletic interpretations of human evolution at the time when, for reasons we have already noted, these interpretations were highly favored in the West. Soviet anthropologists consistently have interpreted the successive grades of fossil hominids as illustrations of the developmental sequence through which modern humans must have passed.

On the other hand, while numerous theoretical discussions of human development have been published, Soviet efforts to develop Engels' theories and apply them to the interpretation of the fossil record have been disappointing. A notable exception is G. A. Bontch-Osmolovski's study of the hand of the Neanderthal man found at Kiik-Koba in the Crimea. This study represents an important attempt to show a relationship between the development of human physiology and technology in prehistoric times. Other scholars, such as Ia. Roginskii, have chosen to stress the development of group life as a primary force in human evolution. These studies view tool production as a major force promoting interdependence, which in turn has caused natural selection to operate in such a way as to adapt human beings to social life, particularly through the suppression of violence. Unfortunately, these studies seem to have made little use of data derived from comparative primatology and contributed little to the development of this discipline. Moreover, the fossil evidence that was used to support many arguments of this sort appears to be limited and tenuous in the extreme.

It is also noteworthy that until recently the early stages of hominid evolution have received less attention from Soviet physical anthropologists than have the later periods. In particular, problems relating to the transition from the Australopithecine to the *Homo erectus* (Pithecanthropine) stage have attracted less attention from Soviet scholars than has "the problem of the primitive human group and the formation of *Homo sapiens*" (Debetz 1961: 142, 147). This is unfortunate, because it is precisely for the earliest periods that Engels' theory is most relevant and could best be applied.

There are a number of reasons for this. To begin with, the area comprising the Soviet Union does not appear to have been a key area in early hominid development and fossil finds there have been few in number and belong to the later phases of human development. Soviet anthropologists have had little opportunity to work outside their country and thus to participate directly in the major human palaeontological work of this century. Hence their interests appear to have focused, not unreasonably, on the problems most relevant to the primary materials they have at hand (Mongait 1959: 63-88).

Other reasons seem to lie in Soviet politics and culture. In efforts to reshape Soviet life, communist ideology tended to stress the plasticity of human nature and minimize the constraints of natural forces. This point of view, which has been popular with socialists and other reform-minded groups elsewhere for a century or more, is in itself no doubt far less dangerous than the views of certain conservatives who justify their opposition to change with the argument that the status quo represents an adjustment to human nature that can be tampered with, if at all, only at great peril to all concerned. Nevertheless, one must count the influence of the neo-Lamarckist doctrines of Trofim Lysenko among the adverse effects of the coercive political support that was given to an anti-heredity position in the field of biology in the Soviet Union. In the social sciences, also, great stress was laid on the freedom of human beings from biological constraints. It would therefore appear that the reluctance of Soviet physical anthropologists to examine the earlier stages of human evolution in more detail during the Stalinist régime also may result in part from the tendency of Soviet officialdom to play down heredity and natural selection and stress the physical and emotional plasticity of humans. Engels' hypothesis that human beings had developed as a result of natural selection favoring tool-using was squared with this position by assuming that at some stage in human development the "predominance of biological laws" had become an obstacle to the further improvement of work. At that point, the rate of cultural evolution came to exceed the rate of biological evolution and as a result human destiny ceased to depend on biological change. This new phase is called the "era of the unlimited rule of social laws" (Debetz 1961: 141). During the Stalinist period, the detailed examination of human physical evolution, even when seen as conditioned by culture, might have been viewed as reactionary and undesirable; at the very least it would have been politically sensitive. Another factor inhibiting research at that time was the canonical status accorded the writings of Marx and Engels by the Communist Party. For a long time, the creative application of Marxist principles to problems of scholarship was fraught with danger. The inhibiting effect of this insistence on general conformity to party-dictated orthodoxy has been noted in other branches of Soviet anthropology (M. Miller 1956). It has also been suggested that at least some of the theoretical weaknesses of Soviet physical anthropology lie in its failure to adopt a genetic viewpoint. This decision has resulted in a "pointless pregenetic insistence on typology" (Brace 1964: 12). Such behavior can be traced back to Lysenkoism and political conditions. It is clear then that for various reasons Soviet anthropologists did not, and perhaps could not, capitalize upon the deductive advantage that their familiarity and sympathy with Engels' theories should have given them.

There is no evidence that French or English-speaking physical anthropologists were familiar with Engels' theories in the past, or are so now. For many years the basic premises that Engels held to be self-evident were rejected by physical anthropologists who were overwhelmingly committed to a mentalist or idealist outlook. Much of the thinking about human palaeontology in the first half of the twentieth century was dominated by the theories of Marcellin Boule (1912), who assigned Neanderthals, as well as Pithecanthropus, to side branches of human evolution that became extinct without issue. This line of interpretation was followed later by the majority of physical anthropologists, among them Henri Vallois, L. S. B. Leakey, W. W. Howells (whose textbooks have been particularly influential), and Pierre Teilhard de Chardin. This position was adopted in spite of the fact that Pithecanthropine finds generally appeared to be earlier than Neanderthal ones and Neanderthal finds earlier than those of the modern form of *Homo sapiens*. The main argument in favor of this theory, when it was first propounded, was that too few remains of fossil human beings had been found for any theory to be adequately tested. By exaggerating formal differences between various skeletal finds, it was possible to construct a disjointed and essentially non-evolutionary picture of hominid development.

In an effort to establish a polyphyletic interpretation of human evolution, a great deal of energy was expended in the search for modern types of human beings that could be shown to be contemporary with, or to precede, the more primitive types. Great importance was attached to the discovery of the remains of various supposed early *sapiens*, such as Fontéchevade, Kanjera, Steinheim, and Swanscombe. Yet, as C. L. Brace (1964: 12) has commented, these finds all turned out to be "either distorted, fragmentary, of dubious date, or downright un-*sapiens*." The general reluctance to accept Australopithecus as a primate that was earlier and still more primitive than the Pithecanthropines no doubt also stemmed from this same preoccupation with the great antiquity of modern humans. Only a few physical anthropologists, such as Franz Weidenreich, Aleš Hrdlička, and Hans Weinert, remained aloof from this general trend (Brace 1964: 11-17).

In the 1950s the prolonged failure of the polyphyletic school to demonstrate its case, and increasing fossil evidence to the contrary, led a growing number of Western physical anthropologists to rethink their basic assumptions. Many were induced to do this by a growing awareness that previous interpretations of human evolution violated many of the principles applied to interpreting the evolution of other forms of life (Le Gros Clark 1955: 1-47). An interest developed in explaining the causes of the skeletal variation in fossil humans instead of simply recording it and attempts were made to view human evolution in terms of its ecological parameters (Washburn 1953).

This dynamic approach to human evolution soon led to the independent reformulation of many of the ideas expressed by Engels. In "Tools Makyth Man," Oakley defined humans as tool-making primates and, surveying the palaeontological and cultural record, suggested that their development during the Australopithecine stage might have taken place because natural selection strongly favored tool-using. This suggestion helped to bring physical and cultural anthropology together in a new and dynamic fashion. In succeeding years, physical anthropologists have advanced an increasing number of hypotheses based on this essentially materialist position and have tested them against an ever growing number of fossil finds. At first a large number of these hypotheses were concerned with the relationship between tool-making and the development of the hand, brain, and other parts of the body. Now an increasing number are concerned with primate behavior and the development of primate social organization (Holloway 1967). While very little archaeological evidence is available to shed direct light on these problems, questions of this sort have helped to stimulate a growing interest in behavioral studies of non-human primates. While much remains to be discovered about human evolution, particularly about its pre-Australopithecine stages, a general theory seems at last to have been formulated that can explain the evidence being collected and generate hypotheses of value for understanding human evolution.

From the point of view of this essay, it is important to note that there is no evidence to suggest that these new Western formulations are in any way the result of the emergence of a new view of human beings and their role in nature, although a materialist orientation has perhaps been gaining ground. The years separating the work of Marcellin Boule from that of Sherwood L. Washburn and F. Clark Howell have seen a deepening appreciation of the nature of evolution among anthropologists, but no fundamental re-orientation in their view of humans that would of itself account for the decline of one theory of human origins and the rise of another. The reasons for the change seem to be technical, not philosophical. We now have much evidence concerning the nature of human evolution and more is appearing every year. At the same time, the study of the evolution of other plants and animals has provided comparative data that can be applied in understanding human origins. Although the deductive basis for the study of human evolution has been altered in the latter sense, the main stimuli towards change can clearly be traced to the evidence itself.

English-speaking social scientists traditionally have prided themselves on the empiricism of their research. They are proud of their ability to observe and trace objective connections between what they observe. In our work we show relatively little awareness that our choice of problems, as well as our attitudes toward what we are studying, are conditioned by our personal and social relations to the values of the society in which we live. To a larger degree than we are probably willing to admit, our professional success depends on our ability to subscribe to the implicit major premises of the bourgeois entrepreneurial society in which we live. In the Soviet Union, on the other hand, the builders of the new society sought to create a mechanical solidarity based on the application of dialectical materialism to public and private life, as well as to the realm of scholarship. Revolutionary exigencies have resulted in a narrow, often formalist, interpretation of Marxism, which in turn has made free scientific inquiry very difficult. It is perhaps then not as ironic as it first appears that the principles originally deduced by the Thomas Huxley of Marxism should have been independently reformulated and confirmed almost a century later by scientists who subscribe to a different philosophical system instead of being developed by his own followers. Linguists frequently remind us that any idea can be expressed in any natural language, although the difficulty of doing so varies according to the nature of the vocabulary and grammar of each. In some ways bodies of theory seem to be like languages. The materialist view of humans was obviously much more capable of generating a farsighted hypothesis of human origins than was the idealist one. Nevertheless the formulation of an hypothesis is not the same as establishing it. The example we have just considered provides some indication that, so long as a diligent search is made for empirical evidence, valid explanations eventually can be arrived at in spite of the manifold illusions and misconceptions that scientists must share as members of functioning, and hence myth-ridden, cultures.

3

Archaeology and the Image of the American Indian

In this chapter, I will argue that the most important single factor that has shaped the long-term development of American archaeology has been the traditional Euro-American stereotype which portrayed America's native peoples as being inherently unprogressive. I will attempt to demonstrate how the influence of this stereotype has caused American archaeology to develop in a fundamentally different manner from European archaeology, which from its beginning was preoccupied with affirming that continuous cultural progress characterized that continent in prehistoric as well as historic times. I do not deny that American archaeologists have been familiar with ethnological research concerning native peoples and that at certain periods ethnological conclusions represented a marked improvement on popular stereotypes. It appears, however, that because of the relative lack of direct contact between archaeologists and native peoples, popular stereotypes have influenced archaeologists more than they have influenced ethnologists.

While I feel that the extreme view that "truth is determined by the cultural context in which it exists" (Fitting 1973: 289-290) fails to take account of the long-term accomplishments of prehistoric archaeology, I accept that the problems social scientists choose to research and (hopefully less often) the conclusions that they reach are influenced in various ways and sometimes to a highly significant degree by the attitudes and opinions that are prevalent in the societies in which they live (Darnell 1971: 85). For this reason, current prejudices may influence the perceptions that archaeologists have of their discipline's past. In any treatment of intellectual history, it is easy to ignore minority opinions or to select data to produce a biased view of past realities. Conversely, when the conclusions that emerge from such studies seem unpleasant or controversial, it is tempting to dismiss them as being unrepresentative or polemical. Yet, the variety of views that have been held simultaneously at any particular time in the past should not lead us to ignore the dominant paradigms that have successively governed research in various disciplines. I do not claim that there are no exceptions to my characterizations; I suggest, however, that these characterizations are sufficiently representative to pinpoint the major factors that have influenced the development of archaeological interpretation in America during the past two centuries.

American Archaeology Prior to 1914

The popular stereotypes about native people that influenced American archaeology during the nineteenth century long antedate the professionalization of the discipline. From the time of earliest exploration of the New World by Europeans, the Indians, whether condemned as brutal murderers or romanticized as noble savages, were held to be inferior to civilized people (Jennings 1975: 59). This concept of inferiority was further elaborated in order to rationalize the seizure of Indian lands, which accompanied the expansion of European settlement. The European colonists in New England argued that the Indians' failure to make adequate use of the land God had given them justified their own technologically more advanced society having laid claim to it. Metaphorically, America became a second Canaan which God was taking away from its original inhabitants to give to his new chosen people. Indeed, in 1783, President Ezra Stiles of Yale University extended the parallel by suggesting, as Spanish and French scholars had done still earlier, that the Indians were literally descended from Canaanites whom Joshua had expelled from Palestine (Haven 1856: 27-28).

As European colonization pressed westward from the 1790s to the end of the nineteenth century, racial myths gradually replaced religious ones as a justification for waging war on the Indians and violating their treaty rights. It was widely maintained that Indians were brutal and warlike by nature and biologically incapable of significant cultural development. They were also pronounced to be incapable of adjusting to a European style of life and hence destined to die out as civilization spread westward. Many white Americans saw these arrangements as the manifestation of "a mysterious Providence" (Thruston 1890: 15). This view of Indians as being primitive, alien, and part of America's past had archaeological implications. It suggested that in prehistoric times Indian cultures had remained static and simple.

As archaeological research developed more systematically following the establishment of the American Antiquarian Society in 1812, it did so within a framework that for several decades continued to be dominated by Biblical concepts. Human beings were viewed as a relatively recent creation, and all the peoples of the world were believed to be derived by migrations from the Garden of Eden, located in the Near East. After the middle of the nineteenth century, American anthropologists began to be influenced by a growing European interest in cultural evolution. This interest accorded with a preoccupation with progress in the United States, which reflected both contemporary economic growth and the strong continuing influence of the philosophy of the Enlightenment.

An enthusiasm for evolution and a pride in things American also prompted some antiquarians to try to demonstrate that the Western Hemisphere could boast indigenous cultural achievements rivaling those of Europe. The most spectacular evidence of ancient glories appeared to be the stone cities that John L. Stephens had discovered in the jungles of Central America in the 1840s. Yet, even so, most American anthropologists tended to doubt that the cultures of Mesoamerica had been as advanced as either their Spanish conquerors or the historian W. H. Prescott had claimed. The influential ethnologist, Lewis Henry Morgan, took great pains to argue that the cultural achievements of the Aztecs and the Iroquois were little different; both were examples of Middle Barbarism, which was the highest stage of development reached by any native people of the New World (Morgan 1881). Moreover, none of the apparently more advanced cultures extended into the territory of the United States. It was agreed that all the Indians who lived north of the Rio Grande had possessed simple Stone Age cultures, which was evidence of their unprogressiveness. Only limited interest was shown in interpreting cultural differences among the Indian societies of the nineteenth century in terms of an evolutionary hierarchy. Toward the end of the century, this view of the American Indians was further reinforced by growing doubts about the inevitability of cultural progress that had begun to influence the interpretation of archaeological data in Europe after 1860 (Trigger 1978a: 64).

The idea that Indian cultures were inherently static and primitive was reflected in a number of ways in the interpretation of archaeological data prior to 1914; several of these are discussed below.

1. There was a general lack of concern with cultural change on a lesser scale than from one major cultural stage to the next, as from the Palaeolithic to the Advanced Stone Age, or from the Neolithic to the Bronze Age (Rowe 1962: 399-400; Warren 1973: 219). This attitude reflected and reinforced the common assumption that the failure of Indian groups to evolve beyond the Stone Age indicated that they had not advanced at all. The lack of awareness of less dramatic changes cannot be attributed wholly to a dearth of stratified sites or lack of knowledge among American archaeologists as to how to deal with them (cf. Willey & Sabloff 1974: 89). As Gordon Childe (1932: 207) pointed out, the lack of stratified post-Pleistocene sites among those that were known in Northern and Western Europe in the nineteenth century did not inhibit the construction of detailed cultural chronologies in that region, mainly using crude forms of seriation. In America, during the latter part of the nineteenth century, shell-heaps were studied, both typologically and stratigraphically, using European archaeological reports as models, and on the basis of these studies cultural changes were noted. In particular, such observations were made by Jeffries Wyman (1875), S. T. Walker (1883), and C. B. Moore (1892) in the southeastern United States; William Dall (1877) in Alaska; and the German archaeologist Max Uhle (1907) in California. The evidence of local cultural change which these archaeologists adduced was generally rejected or dismissed as being of trivial importance by contemporary archaeologists (Thomas 1898: 30-36). Discussing Uhle's evidence for "the gradual elaboration and refinement of technical processes" within the Emeryville shell mound, A. L. Kroeber (1909: 16) proposed that the native cultures of central California had been so primitive even in historic times as to rule out on a priori grounds the idea that there could have been significant cultural change in the past.

2. The systematic study of cultural variation in the archaeological record was oriented primarily toward defining geographical rather than chronological patterns. This paralleled the tendency of American ethnologists, late in the nineteenth century, to organize the study

of cultural similarities and differences in terms of cultural areas. In 1887, Franz Boas had argued that the ethnological material from across the United States that was accumulating in major museums should be exhibited according to geographical areas and tribes rather than in terms of hypothetical evolutionary sequences or typological divisions applicable to the entire continent. The ethnologist, Otis T. Mason, although interested in cultural evolution as a universal phenomenon (Mason 1895), published the first detailed treatment of the cultural areas of North America in 1896 and was followed in this approach by Clark Wissler (1914). Archaeologists had long been aware of geographical variations in the distribution of some classes of archaeological data. In 1848, E. G. Squier and E. H. Davis assigned the mounds of the eastern United States to three zones: the effigy mound region of the Upper Great Lakes, the area of symmetrical enclosures in the Ohio Valley, and a belt of truncated mounds farther south. Cyrus Thomas (1894) later divided these mounds into eight geographical units, which he suggested represented more than one nation or group of tribes. Still later, in his *Introduction to the Study of North American Archaeology*, he divided all of North America into three major cultural zones: Arctic, Atlantic, and Pacific, the latter being subdivided into several districts (Thomas 1898). J. D. McGuire (1899) examined the distribution of different types of Indian pipes, separating the United States into fifteen geographical divisions; in 1903 W. H. Holmes, utilizing detailed stylistic analysis, defined a series of pottery regions for the eastern United States. In 1914, Holmes divided the whole of North America into twenty-six "cultural characterization areas" on the basis of archaeological data in a manner which paralleled the procedures then being followed by ethnologists. It was characteristic of this approach that, although Thomas (1898: 13) accepted the universality of certain broad general categories, he believed that any detailed typological classification could apply only in a single geographical region. This was the opposite of trends in Europe, where Oscar Montelius and other archaeologists had applied developmental typologies on a continental scale (Gräslund 1974).

3. The third characteristic of this period was a tendency to see individual cultural patterns as the exclusive possessions of particular peoples. This also became characteristic of European archaeology late in the nineteenth century, when considerable attention was

paid to tracing the prehistory of various ethnic groups in the archaeological record, but it had not been a prominent feature of European archaeology prior to the 1880s (Trigger 1978a: 80-81). There was also a tendency to assume that the culture of each prehistoric Indian tribe tended not to change through time. Evidence of change in the archaeological record generally was interpreted as resulting from movements of people rather than from alterations within individual cultures. For example, late in the nineteenth century the change from what would now be called Middle to Late Woodland cultures in upper New York State was attributed to an incursion of Iroquoian-speaking peoples who brought their own distinctive culture from the south and displaced the Algonkians who were believed to have lived in the region previously (Beauchamp 1900; Parker 1907). R. B. Dixon (1913) saw the complexity of the archaeological record in eastern North America as a palimpsest resulting from repeated shifts of population in antiquity. Much later, the economic historian, George T. Hunt (1940: 13), characterized such movements as a "slow flux of native population, the advance and recession of tribes and cultures, which is always found in and is perhaps an inevitable characteristic of aboriginal life on a large and thinly populated continent." The implication was that such movements were neither particularly comprehensible nor significant. This was precisely the view that archaeologists had held much earlier.

4. It was also generally accepted that, where there had been no major shifts in population, it was a relatively simple matter to use ethnographic data concerning tribes that had lived in a region in historic times to explain prehistoric archaeological data from that region (Fewkes 1896). Cyrus Thomas (1898: 23) argued that once America had been settled, people tended to remain in the same place; hence the archaeological record of a particular region had been mostly produced by the same peoples who had lived in that region in historical times. He further proposed that such stability might be assumed unless clear evidence to the contrary were forthcoming. Archaeologists, such as Frank H. Cushing (1886) in his Southwestern Pueblo studies, paid much attention to determining by means of close ethnographic parallels what artifacts had been used for and how they had been made. This brought such archaeologists into contact with ethnologists and sometimes with Indians. Harlan I. Smith (1910) attempted to view the artifacts from the Fox Farm site in Kentucky

as illustrative of the life of a prehistoric community. Studies of this sort constitute early examples of the direct historical approach to the interpretation of archaeological data (Thomas 1898: 27; Dixon 1913).

5. It was generally agreed that the archaeological record supported claims that Indian cultures had not experienced major developmental changes in prehistoric times and that Indians were perhaps incapable of such changes. A few archaeologists admitted the likelihood that minor, principally stylistic, changes had taken place among some Indian groups, although they generally believed that little specific could be ascertained about these. Warren K. Moorehead (1910, I: 331), for example, believed some progress likely because "the Indian brain is finer than the Australian or African brain." In the midwestern United States, however, where more archaeological work had been done than anywhere else, it was generally admitted that the evidence indicated that different, and apparently more complex, cultures had flourished in prehistoric times than were observed by the first Europeans to visit that region. The earlier remains were frequently attributed not to prehistoric American Indians but to the "Mound Builders," a non-Indian race that was alleged to have been "more enlightened than the present Indians" (Silverberg 1968: 48). The Mound Builders were believed to have been a people related to the prehistoric Mexicans (or in some views to have had more exotic origins) who, after living in the eastern United States for a considerable period of time, had either withdrawn southward or been exterminated by the ancestors of the American Indians. The latter claim reflected the widespread belief that the Indians were genocidal savages and made the archaeological record appear to be further justification for waging war on them and the seizure of their land. A number of capable archaeologists either rejected or were skeptical about the claim that the Mound Builders had constituted a different racial or ethnic group from the Indians (e.g., Haven 1856; Thomas 1894). Yet in general, archaeologists either credited the Mound Builders with possessing a more advanced culture and denied that they were Indians or accepted them as Indians and claimed that their culture was no more advanced than that of any other Indian group living north of Mexico. Cyrus Thomas (1894), for example, sought to demonstrate that the cultures of the so-called Mound Builders in no way excelled those of the Indian groups who lived in the eastern United States in historic times. Thus the refutation of the Mound Builder

myth tended to involve the wholesale rejection not only of inflated claims that had been made about them (such as that they were able to work iron) but also of many genuine accomplishments of the various Indian groups who had built mounds.

6. Finally, most archaeologists either believed that the Indians had arrived in the New World fairly recently or were disinterested in their very early prehistory. Their recent arrival was sometimes said to explain their lack of cultural development, but in a curious way nineteenth-century Euro-Americans also saw it as lessening the Indians' claims to the land they occupied. During the nineteenth century, some supporters of the theory of polygenesis, which maintained that the fauna of the New World, including humans, represented a separate creation, favored a considerable antiquity for humans in the New World (Haven 1856: 81-105). Yet most polygenists interpreted the separate creation of Indians and Africans as further reason to believe that these groups were different from and inferior to Europeans. Other archaeologists who believed in the high antiquity of humans in the New World thought that the Mound Builders, but not the Indians, had been coeval with Pleistocene fauna; hence the credibility of platform pipes representing prehistoric elephants. Frederic Putnam and C. C. Abbott sought in the Trenton Gravels of New Jersey evidence that would rival in age the Palaeolithic finds that were being made in Europe (Willey & Sabloff 1974: 54-56). Yet many leading archaeologists, such as W. H. Holmes and Cyrus Thomas, remained skeptical about such evidence and on the whole rejected it. Aleš Hrdlička's systematic rejection of all of the Early Man claims that had been proposed into the early part of the twentieth century was effective in large part because it accorded with the opinion generally prevailing among professional archaeologists at that time.

During the nineteenth century, American archaeologists made their greatest contributions to the functional interpretation of Indian artifacts and to defining geographical variations in artifact distributions. They also produced factual evidence which laid to rest the Mound Builder hypothesis, a popular myth which reflected Euro-American contempt for Indians and had helped to justify the seizure of their lands. It was probably not a coincidence that John Wesley Powell, who spearheaded the demolition of this myth, was a Euro-American who acknowledged that "cruel and inexcusable" wrongs had been inflicted on the Indians (Silverberg 1968: 170). Most archaeologists, whether favorably disposed toward living Indians or not, tended to regard them as static and primitive. Some limited awareness had been gained of cultural change in prehistoric times, but in general this evidence was either ignored or explained in terms of shifts in population rather than as internal cultural transformations. In 1913, B. Laufer was to identify a lack of chronological perspective as the main weakness of American archaeology. Willey and Sabloff (1974: 88) see the efforts to correct this deficiency as marking the beginning of their Classificatory-Historical period (1914-1960).

Chronological Archaeology

The interest in cultural chronology that characterized American archaeology after 1914 at least partly reflected recent developments in European archaeology and American ethnology. These developments involved the rejection of unilinear evolution and an increasing emphasis on inductive and historical approaches. We have already noted that after 1880 Neolithic and Bronze Age archaeology in Europe largely focused on tracing the prehistoric development of various ethnic groups. This preoccupation reflected the growing political importance of nationalism in Europe at that time. The new "historical" rather than "evolutionary" approach to the analysis of archaeological data resulted in growing attention being paid to the significance of geographical as well as chronological variation in the archaeological record. About the beginning of the twentieth century, this led archaeologists for the first time to define archaeological cultures, starting in central Europe (Meinander 1981). These cultures were associated with specific peoples and formed the basis of spatio-temporal mosaics which replaced evolutionary stages as the basic framework of archaeology (Trigger 1978a: 75-95). The potential of this new approach was strikingly exemplified in the works of Gustaf Kossinna (1911) and V. G. Childe (1925). Studying the past in terms of cultures also resulted in greater attention being paid to small-scale changes in the archaeological record, since these were of more interest in terms of ethnic history than they had been from an evolutionary perspective.

Some awareness of the new fashions in European archaeology began to be transmitted to America, after 1890, by Franz Boas (Willey & Sabloff 1974: 89). More importantly, Boas brought to American anthropology a broader awareness of the special concern that German ethnologists had developed for systematically comparing cultures and culture complexes. Such studies had been fostered by the publications of the ethnologist and geographer Friedrich Ratzel in the 1880s. These had originally stimulated the elaboration of the concept of the archaeological culture in Europe. Boas also encouraged an archaeological concern with small-scale change by advocating the value of a historical approach as a technique for explaining cultural variation, even if he and his students did not assign archaeology an important role within this approach (Sapir 1916). In addition, his persuasive advocacy of cultural relativism and his wholehearted rejection of prevailing racist interpretations of human behavior encouraged the view that Indians were capable of change.

These developments encouraged American archaeologists to try to construct cultural chronologies and to delineate small-scale changes that had taken place in prehistoric times. While pejorative comments about the nature and ability of Indians became less overt in archaeological publications, functional interpretations also grew less important, and archaeological interest tended to focus almost exclusively on the formal analysis of artifacts, with scarcely any consideration being given to the Indians who had made them. Thus, at the same time that American archaeology began to study cultural change, it entered a phase in which archaeologists ceased to be interested in Indian ethnography. The resulting failure of archaeologists to reassess their views about American Indians permitted many of the traditional negative stereotypes that had been formulated prior to 1914 to continue influencing the interpretation of archaeological data. This impeded the progress of the discipline in many ways.

In America, archaeological cultures were first defined as information concerning regional cultural chronologies began to transect existing knowledge of geographical variations in the archaeological record. This was the opposite of what happened in Europe, where archaeological cultures were defined as data concerning geographical variations in culture supplemented well-established sequences of cultural development. The differing manner in which the concept of cultural units was applied to archaeological data in Europe and in America indicates that this concept had evolved independently, though from a common stock of anthropological ideas, in the two hemispheres. Such a separate evolution explains why the concept of the archaeological culture was already being used in parts of America before it had spread from Central to Western Europe (Trigger 1978a: 80-93).

It was not accidental that the concept of the archaeological culture was first, though rather unsystematically, applied in the American Midwest, the one area where an awareness of sequential cultural change had been well established in the nineteenth century. In 1832, William Henry Harrison had pointed out that in the interval between the Mound Builders and the unsettled Indian refugee population that had lived in the Ohio Valley in historic times, the region had likely been inhabited by another group of farming Indians; while, in 1888, Frederic Ward Putnam had argued that there had been a succession of mound-building races in the Ohio Valley (Silverberg 1968: 78, 198-199). In 1890, G. P. Thruston described the material associated with the stone grave cemeteries of Tennessee and neighboring states as the remains of a single tribe or group of related tribes, hence as a de facto archaeological culture (1890: 5, 28). By 1902, William C. Mills was using cultural similarities to define geographically and temporally bounded entities that he specifically labeled the Fort Ancient and Hopewell cultures, although the chronology of these cultures remained uncertain. In 1909, W. K. Moorehead isolated the Glacial Kame culture, while by 1920 H. C. Shetrone had designated still other prehistoric cultures in the Ohio Valley.

In 1913, the cultural chronology of the American Southwest began to be studied systematically; N. C. Nelson and A. V. Kidder did this by means of extensive stratigraphic excavations. Nelson, although he had observed traditional stratigraphic excavations in Europe, initiated digging in arbitrary levels. In 1916 and 1917, A. L. Kroeber and Leslie Spier used seriation techniques to determine the chronological ordering of sites. While they may have known something about the work of the British Egyptologist W. M. F. Petrie (1899), the quantitative method they employed was fundamentally different from Petrie's co-occurrence technique. In technical matters, as with abstract concepts, European influence on American archaeology appears to have been indirect (Willey & Sabloff 1974: 92-102).

In 1924, Kidder defined four sequential cultural stages as being applicable to the Southwest. These periods were refined to become the basis of the Pecos classification that was devised in 1927 (Willey and Sabloff 1974: 110-111). In 1934, Harold and Winifred Gladwin introduced regional differences into this system to produce a series of "phases," which were units closely resembling archaeological cultures. Indeed, they referred to their system as a "method for the designation of cultures and their variations." The Gladwins' hierarchical or dendritic scheme of cultural classification and their identification of major groupings of phases with specific ethnic groups implied that cultures had tended to evolve locally by means of a gradual process of differentiation. This produced ever more cultures, but each was of decreased geographical extent.

In 1932, William C. McKern (1939), building on Shetrone's work, formulated the Midwestern Taxonomic Method, a dendritic system of classification that was applied to the archaeological material of the central United States. Its basic unit was the focus. Although it was maintained that this system was based on typological similarities only and that its taxons did not imply genetic relationships (Griffin 1943:328-338), many archaeologists were tempted to read historical and ethnic implications into its classificatory hierarchies. Like those of the Gladwin system, they were interpreted as implying cultural development in the form of increasing differentiation. In New York State, for example, McKern's Woodland pattern embraced cultures that archaeologists traditionally had associated with Algonkian-speakers, while his Mississippian pattern embraced the cultures of the linguistically unrelated Iroquoians. The assumption that cultures could not evolve from one pattern to another, any more than their people could evolve from one language family to another, severely hindered acceptance of the theory which postulated the gradual development of the historic Iroquoian cultures from local Middle Woodland antecedents (Trigger 1970b). By discouraging the perception of this sort of major cultural transformation in the archaeological record, the Midwestern Taxonomic Method continued to accord with and perpetuate an essentially pessimistic view of the Indian's capacity to change.

Archaeological cultures tended to be defined by trait lists of surviving material culture. The main emphasis in preparing these lists was on the formal definition of artifact types. Not infrequently the lists consisted simply of presence or absence of traits rather than individual abundance (Taylor 1948: 130-135). Archaeologists sought to relate cultures by mechanically comparing the number of traits that they shared or did not share. With this growing preoccupation with the typological procedures involved in the construction of trait lists, the functional ethnographic interpretation of archaeological data ceased to be of importance and was even shunned as speculative and unscientific. Walter Taylor (1948: 73-80) has documented the declining interest in cultural interpretation in the work of W. S. Webb, William A. Ritchie, and other archaeologists during the 1930s and 1940s and has attributed this to the influence of the Midwestern Taxonomic Method. While this explanation is no doubt fundamentally correct, it is worth noting that as early as 1910, Moorehead in *The Stone Age in North America* argued that European contact had so altered Indian life that prehistoric arts and crafts were not to any appreciable extent the same as those recorded by ethnographers or early white travelers. Moorehead (1910, I: 31) used this argument to justify his claim, also made in 1908 by the American Anthropological Association's Committee on Archaeological Nomenclature, on which he had served, that artifacts should be classified by form and material rather than according to supposed use.

A few archaeologists protested that this approach excluded any feeling for archaeological material as the product of human behavior (F. Johnson 1944: 535). Some concern with the behavioral context of archaeological data was also encouraged by a new interest in recovering house plans and community patterns (Lewis and Kneberg 1946). Yet, while the direct historical approach remained important, an increasing awareness of discontinuities in American prehistory limited the situations in which it was believed that this approach could be applied. This too meant that archaeology tended to become more divorced than ever before from ethnography and association with living Indians.

The "classificatory-historical" archaeology that developed early in the twentieth century clearly demonstrated that cultural changes had taken place on a significant scale in many parts of North America in prehistoric times. It thus corrected the erroneous claim that indigenous cultural change had never characterized the American Indians and contributed to a more positive view of the development of native cultures. In spite of this, the new approach exhibited a number of significant limitations in the interpretation of cultural change, which reflected the continuing influence of earlier modes of analysis and unwittingly perpetuated significant aspects of the stereotypes on which these modes of analysis had been based.

1. In spite of their concern for constructing local and regional sequences of prehistoric cultures, archaeologists frequently continued to interpret these sequences in a nondevelopmental fashion and hence to underestimate the degree of internal sociocultural change that they represented. While acknowledging cultural change, both the Gladwin and the McKern systems preserved important elements of the static culture area approach to archaeology. Cultural variation was interpreted mainly as a product of differentiation within a fixed geographical framework (Willey & Sabloff 1974: 111-113). The process these systems had in mind seems to have been closer to random genetic drift in biology than it was to the mechanisms of cultural evolution. Gradually, however, the classificatory hierarchies were abandoned and their basic units—phases and foci—were ordered into local and regional sequences that were empirically determined.

2. This development permitted archaeologists to credit diffusion with having played a major role in cultural development. Nevertheless, diffusionist explanations were employed in a manner which severely restricted the degree of creativity that was seen as characterizing North American Indians. These explanations suggested that the Indians were essentially imitative, with creative impulses coming from elsewhere. In the latter part of the Classificatory-Historical period, the diffusion of culture from source areas as far away as East Asia and Mesoamerica played an important role in explaining cultural change (Spinden 1928; Ford & Willey 1941; F. Johnson 1946).

3. While allowing that cultural change had taken place, many archaeologists still tended to view cultures as the possessions of particular peoples and attributed major cultural changes to migrations. For example, the transitions from the Archaic to the Woodland pattern and from Woodland to Mississippian in the northeastern United States were interpreted as resulting from the entry of new populations into that region. Transitional cultures, when recognized, were often interpreted as ones that had been produced when an invading group mingled with the indigenous inhabitants (Wintemberg 1935).

4. Interpretations of archaeological data were characterized by a lack of will to discover, or even to search for, any overall pattern to American prehistory. By contrast, European prehistory continued to be studied as a chronicle of the progressive development and achievements of the ancestors of particular European peoples, or of Europe-

ans as a whole, even after a concern with ethnic groups had replaced evolutionary progress as the major focus of archaeological interest. However disreputable or naive these motivations for research may now appear to have been, they frequently stimulated detailed analysis and a sharply focused interpretation of the archaeological record. The benefits are evidenced by comparing V. G. Childe's *The Dawn of European Civilization* (1925), which had as its main theme the novel and creative uses to which prehistoric Europeans had put the technological innovations that reached them from the Near East, with *Indians before Columbus* by Martin et al. (1947). The latter is basically a catalogue of prehistoric cultures; it makes some limited attempts at cultural reconstruction and the delineation of regional sequences, but it does not attempt to discern or account for any significant developmental patterns. J. A. Ford and G. R. Willey (1941) did try to do the latter for eastern North America in their "An Interpretation of the Prehistory of the Eastern United States," but, as Willey later noted, they attributed the cultural development of this region almost entirely to successive influxes of people and ideas from Mesoamerica. They, as well as other archaeologists, stressed exotic influences rather than the richness of the local heritage as the principal source of change (Willey & Sabloff 1974: 122).

Hence, while between 1914 and 1960 cultural change and development were perceived for the first time as being a conspicuous feature of the archaeological record for North America, the main product of this period was a series of regional cultural chronologies. The stereotypes of the American Indian that had been formulated before 1914 remained, for the most part, unchallenged. Cultural change continued to be attributed largely to migration and diffusion, and little importance was attached to understanding the dynamics of internal development. In general, there was less concern than there had been previously with reconstructing prehistoric patterns of life, so that the links between archaeology and ethnology were also weakened. It is perhaps misleading to describe this as being a "classificatory-historical period"; it was essentially a "classificatory-chronological" one.

Processual Archaeology

Beginning in the late 1930s, a few archaeologists and interested ethnologists, notably W. D. Strong, Paul Martin, J. H. Steward, F. M.

Setzler, and Clyde Kluckhohn, began to express dissatisfaction with the chronological and descriptive objectives of American archaeology and to urge the need for more functional analyses of archaeological data. They also stressed the desirability of closer cooperation between archaeology and ethnology in order better to understand cultural change and development (Willey & Sabloff 1974: 133-134). Their concerns were elaborated by Walter Taylor (1948), Gordon Willey (1953), and others and helped to produce the routine concern with elucidating process that now characterizes New or processual Archaeology. A major objective of this approach is to understand the internal dynamics of changes that are observed in the archaeological record. This has encouraged some archaeologists to conduct extensive ethnographic research in an effort to acquire a better understanding of regularities that are relevant for interpreting archaeological data. In particular, they are concerned with regularities relating to material culture, which ethnologists have generally ignored. Ethnoarchaeological research of this sort has brought a larger number of archaeologists into contact with living native peoples than ever before (Binford 1977a; Gould 1978a).

Yet, in spite of this, relations between archaeology and native peoples are not good. As Indians and Inuit have become politically more active, they have become increasingly articulate about the white man's treatment of their heritage. They have denounced archaeologists for desecrating the graves and village sites of their ancestors and for failing to respect their cultural values (Johnston 1976; Swinton 1976). In many jurisdictions they have sought to stop or to control archaeological research and have won much sympathy and support both from the general public and from politicians. More significantly, their actions have created a moral as well as a legal crisis for many archaeologists. While individuals have attempted to deal with this challenge in a piecemeal fashion, and in some instances have done so successfully, archaeologists have so far largely failed to grapple collectively with the more fundamental implications of the challenge they are confronting. They have not begun seriously to assess archaeology's moral and intellectual responsibility to native people.

The past history of American archaeology does not provide the basis for a convincing refutation of many of the charges that native people have leveled against the discipline. In the nineteenth century, much archaeological interpretation had close affinities with popular Euro-American myths which alleged that the Indians were savages who lacked the will and even the biological capacity to progress. Indeed, archaeological research did much to provide these myths with seeming substance. Later, as archaeologists became more interested in cultural chronology, they tended to treat prehistoric data typologically and to ignore the connection between these data and living native peoples.

In spite of a renewed interest in ethnoarchaeology, processual archaeology has not provided the basis for an improved relationship between archaeology and native people. A. V. Kidder (1935: 114) and Clyde Kluckhohn (1940) were among the first to propose that the ultimate goal of archaeological research should be to establish generalizations about human behavior and cultural change. Walter Taylor (1948: 156-157) and G. R. Willey and P. Phillips (1958: 5-6) also saw such generalizations as providing a common anthropological focus for archaeological and ethnological research. In the United States social scientists have tended to treat historical research as being of little importance (Bronowski 1971: 195). Instead, they have sought to produce universally valid generalizations (or indeed any kind of generalizations) that might be claimed to be of practical value for the improvement and management of contemporary societies. Hence it is not surprising that the New Archaeology has generally stressed the production of such knowledge as being its ultimate objective. Nor is it surprising that most American archaeologists should now feel it appropriate to pay at least lip service to this utilitarian and socially prestigious goal as being the appropriate one for their discipline. Historical interpretation has been dismissed as unsuitable to play more than "a role in the general education of the public" (Binford 1967a: 235).

Yet, by treating generalizations about human behavior as being the primary or even the only significant goal of archaeological research, archaeologists have chosen to use data concerning the native peoples of North America for ends that have no special relevance to these people. Instead, they are employed in a clinical manner to test hypotheses that intrigue professional anthropologists and to produce knowledge that is justified as serving the broader interests of Euro-American society.

It is instructive to compare the positivist and antihistorical attitudes that many American archaeologists persist in adopting toward their data with the strong ties that continue to link archaeology and history in Europe, even among archaeologists who are strongly influenced by American New Archaeology (Clarke 1968: 12, 358). There archaeological data continue to be valued for the far from neutral interpretations they allow of the prehistoric cultural development and ethnic history of Europe. It is significant in this respect that the major controversies in European archaeology during the past decade have centered primarily on the implications of bristlecone pine calibrations of radiocarbon dates. These calibrations have been interpreted by some archaeologists as minimizing the role of cultural stimuli from the Near East and implying greater primacy for Central and Western Europe in prehistoric as well as modern times (Renfrew 1973a). While it must be allowed that the social sciences as a whole are generally less favorably disposed toward a historical approach in the United States than they are in Europe, it seems not unjust to interpret the emotionally detached and ahistorical attitude that many modern American archaeologists have adopted toward their data as also reflecting Euro-American archaeology's continuing alienation from the native peoples whose cultural and physical remains are being studied. Viewing the Indians' past as a convenient laboratory for testing general hypotheses about sociocultural development and human behavior may be simply a more intellectualized manifestation of the lack of sympathetic concern for native peoples that in the past has permitted archaeologists to disparage their cultural achievements, excavate their cemeteries, and display Indian skeletons in museums without taking thought for the feelings of living native peoples. If prehistoric archaeology is to become socially more significant, it must learn to regard the past of North America's native peoples as a subject worthy of study in its own right, rather than as a means to an end.

This can be accomplished without sacrificing any of the scientific rigor or the urge to explain archaeological data that characterizes the New Archaeology. Prior to the 1930s, ethnologists were generally uninterested in systematically studying the transformations that Indian societies had experienced since European contact. Indeed, these transformations often were viewed as an impediment to ethnographic research, which sought to reconstruct what Indian societies had been like prior to having been disrupted by European contact. A significant interest in postcontact Indian history began with studies of acculturation during the 1930s (Redfield et al. 1936; Linton 1940). These studies later evolved to become ethnohistory or what has recently been labeled Indian or native history (Trigger 1978b: 20). This development, together with the greater urgency that is being accorded to studies of contemporary changes among native peoples, has led ethnology away from its traditional concern with Indian cultures as static entities which exist in a timeless historic present. It is now realized that Indian cultures must be studied as undergoing a continual process of adjustment and change. Ethnologists have also become aware of the naiveté and anachronistic nature of many previous attempts to reconstruct native cultures as they were assumed to have been prior to European influence and domination (Brasser 1971). An analogous development of interest in social change among British social anthropologists is tending to eliminate the distinction between social anthropology and social history (e.g., Macfarlane 1970).

Archaeological findings are in accord with this trend in that they have long made it clear that cultural change did not begin for American native peoples as a result of European contact. On the contrary, change and re-adaptation have characterized all periods of Indian prehistory. It also seems that in many instances native responses to the challenge of European contact were shaped by experiences of cultural change in prehistoric times (Trigger 1976: 175-176). The New Archaeology has provided, and will continue to provide, valuable insights into the significance of archaeological data. These insights permit archaeologists to formulate more detailed and better-informed explanations of temporal changes in the archaeological record than were possible before 1960. Archaeologists are hence better able to interpret their data as an extension of document-based Indian history, just as European archaeologists treat their prehistory as an extension into the past of European history. To do this effectively, however, American archaeologists must learn to understand that historical research when applied to prehistory does not consist only of establishing cultural chronologies and studying stylistic configurations. It must be accepted that explaining historical events is (or can be made) a scientific process involving functional and systemic analysis which is closely linked to, though different in its primary objective from, establishing generalizations about human behavior (Trigger 1978a: 19-52). Contrary to Spaulding's (1968) claim, scientific history seeks whenever possible to base its explanations, not on personal opinion, but on well-established theories of human behavior. Some sense of what can be accomplished in explaining regional prehistory can be gained from Martin and Plog's (1973) *The Archaeology of Arizona*, if that work is considered stripped of its dogmatism, polemic, and simplistic assertions about the possible contemporary applications of archaeologically derived regularities. Yet even that book makes little attempt to explain specific historical events that are of interest to current Indian groups. Good examples of the historical use of archaeological data can also be found in some ethnohistorical works, such as Alfonso Ortiz's *New Perspectives on the Pueblos* (1972).

Archaeological research stands to gain by adopting a historical perspective. Despite the limited unifying effect of its considerable commitment to the study of cultural ecology, New Archaeology consists of groups and individuals innovating along many different lines and in respect of problems that are very different from one another. Because of this, New Archaeology tends toward a display of idiosyncratic intellectual virtuosity, without more long-term substantive goals being clearly in evidence. The special importance that New Archaeology has attached to the deductive approach has encouraged many archaeologists to use their data to examine closely only the particular hypotheses that interest them. Some have gone so far as to argue that these hypotheses alone should determine the types of data that are being collected (Brown & Struever 1973). Such attitudes have led to less attention being paid than formerly to such basic operations as defining regional chronological sequences (Trigger 1978a: 16). Even when archaeological studies seek to explain regularities in cultural change over a long period of time, a limited number of variables are generally selected for examination (Plog 1974). In general, relatively little interest is shown in examining broad functional contexts, patterns of diffusion, or regional patterns of development.

I am not suggesting that processual archaeologists should abandon their efforts to use archaeological data to formulate and test general propositions about human behavior. Nor do I suggest that a greater concern with Indian history would by itself eliminate all the problems that beset archaeology's relationships with native peoples. Those native people who base their opposition to archaeology on strong religious convictions are unlikely to alter their beliefs. On the other hand, native people who associate archaeology with the denigration of their past or who have been made to feel genuinely ashamed of that past may eventually be persuaded that archaeology has something more positive to offer them. The fact that some native groups, such as the Pueblo of Zuni, have showed themselves anxious to work with, or even to hire, archaeologists to study their past is a hopeful augury. As a first step, archaeologists must convince native Americans that archaeology has an important contribution to make to the study of Indian history, by enriching knowledge of the Indians in early historic times, helping to resolve what Indian cultures were like at the time of European contact, and, most importantly, by determining how Indian cultures developed over many prehistoric millennia. It must also be made clear that archaeological data have an important role to play in freeing Indian history from an exclusive reliance on written sources, which are overwhelmingly a product of Euro-American culture.

More active participation in the study of Indian history will provide prehistoric archaeology with one important focus for its research. It may also stimulate archaeologists to ask new kinds of questions and to see significant new implications in their data. In particular, as native people come to value archaeological research as a source of information concerning their own history, they may begin to pose questions that will alter and expand the focus of archaeological interpretation in new and exciting directions. Such questioning will be particularly effective if more native people are attracted to become professional archaeologists (Trigger 1978b).

While some archaeologists may fear that a historical approach cannot be objective, especially if particular groups seek to use the findings to promote their own interests, it is doubtful that a scientifically oriented history is any less objective than a nomothetic approach. At a time when the boundaries between social anthropology or ethnology and history are becoming increasingly blurred and when many scholars in both fields see themselves as pursuing common scientific goals, archaeologists need no longer assert a false dichotomy between history and science in order to defend their discipline's scientific credentials. By eliminating the white man's definition of history as studying themselves and of anthropology as the science of allegedly simpler peoples, archaeology may at last transcend some of the false consciousness that is a heritage from America's colonialist past. It is our duty to recognize this heritage for what it is and to overcome it.

4

Alternative Archaeologies: Nationalist, Colonialist, Imperialist

It has long been recognized that there is considerable variation from one country or part of the world to another in the kinds of problems that archaeologists think it worth investigating and in what they are predisposed to regard as acceptable interpretations of evidence. It is widely believed that this variation represents the infancy of the discipline and that in due course what D. L. Clarke (1979:154) called the "unformulated precepts of limited academic traditions" will be winnowed and consolidated to produce a "single coherent empirical discipline of archaeology." It may be questioned whether, in the long run, such "coherence" would be in the best interests of archaeology or whether variability is a better guarantee of scholarly vitality and adaptability. The issue addressed in this chapter is rather whether it is remotely possible to achieve such unity. While the accumulation of hard evidence and the development of new techniques for interpreting these data inevitably constrain wild speculation among professionally responsible archaeologists, it does not appear that national variations in archaeology are disappearing or even significantly diminishing as Clarke's view would imply. A survey of national traditions in archaeological research indicates that they are far from random, which would be the case if they were simply the result of historical accidents. Similar orientations were found in diverse parts of the world that were not especially closely connected in terms of archaeological practice or academic interaction (Trigger & Glover 1981a; 1982). This suggests that something more fundamental than local idiosyncrasies and historical accidents is at work and that examining this variation more closely might reveal important factors that influence the nature of archaeological research.

As a result of these observations, I began to consider what factors might shape similarities and differences in the general orientation of archaeology from one country to another. This chapter presents the conclusions that have been reached so far. I do not claim to be able to explain all the variations of this sort or even to do summary justice to many complex issues that are involved. Doing so would involve considering factors such as differences in the funds and technical resources available to archaeologists in different countries and in the dynamism, charisma, and capacity for innovation among those archaeologists whose research sets the standard for work in various parts of the world. Yet my investigation leads me to believe that there is a close relationship between the nature of archaeological research and the social milieu in which it is practiced. More specifically, I would suggest that the nature of archaeological research is shaped to a significant degree by the roles that particular nation-states play, economically, politically, and culturally, as interdependent parts of the modern world-system (Wallerstein 1974: 3-11). I do not rule out the possibility that different kinds of archaeology (Palaeolithic, prehistoric, ancient, medieval, industrial) may have different social orientations within the same country, but investigating these differences is beyond the scope of this paper. The emphasis is placed primarily on prehistoric and early historical archaeology, which are the two types of most general interest to anthropologists.

It is generally recognized that the development of scientific archaeology corresponds with a specific stage of social development. A systematic antiquarian study of material artifacts as a supplement to written records has been traced back to the Song Dynasty (A.D. 960-1279) in China (Chang 1981: 158-61), to the Italian renaissance in Europe (Daniel 1950: 17-18), and apparently as an independent phenomenon to the Tokugawa period (A.D. 1603-1868) in Japan (Ikawa-Smith 1982: 297-8). A less systematic and perhaps less specifically historical interest in the material remains of the past has been noted for Classical Greek and Roman civilizations and for the later phases of the still earlier Egyptian and Mesopotamian ones (Rouse 1972: 29-30). Yet the notion that the material remains of the past could be a source of information about human history independently of written records had to await the replacement of cyclical and degenerationist views of human development by the widespread intellectual acceptance of an evolutionary perspective (Daniel 1950:

38-56). This occurred within the context of accelerating technological change that characterized the Industrial Revolution in Europe (Toulmin & Goodfield 1966). It was also accompanied by the development of modern nationalism, in which a sense of the solidarity of states became focused less on kings or princes and more on its citizens as a collective group (Wallerstein 1974: 145). At least in Western Europe, the leading role in the development of prehistoric archaeology was played by the middle classes, which benefited the most, economically and politically, from the social changes that were being brought about by the Industrial Revolution. It is perhaps significant that, as early as the sixteenth century in Northern and Western Europe, local antiquarian studies had been an activity of the gentry and middle classes, even if in some areas, such as Scandinavia, they enjoyed royal patronage, by virtue of which they were also to some degree subject to royal control (Daniel 1950: 17-19; Klindt-Jensen 1975: 14-31). In various forms and combinations, nationalism, social evolutionism, and the interests of the middle class have proved to be significant variables in the development of various traditions of archaeological research.

Today archaeologists are employed in most countries or regions of the world. Since 1945, there has been a considerable expansion of archaeological research even in third world countries where economists might consider it a wasteful luxury. The spread of archaeology as a locally based activity throughout the world appears to correlate with the emergence of nation-states within the modern world-system. Yet we are not witnessing parallel developments. Scientific archaeology originated early in the nineteenth century in Scandinavia and diffused from there to Scotland and Switzerland and eventually throughout Europe as a whole (Morlot 1861). Prehistoric archaeology developed in America within the context of an awareness of what was happening in Europe, while Europeans initiated archaeological research in many other parts of the world within colonial or semi-colonial settings, often carrying out the first archaeological investigations and training (as in India) the first generations of local archaeologists. The rapid spread throughout the world of technical innovations in archaeological research, such as radio-carbon dating or flotation, demonstrates the continuing interconnectedness of archaeological investigation on a planetary scale, while the leading role of certain countries in training archaeologists and supplying them to others further reinforces such ties (Murray & White 1981). It is simply not true that local traditions of research reflect the isolation of archaeologists from each other, either in the past or at present.

A final introductory observation is that, while archaeologists generally are caricatured as embodiments of the myopic, the unworldly, and the inconsequential, the findings of archaeology have always been sources of public controversy. Many of these controversies have centered around conflicting claims of national priority and superiority. Scandinavian antiquarians, such as Ole Worm and Johan Bure, engaged in such disputes long before the development of scientific archaeology (Klindt-Jensen 1975: 15-16). Other disputes have been about matters of more general interest. Archaeological evidence has played, and continues to play, a major role in the struggle between evolutionists and creationists, which in turn has a host of additional ideological implications (Grayson 1983). It is also looked to for support by those who believe in or deny the literal truth of the Bible or the Book of Mormon. The widespread belief among supporters of Erich von Däniken that professional archaeologists are willfully concealing evidence of the existence of extraterrestrial benefactors is an extreme example of the bizarre passions that interpretations of archaeological evidence currently arouse. Further evidence of the significance of archaeology is provided by the fact that many totalitarian governments have thought it worthwhile to control the interpretation of archaeological data. A striking example occurred in Japan during the 1930s and early 1940s, when restrictions were placed on prehistoric and protohistoric research that might touch on sacrosanct traditions concerning the origin and early history of the royal family (Ikawa-Smith 1982: 302-4). In some other countries, public beliefs and expectations have been scarcely less constraining. Such examples clearly demonstrate that archaeology operates within a social context. It is reasonable to conclude that, if archaeology is highly relevant to society, society has played an important role in shaping archaeology.

I will now attempt to distinguish three different social contexts, each of which produces a distinctive type of archaeology. I will label these contexts and the archaeology associated with them nationalist, colonialist, and imperialist or world-oriented. These formulations capture only certain broad features of very complex situations. As ideal types, they also fail to express the varying intensity with which the characteristics of each type are realized in specific cases.

Nationalist Archaeology

Most archaeological traditions are probably nationalistic in orientation. The development of European prehistoric archaeology was greatly encouraged by the post-Napoleonic upsurge of nationalism and romanticism. Some of this archaeological activity was directed towards strengthening patriotic sentiments and in these cases it often received substantial government patronage. For example, Napoleon III ordered the excavation of the Gallic fortresses at Mont Auxois and Mont Réa, which illustrated Celtic life in France at the time of the Roman conquest (Daniel 1950: 110). In Eastern Europe, representatives of suppressed nationalities, such as the Czechs, turned to archaeology as a means of glorifying their national past and encouraging resistance to Habsburg, Russian, and Turkish domination (Sklenar 1981; 1983). After the 1880s, as class conflicts became more pronounced in Western Europe, archaeology and history were used to glorify national pasts in an effort to encourage a spirit of unity and cooperation within industrialized states. In so far as it was concerned with Europe, prehistoric archaeology was regarded as a historical discipline.

Denmark provides a precocious example of the development of prehistoric archaeology in Europe. Danish national pride had suffered badly during the Napoleonic period and was to receive further blows from the Germans in the course of the nineteenth century. It is not surprising that the Danes (at first largely upper-middle-class functionaries but later, as they grew more powerful, the lower middle class [Kristiansen 1981]) turned to history and archaeology to find consolation in thoughts of their past national greatness. In particular, they took pride in the fact that Denmark, unlike its southern neighbors, had not been conquered by the Romans. They were also powerfully attracted to the Viking period. Scandinavian archaeologists attempted to reconstruct what life had been like in the past and to that degree their research projected a nationalistic interest in folklore into prehistoric times. Throughout southern Scandinavia, it was assumed that ethnic continuity extended back into the prehistoric period, so that Iron Age, and possibly Bronze Age and Neolithic archaeology as well, were studying the ancestors of the modern Scandinavian peoples. Moberg (1981) has noted the continuing fascination with the Viking period and the disproportionate time and resources that are still devoted to its study.

In modern Israel, archaeology plays an important role in affirming the links between an intrusive population and its own ancient past and by doing so asserts the right of that population to the land. In particular, Masada, the site of the last Zealot resistance to the Romans in A.D. 73, has become a monument possessing great symbolic value for the Israeli people. Its excavation remains one of the most massive archaeological projects undertaken by Israeli archaeologists. For the most part, Israeli archaeologists are trained in historical and biblical research and devote much time to studying history, philology, and art history. Palaeolithic archaeology is much less important and the impact of anthropological archaeology has generally been limited to encouraging the use of technical aids in the analysis of data (Bar-Yosef & Mazar 1982).

In some countries, where the emphasis of archaeology is on the historical period, the situation is more ambiguous. In particular, Egypt and Iran tend to emphasize the glories of pre-Islamic times in periods when nationalistic and relatively secular politics prevail, but de-emphasize them in favor of the Islamic period when political movements favor a pan-Islamic or (in the case of Egypt) a pan-Arab orientation (J. Wilson 1964). During the latter periods, attitudes towards the pre-Islamic period can vary from lack of interest to hostility. In recent years, such shifts have been dramatically displayed with respect to the monuments of Achaemenid Persia.

In Mexico, since the Revolution of 1910, it has been official policy to encourage archaeologists to increase knowledge and public awareness of the pre-Hispanic civilizations of that country. This is done to promote national unity by glorifying Mexico's past and honoring the achievements of the native people, who constitute a large part of the population. It is also intended to assert Mexico's cultural distinctiveness to the rest of the world. An important part of this policy is the development of major archaeological sites as open-air museums for the entertainment and instruction of Mexicans and tourists alike (Lorenzo 1981; Bernal 1980: 160-89). To some degree, however, this policy of integrating Indian peasants into Mexican life by dignifying their past seems to have become a substitute for the far-reaching economic and social reforms that were promised by the revolution.

Despite China's size and potential political importance, its archaeology has been of the nationalistic variety. It remains so today, even though the discipline's very right to exist was attacked during the

Cultural Revolution. During that period, the view that the study of the past was itself reactionary led to the disruption of archaeological excavations and publications and to attacks on some archaeological sites. Today archaeology is extensively encouraged as a means of cultivating national dignity and confidence, though at least lip service is paid to a socialist ideology by interpreting the past in terms of a Marxist perspective and by lauding cultural achievements as testimonials to the skills of worker-artisans in ancient times. As of 1984, the interpretation of the archaeological record remained in accord with the northern-centered views of traditional Chinese historiography and centrist politics (Chang 1981; W. Watson 1981). The importance of southern China as an area of independent cultural development was recognized only by some Western archaeologists and by Vietnamese archaeologists who rejected the view that northern China was the only significant center of cultural development in East Asia. The latter see in the archaeological record of southeast Asia evidence of a "deep and solid basis" for Vietnamese culture which, despite heavy pressure, "refused to be submerged by Chinese culture while many other cultures ... were subjugated and annihilated" (Van Trong 1979: 6).

Although Germany had imperialist ambitions, its prehistoric archaeology never transcended the limits of a nationalistic tradition. In the nineteenth and early twentieth centuries, patriotic German archaeologists sought to project far back into prehistoric times the ethnic continuity that historians maintained had characterized their homeland throughout the historic period. Gustaf Kossinna (1911; 1912) sought to demonstrate archaeologically that Germany was the homeland of the Indo-European peoples and the center of cultural creativity in prehistoric times. While the other Indo-European-speaking peoples had moved off and interbred with allegedly inferior races, the Germans alone had preserved their racial purity and hence their full powers of creativity (Klejn 1974). While such views were a powerful stimulus to nationalism and were enthusiastically endorsed by prominent Nazi leaders, they failed because of their parochial nature to attract major support among archaeologists elsewhere.

The primary function of nationalistic archaeology, like nationalistic history of which it is normally regarded as an extension, is to bolster the pride and morale of nations or ethnic groups. It is probably strongest amongst peoples who feel politically threatened, insecure, or deprived of their collective rights by more powerful nations or in countries where appeals for national unity are being made to counteract serious divisions along class lines. Nationalistic archaeology tends to emphasize the more recent past rather than the Palaeolithic period and, in particular, to draw attention to the political and cultural achievements of ancient civilizations or other societies. There is also, as Daniel Wilson (1876, 1: 247) noted long ago, a tendency to glorify the "primitive vigor" and creativeness of peoples assumed to be national ancestors.

Colonialist Archaeology

By colonialist archaeology I mean archaeology that developed either in countries whose native population was wholly replaced or overwhelmed by European settlement or in ones where Europeans remained politically and economically dominant for a considerable period of time. In these countries, archaeology was practiced by a colonizing population that had no historical ties with the peoples whose past they were studying. While the colonizers had every reason to glorify their own past, they had no reason to extol the past of the peoples they were subjugating and supplanting. Indeed, they sought by emphasizing the primitiveness and lack of accomplishments of these peoples to justify their own poor treatment of them. While history and the specialized social sciences, such as economics and political science, studied the accomplishments and behavior of white people in Europe and around the world, the study of colonized peoples, past and present, became the domain of anthropology. Modern native peoples were seen as comparable only to the earliest and most primitive phases of European development and as differentiated from Europeans by possessing no record of change and development and hence no history.

The oldest and most complex example of colonialist archaeology was that which developed in the United States. Long before the beginnings of significant antiquarian research in the late eighteenth century, native people were regarded as being inherently unprogressive and incapable of adopting a civilized pattern of life (Vaughan 1982). Hence, from the start, archaeologists assumed that their work would reveal little evidence of change or development in prehistoric times. Past and present were not seen as qualitatively distinct and much effort was expended using local ethnographic knowledge to interpret the archaeological finds for a particular region (Meltzer 1983: 38-40). When cultures that were strikingly different from those known in historical times and seemingly much more elaborate were discovered in the Ohio and Mississippi Valleys beginning in the late eighteenth century, it was fashionable to assign these to a lost race of Mound Builders who were distinct from the North American Indians and had been either destroyed by the latter or driven out of North America by them (Silverberg 1968). Archaeology thus identified the Indians not only as being unprogressive but also as having willfully destroyed a civilization, which made their own destruction seem all the more justifiable. Where cultural change was obvious in the archaeological record, it was assumed to reflect not internal development but one static tribe replacing another as a result of warfare or migration. In the absence of satisfactory chronological data, it was widely accepted that elaborate artifacts had been made by the Indians only after they had obtained the metal tools and inspiration necessary for doing so from white intruders. Finally, while some archaeologists sought to discover a North American equivalent for the Palaeolithic period, convincing evidence was not forthcoming until the 1920s, in part as the result of a general reluctance to believe that native people had been established in North America that long (Meltzer 1983).

After 1910, American archaeology became chronologically orientated and it also became obvious that internal changes had taken place within native cultures. Yet, until the 1960s, these changes generally were attributed to cultural diffusion. Moreover, all the major innovations that loomed large in the archaeological record, such as pottery, agriculture, and burial mounds, were habitually traced to a point of origin outside of North America, either in Mesoamerica or in eastern Siberia. This suggested that, while North American Indians were flexible enough to adopt innovations coming to them from abroad, they were not capable of innovating on their own. Throughout what has been called the culture-historical period (1910-1960), major changes continued to be attributed to diffusion and migration (Willey & Sabloff 1980: 109-21; Trigger 1981a).

Archaeology began later and, until recently, was practiced on a much smaller scale in Canada, Australia, and New Zealand than it was in the United States. Canadian anthropologists argued that because of the limited funds that were available for research, it was more important to record the vanishing customs of living Indian peoples than to excavate their prehistoric remains, which it was wrongly thought would survive in the ground for centuries (Jenness 1932: 71). Yet the history of archaeology in these countries has much in common with that of American archaeology. In Australia, the image of the "unchanging Aborigine" (fostered by social anthropologists, by the evolutionist belief that hunter-gatherers possessed the simplest of human life-styles, and by an apparent lack of evidence for a high antiquity of human occupation) discouraged the archaeological study of changes in cultural patterns and ecological adaptations. W. B. Spencer interpreted all differences in the form and function of Australian tools as synchronic responses to raw materials and local conditions and it was thought that a harsh environment rendered the stratigraphic interpretation of deeply buried materials hazardous. The building of chronologies and a more dynamic view of Australian prehistory had to await the 1960s (Mulvaney 1981; Murray & White 1981).

Prior to 1950, such archaeological work as was done in New Zealand tended to be focused on whether or not the prehistoric "Moahunters" were related to the historic Maori. It was generally assumed that everything else that needed to be known about the Maori could be learned from ethnology and oral traditions. Although oral traditions conveyed an awareness of historical events, New Zealand archaeologists did not develop an accompanying sense of change in material culture that would have stimulated the archaeological investigation of Maori (i.e., post-Moa-hunter) prehistory. Culture change was attributed almost entirely to migration (Gathercole 1981).

During the colonial period, archaeologists and ethnologists regarded the so-called tribal cultures of sub-Saharan Africa as a living but largely static museum of the past (Clark 1969: 181). They also tended to underestimate the technological, cultural, and political achievements of African peoples past and present and to attribute such accomplishments as were recognized to diffusion from the north. The role that was assigned to prehistoric Hamitic peoples in transmitting to sub-Saharan Africa a smattering of more advanced traits that were assumed to be ultimately of Near Eastern origin bore a striking resemblance to the civilizing missions that European colonists were claiming for themselves (MacGaffey 1966). There was also a tendency for European archaeologists to devote a larger share of attention to Palaeolithic archaeology than to studying the Iron Age. While there "were few incentives to study cultures that were considered to be 'native' or 'recent'" (Fagan 1981: 49), Palaeolithic cultures were valued because they were judged to be ancestral to European societies no less than to African ones. Later phases of African history were generally regarded as ones of stagnation that were of little general interest (Posnansky 1982).

The most spectacular example of the colonialist mentality operative in African archaeology is provided by the controversies surrounding the Zimbabwe ruins. Early white investigators of these monuments, beginning in 1868, saw them as proof of ancient white settlement in Southern Africa, by Sabaeans or Phoenicians. Cecil Rhodes appreciated the propaganda value of such speculations. When, in 1904, the archaeologist D. Randall-MacIver dated these ruins to the second millennium A.D., he so angered local white settlers that it was almost twenty-five years before serious archaeological research was again carried out there. Although Gertrude Caton Thompson confirmed Randall-MacIver's work and the Bantu origins of Zimbabwe in 1930, local amateur archaeologists kept alive the notion that Zimbabwe was the work of foreign invaders, merchants, or metalworkers. For white settlers, such claims served to deprecate African talents and past accomplishments and to justify their own control of the country. Extraordinarily, in 1971, P. S. Garlake was forced to resign as a Rhodesian Inspector of Monuments because he was unwilling to interpret Zimbabwe to the satisfaction of the white settler government of the day (Fagan 1981: 45-6; Posnansky 1982: 347).

In post-colonial Africa there has been a considerable reorientation of archaeology. As Posnansky (1982: 355) points out, African archaeologists are not necessarily interested in the same problems as are foreign scholars. They tend to be concerned more with recent prehistory than with Palaeolithic archaeology and with problems that relate to their national history. These include the origin of states, the early development of trade, the evolution of historically attested social and economic institutions, and relations among ethnic groups that live within the boundaries of modern African states. There is also an interest in the excavation of famous sites and monuments that relate to the national past. At the same time, anthropology is not well regarded and archaeological research is being increasingly aligned with history, just as ethnological studies are being redefined as sociology (Ki-Zerbo 1981). In terms of the categories being used in this paper, the archaeology of post-colonial Africa is being transformed from a colonialist into a nationalist type.

Colonialist archaeology, wherever practiced, served to denigrate native societies and peoples by trying to demonstrate that they had been static in prehistoric times and lacked the initiative to develop on their own. Such archaeology was closely aligned with ethnology, which in the opinion of the general public documented the primitive condition of modern native cultures. This primitiveness was construed as justifying European colonists assuming control over such people or supplanting them. In Africa and elsewhere where native peoples have regained control of their own lands, archaeology is now severing its connections with anthropology and is being transformed into a branch of history. The situation for archaeology in countries where native peoples have been largely or wholly supplanted by European colonists is considerably more complex and involves new ways of either symbolically co-opting or continuing to ignore native people in changing social conditions.

Imperialist Archaeology

Imperialist or world-oriented archaeology is associated with a small number of states that enjoy or have exerted political dominance over large areas of the world. As one aspect of this hegemony, such nations exert powerful cultural, as well as political and economic, influence over their neighbors. The archaeologists in two of the three cases we will be examining engage in much research in other countries, and play a major role in training students who find employment abroad (this is also true of some nonhegemonous countries). Through their writings, archaeologists in these countries also exert a disproportionate influence on research throughout the world.

The first imperialist archaeology developed in the United Kingdom. Scientific archaeology was introduced there from Scandinavia in the 1850s, at a time when the British middle class was fascinated by technological progress. Britain had become the "workshop of the world" and industrialization promoted by individual enterprise had greatly strengthened the middle class both economically and politically. By offering evidence that such progress was the continuation of what had been going on more slowly throughout human history, prehistoric archaeology bolstered the confidence of the British middle class and strengthened their pride in the leading role that Britain was playing in this process (Trigger 1981a: 141-2). With the development of Palaeolithic archaeology, beginning in 1859, archaeology became more than ever the science of progress in prehistoric times. It is no accident that British archaeologists and geologists played the leading role in winning scientific recognition for this new field (Grayson 1983). The popularizer John Lubbock, whose book *Pre-historic Times* went through seven editions between 1865 and 1913, assured his readers that progress was inevitable and ultimately benefited every facet of human life. He asserted that, as a result of technological progress, future generations of humanity would be wiser, healthier, happier, and more moral than are present ones (1913: 594). Yet in order to counteract anti-evolutionary arguments, he adopted a position that was similar to, and reinforced, that of colonialist archaeology. He believed that technologically less evolved peoples were also intellectually and emotionally less advanced than were civilized ones, to the extent that the most primitive groups could never catch up with more advanced ones and, because of that, were doomed to extinction as a result of the spread of civilization. The study of prehistory was interpreted as proving that, among European peoples, culture had evolved rapidly, while elsewhere it had either developed more slowly or remained static. Through this version of cultural evolution, prehistoric archaeology was linked to a doctrine of European pre-eminence. Lubbock's formulation, which was not conceived in a narrowly chauvinistic fashion, but rather sought to explain the expanding world-system that was dominated by western Europe with Britain at its head, had appeal far beyond Britain itself and served to integrate much archaeological interpretation. Above all, it was echoed in the unilinear evolutionary views of Gabriel de Mortillet in France and provided a broader perspective and greater intellectual respectability for colonialist archaeology, especially in the United States.

By the 1880s, growing economic competition abroad, the proliferation of slums and discontent among the lower classes, and the incipient challenge of working-class political movements caused many middle-class intellectuals in Britain and elsewhere in Europe to have grave doubts about the inevitability of technological progress or its beneficial effects (Trevelyan 1952: 119). British archaeologists grew increasingly uncertain about the creativity even of Europeans, doubted that there was a fixed order to history, and explained cultural variation to an ever-greater degree in terms of biological differences. All this encouraged increasing belief in diffusion as a mechanism of change.

Towards the end of the nineteenth century, British archaeologists accepted the view of the Swedish archaeologist Oscar Montelius that the prehistoric development of Europe had been stimulated by the diffusion of culture from the Near East. Their reactions to this view were deeply influenced by the understanding of more recent British history, when successive waves of invaders and settlers were portrayed as having brought fresh ideas to Britain, which in the long run accounted for British preeminence in world affairs. They did not, as Kossinna had done for Germany, attribute national greatness to their ethnic and cultural purity (Rouse 1972: 72). The achievements of ancient Near Eastern civilizations were appropriated for Western Europe by claiming that Western Europeans, rather than the people who lived in the Near East today, were their true spiritual heirs. British archaeologists also stressed that Britain was located where several streams of cultural influence from the Near East had converged; hence Britain, and especially England, had been able to develop more rapidly than its neighbors (Myres 1911; Childe 1925). Thus, despite growing pessimism about human creativity, British archaeologists continued to stress the capacity of Europeans, and especially of the British, to use innovations creatively. One is tempted to see these developments as evidence of a shift towards a more nationalistic archaeology, and this in turn as a reflection of the growing insecurity of the British middle class.

The second archaeology with a world mission was created by government decree in the Soviet Union beginning in 1929. Prior to that time, many Russian archaeologists had continued the nationalistic approach to archaeology of the tsarist period. While stressing the spectacular achievements of the inhabitants of Russia in prehistoric times, these archaeologists had hoped that, because they studied material culture, their work would satisfy the new political order. In 1929, existing theories and methods were subjected to severe criticism and pronounced to be unacceptable. Archaeologists were called upon to explain change not simply in terms of technological development, as the disciples of Montelius had done, but within the context of social organization. They were required not only to describe archaeological remains but also to reconstruct the society that had produced them. This involved defining that society's mode of production and determining as much as possible about its technology, social organization, and ideological conceptions. Changes were to be seen as coming about as a result of the development of contradictions within societies between different social classes and ultimately between the forces and relations of production (M. Miller 1956: 79).

Marxist archaeologists had to labor under severe ideological constraints. A belief in psychic unity was reasserted and with it a unilinear scheme of socio-economic formations or stages of development that was loosely derived from Friedrich Engels's *The Origin of the Family, Private Property and the State*. No criticism of this scheme was allowed. Under the influence of Nikolai Marr, a linguist turned prehistorian, all discussion of diffusion and migration was suppressed in favor of the belief that each ethnic group had evolved spontaneously in its historical homeland from earliest times to the present. Finally, too much concern with typology and chronological detail was likely to be viewed as evidence of lingering anti-Soviet attitudes (Bulkin et al. 1982: 274-6).

Soviet archaeology presented a world scheme which, while not denying creative powers to any ethnic group, implied that the Soviet Union represented the direction in which all other societies were evolving, thus giving it preeminence in a world-historical sense. Despite the limitations under which it labored, early Soviet archaeology was innovative in many ways. By directing the attention of archaeologists to studying how ordinary people had lived in prehistoric times, it pioneered the careful excavation of settlements, campsites, and workshops. Archaeologists were also encouraged to try to explain cultural change internally in terms of the development of social systems, rather than to attribute it to diffusion and migration. In addition, an interest in the processes of labor encouraged the development of use-wear analysis.

In the period immediately prior to and following the Second World War, the external threat to the Soviet Union produced a strong emphasis in archaeology on tracing the origins of the various national groups that made up the Soviet federal state and in particular on lauding the prehistoric achievements of the Slavic peoples. This attempt to counteract German archaeologically based propaganda had much in common with the nationalistic archaeologies of central Europe (M. Miller 1956: 107-56; Klejn 1977: 13-4). In the post-Stalin era, Soviet archaeology reacquired a more distinctively Marxist orientation, but Soviet archaeologists rejected the excesses of the 1930s. Unilinear views of cultural evolution were muted, diffusion and migration were accepted as historical realities, and there was increasing emphasis on the formal analyses of archaeological data and on ecology. Soviet archaeologists proclaimed that these developments made archaeological findings even more useful for a Marxist analysis of history (Bulkin et al. 1982).

Soviet archaeology counts as a world archaeology not only because it influenced archaeological practice in countries allied to the Soviet Union but also because it offered a view of the significance of archaeological data that, both directly and through the works of western archaeologists such as A. M. Tallgren and V. Gordon Childe, influenced archaeological research far beyond the Soviet sphere of political control.

American archaeology remained colonialist in orientation until the advent of the New Archaeology in the early 1960s. By stressing internal change and adaptation, the New Archaeology eliminated the previous tendency of American archaeology to stigmatize native peoples by failing to recognize their creativity. Yet the New Archaeology took no more serious account of native peoples than earlier versions of American archaeology had done. The goal of the New Archaeology was not to understand prehistory but to use archaeological data to establish universal generalizations about human behavior that would be of practical value in modern society (Martin & Plog 1973: 364-8). That it studied data produced by native peoples was a matter of only incidental concern. The New Archaeology's emphasis on generalizations in part reflects the low prestige accorded to historical studies by American social scientists. It also reflects a general tendency in American society to prefer knowledge that has specifically utilitarian applications (Gardin 1980: 178).

In a more general sense, however, the New Archaeology can be seen as the archaeological expression of postwar American imperialism. Its emphasis on nomothetic generalizations implies not simply that the study of native American prehistory as an end in itself is trivial but also that this is true of the investigation of any national tradition. By denying the validity of studying the prehistory of specific parts of the world, the New Archaeology asserts the unimportance of national traditions themselves and of anything that stands in the way of American economic activity and political influence. Of the three imperialist archaeologies we have examined, the American is the only one that is also explicitly anti-national. Lest this seem too strong a claim, one may point to the aggressive American promotion after the Second World War of abstract expressionist art as the dominant international style, apparently with financial support from the American government as well as from private foundations. As a result of this activity, many national or regional artistic traditions were suppressed or trivialized (Fuller 1980: 114-15; Lord 1974: 198-214).

The impact of the New Archaeology throughout the Western world and in particular in Britain has been very considerable. In recent British symposia, it has become fashionable to invite leading American exponents of the New Archaeology to pass judgment on the proceedings; which usually involves their pointing out to what degree British archaeologists, despite their good intentions, have failed to live up to the exacting standards of the new "international archaeology" (Renfrew & Shennan 1982; Hodder 1982a). Yet, in Britain and the rest of Europe, the New Archaeology has not succeeded in dissolving the sense of an important relationship between past and present and hence of a historical perspective as a significant part of archaeology.

Within American archaeology, interesting developments have taken place in the 1970s. The New Archaeology was primarily a technical innovation concerned with what archaeologists should do and how they should do it. Its view of humanity in relationship to a broader context was provided at first by neoevolutionism; an anthropological paradigm that expressed an optimistic view of technological progress, well suited for a period of economic prosperity and unchallenged political power. During the 1970s, however, this view gave way to a pessimistic and even tragic version of cultural evolution that sees population growth and other factors constraining cultural change to take place along lines that most people do not regard as desirable. The development of food production and urbanism, which previous generations of archaeologists interpreted as desirable products of humanity's ability to solve problems and make life easier and more fulfilling, is now widely viewed as a response to forces that are beyond human control and which throughout history have compelled the majority of people to work harder, suffer increasing exploitation, and degrade their environment. In place of the belief that most important changes took place in a slow and gradual fashion, catastrophic reversals are now seen as common occurrences. Humanity is imagined to be the victim of forces that lie beyond its understanding or control. There is more than a hint in this eschatological materialism that the future is likely to be far worse than the present and that humanity is moving from a primitive Eden, filled with hunter-gatherers, to an atomic hell (Trigger 1981a: 149-51).

This cataclysmic evolutionism is all too clearly a reflection of the growing insecurity of middle-class Americans, who have been troubled since the late 1960s by deepening economic crises and the increasing ineffectiveness of American foreign policy. More specifically it has been influenced by the key expressions of this anxiety: fear of catastrophic environmental pollution, fear of unchecked population growth, and fear of the depletion of non-renewable resources. It is significant, however, that American archaeologists, and the American public, do not treat these problems as national ones that they can debate and solve politically. Rather they situate them within a universal context. Hence cataclysmic archaeology has become part of the imperialistic formulation of American anthropology, with a willing audience amongst the insecure middle classes of other Western nations. This surely reflects the strength of America's conception of its international mission, even in the midst of a serious internal crisis.

Conclusion

The classification I have proposed is not without its problems. Israeli archaeology might be classified as being of the colonialist type, were it not that Israelis claim substantial historical roots in the land they are occupying. Mexican archaeology might also be thought of as an example of colonialist archaeology, as archaeology clearly is in many other Latin American countries. Yet this view does not accurately take account of the complex political and social realities of modern Mexico. German archaeology of the Kossinna school had some of the characteristics of an imperialistic archaeology and these features would undoubtedly have become more pronounced had

National Socialism been militarily successful. Yet this archaeology was nationally too specific and its treatment of the evidence too obviously biased to command respect abroad. It is also clear that nationalistic themes have been strong at certain points in both British and Soviet archaeology. These characteristics tend to blur the distinctions between different types of archaeology and serve to remind us that we are dealing with ideal types. On the other hand, the rapid transitions of American archaeology from a colonialist to an imperialist type or of African archaeology from a colonialist to a nationalist one do not pose problems. Instead, they show the utility of these concepts.

There are also clearly unanswered problems. Why has a country as nationalistic and proud of its past and possessing such important sites as the Republic of Ireland shown relatively little interest in its prehistoric archaeology (Clark 1957: 256-7)? Why does archaeology in India, in spite of its impressive development, continue, as of 1984, to appear so foreign to India and so attached to its European origins (Chakrabarti 1982)? In both cases, religion may provide part of the answer. The present model requires many kinds of elaboration and clarification. Nevertheless, the regularities that have been noted provide evidence that archaeology does not function independently of the societies in which it is practiced. The questions that are asked and the answers that appear reasonable reflect the position that societies occupy within the modern world-system and change as the positions of countries alter within that system. It does not appear likely that the present diversity of views represents merely the immaturity of archaeology or that in the future an objective and value-free archaeology is likely to develop. Instead the past will continue to be studied because it is seen to have value for the present, the nature of that value being highly variable.

This does not mean that archaeologists should abandon the search for objectivity. The findings of archaeology can only have lasting social value if they approximate as closely as possible to an objective understanding of human behavior. But such understanding requires not only paying scrupulous attention to archaeological and other relevant sources of information but also a deeper awareness of why archaeologists ask the kinds of questions and seek the kinds of knowledge that they do. This, in turn, necessitates investigating the behavior of archaeologists not simply as individuals but as researchers working within the context of social and political groups. Understanding of this sort at the level of the world system is both a point of departure and the ultimate synthesis of such research.

5

Archaeology at the Crossroads: What's New?

In the mid-1980s, archaeology was changing and archaeologists were asking the perennial question: was their discipline in serious trouble or did it stand on the threshold of brilliant new accomplishments? What follows was my answer to that question.

* * *

Many prehistoric archaeologists view with considerable trepidation the varied and seemingly disparate directions in which their discipline appears to be developing. There is also growing uncertainty about the theoretical propositions relating to human behavior that have guided the interpretation of archaeological data for the past twenty-five years. Yet, at the same time, acrimonious debates are yielding to profitable dialogues, while archaeology as a whole is coming to appear less sectarian within the broader context of anthropology (Dunnell 1979; 1980a; 1981; 1982; Moore & Keene 1983; Renfrew 1983). All the major changes that are taking place with respect to the interpretation of archaeological data influence to some degree the relationship between archaeology and sociocultural anthropology. To understand where current developments may lead, it is therefore essential to consider how these trends have already altered the relationship that Binford and Clarke defined between these disciplines in the early 1960s (Binford 1962; 1965; Clarke 1968). Paying more explicit attention to this relationship may also help archaeologists to cope more effectively with the problems being posed by the unparalleled accumulation of archaeological data (Gardin 1980), the accelerating destruction of archaeological sites (Wildesen 1982), and the proliferation of expensive and time-consuming new techniques for analyzing archaeological data. It may also assist in finding "compatible goals and field methods" that will bring cultural resource management and academic archaeology closer together (Dunnell 1981: 431).

In the 1950s and 1960s, prehistoric archaeologists emphasized the similarities between their field and the rest of anthropology (Binford 1962; Willey & Phillips 1958: 1-7). Today, whether archaeology and ethnology or social anthropology are thought of as separate disciplines or as two branches of anthropology, it is once again being acknowledged that they exploit different categories of data, which differentiate what each can do and how it does it (Binford 1981a; 1983: 19-26; Clarke 1968; Dunnell 1982: 528; Schiffer 1976). Ethnologists can study directly the complete range of human behavior. They can document the total extent of material culture at every stage of its manufacture, use, and disposal. They can also observe how human beings behave and through the medium of language learn something about other people's beliefs and aspirations. Archaeologists can study only the material culture that has survived varied and often poorly understood processes of cultural recycling and natural destruction to become part of the archaeological record. It is now also widely acknowledged that because of the reuse and disposal of artifacts prior to their becoming part of the archaeological record, archaeological data reveal even less about the contexts in which artifacts were used than was formerly believed. Yet if archaeology must be based to a considerable degree on the study of refuse, it is generally agreed that, if it is to have any broad significance, it must strive to be more than a science of garbage.

The principal challenge that has always faced archaeologists has been to infer human behavior and ideas from material culture. It is now effectively argued that realizing that goal requires a detailed understanding of the archaeological contexts from which data are recovered and also of the systemic relations between material culture and behavior. Binford has labeled generalizations of the latter sort middle-range theory (Binford 1977a; 1981a). His distinction between middle-range theory, which supplies archaeologists with behavioral information, and general theories, which seek to explain cultural change, while challenged on theoretical grounds (Tilley 1982: 36), is of great practical importance because it distinguishes theoretical problems that are of particular interest only to archaeologists from those which are of general interest to the social sciences. Social anthropologists have generally not bothered to search for regularities between material culture and human behavior, since they can observe the latter directly. In recent years this has led an increasing number of archaeologists to do ethnographic research, under the rubric of ethnoarchaeology (Binford 1978; Gould 1978a; 1980; Kramer 1979; Yellen 1977). This involves searching for regularities that will permit them to infer human behavior from archaeological data. Such an allocation of resources is particularly difficult at a time when the archaeological record is being threatened with destruction as never before.

Yet what archaeology lacks in the limited variety of its data is compensated for by its ability to study change over long periods of time. Ethnology is limited by the nature of its data to the present or the near present, although by using external sources of information, such as historical records or oral traditions, some time depth may be obtained. Where specific groups have been restudied, ethnographic field notes and monographs also become historical sources. Yet, even under the best conditions, ethnologists can study change only over very short periods of time. Only by using historical and archaeological data, is it possible to study actual processes of change that occur over long periods (Binford 1983a: 194; Childe 1946b).

New Archaeology

Between 1910 and the 1950s, American archaeology passed through its "culture-historical" phase (Willey & Sabloff 1980: 83-180). Three important features distinguished the archaeology of that period. Most importantly, archaeologists sought to define individual archaeological cultures and to use these units to construct local chronologies or cultural sequences. Second, many archaeologists aimed to learn as much as possible about the way of life that was associated with each of these cultures. This interest had persisted from a still earlier phase of American archaeology, despite a growing feeling among the stricter advocates of formal classification that it was no longer scientific to speculate about what artifacts had been used for (Taylor 1948: 73-80). The third characteristic of culture-historical archaeology was its much-criticized tendency to account for change by invoking external factors operating by means of diffusion and migration.

In the 1950s, there were two important developments in American archaeology. The first was a growing interest in cultural ecology, exemplified in works such as Caldwell's (1958) *Trend and Tradition in the Prehistory of the Eastern United States*. The second was the emergence of settlement archaeology, which was heralded by Willey's monograph on changing settlement patterns in the Viru Valley, Peru (Willey 1953). These developments signaled the start of major efforts to study the adaptive patterns and social organization of prehistoric societies. Settlement archaeology drew attention to the importance of a class of data that had suffered relatively little distortion in the course of abandonment and hence provided valuable information about the contexts in which human beings had lived in prehistoric times. Both approaches encouraged the study of change as processes that were internal to prehistoric societies and enhanced an understanding of their internal structure. There were precedents for these approaches in European archaeology, especially in the work of Grahame Clark (1952; 1954) on ecology and of Clark (1939), Childe (1946a; 1951; 1958), Tallgren (1937), and Soviet archaeologists (Kruglov & Podgayetskiy 1935; M. Miller 1956) on social organization.

The New or processual Archaeology that was formulated in the 1960s maintained that the highest goal of archaeology was not to understand history but to emulate social anthropologists by trying to formulate and test general laws of human behavior. This view had already been enunciated by Kidder (1973: 138), Taylor (1948: 154-157), and Willey and Phillips (1958: 5), although when the latter published they felt that little had been achieved along these lines. By the 1950s, a growing number of archaeologists were smarting from the charge that their discipline was descriptive rather than theoretical in orientation and that they were the not very intelligent playboys of anthropology. Some ethnologists were claiming that their own work was more nomothetic in orientation than it appears to be today (Kluckhohn 1940). This made many archaeologists anxious to prove that they could do whatever ethnologists could. Among this group, the New Archaeologists dedicated themselves to using archaeological data to contribute to the development of a body of generalizing social science theory (Martin & Plog 1973: 364-68; Watson et al. 1971). At the same time, they borrowed from general anthropology, and in particular from the work of Steward and White, a set of concepts that were not shared at that time by a majority of ethnologists and which remain controversial (Harris 1979: 117-341). These concepts were chosen, not because they were demonstrated to be better founded than other ones, but because they appeared to enhance the theoretical importance of archaeological data.

The first of these concepts was the doctrine of neoevolutionism (Harris 1968: 634-53). Neoevolutionism shared with the cultural evolutionary beliefs of the nineteenth century the conviction that all significant differences among cultures can be regarded as differing states of development from simple to complex. Therefore, in accounting for cultural variation, development is the main factor to be explained. Sahlins and Service (1960), in distinguishing between general and specific evolution, allowed a significant role for specifically adaptational as well as evolutionary factors in creating cultural variation. Yet, despite their interest in ecology, archaeologists have been more fascinated by the neoevolutionists' unilinear scheme of development from band through tribe and chiefdom to civilization (Sahlins 1968; Service 1962; 1975). While paying lip service as an ecologist to the concept of multilinear evolution, Steward played a major role in promoting this unilinear perspective with his argument that only parallels (not differences) among cultures are an appropriate object of scientific study (Steward 1955: 209). He also set a bad example by claiming that only one set of circumstances could account for the earliest development of civilizations in different parts of the world. All other complex societies were secondary ones that would not have evolved had the primary ones not already existed (Steward 1955: 178-209). Despite Steward's disclaimers (1953), his treatment of the origins of civilization must be seen as strongly unilinear.

The New Archaeologists also emphasized a systemic view of culture, as settlement and ecologically oriented archaeologists had done previously. Binford stressed that culture was something that individuals participated in differentially, and he adopted from White (1949: 364-369) the concept of individual cultures as functionally integrated thermodynamic systems. He also rejected the Durkheimian view of society that simplistically defined function as the positive contribution that a part makes to the operation of the whole. Durkheim and the British social anthropologists who adopted his ideas had assumed that the various institutions of a society were harmoniously integrated in the same manner as were the various organs that composed a living creature, and they interpreted the lack of such harmony as evidence of social pathology and decay (Harris 1968: 515-67). The New Archaeology quickly replaced this static view of integration, as well as White's rather simplistic concept of systems change, with a model derived from cybernetics that had subsystems integrated by means of positive and negative feedback (Watson et al. 1971: 61-87). This seemed particularly advantageous because it allowed a systemic understanding of cultural change. In general, at that time, social anthropologists were still experimenting very cautiously with a systems theory approach (Rodin et al. 1978). Like social anthropologists, the New Archaeologists continued to view sociocultural entities as systems that are both integrated and clearly bounded.

The third commitment of the New Archaeology was to a materialist perspective that had been introduced into American archaeology not long before as the result of a growing interest in ecology. Yet the formulation of this perspective remained unclear. Archaeologists invoked the technological determinism of White and the ecological determinism of Steward without noting the logical incompatibility of the two (Binford 1962). These views were soon joined by a demographic determinism inspired by the work of the economist Ester Boserup (Cohen 1977; P. Smith 1976), while the economic determinism of Marvin Harris (1979) sought to reconcile all three of the above. All of these formulations are very narrow by comparison with the classical Marxist determinism of the mode of production, and from a Marxist perspective constitute examples of vulgar materialism (Kohl 1981).

The fourth commitment of the New Archaeology was to a deductive mode of explanation and a related insistence upon the equivalence of explanation and prediction (Spaulding 1968; Watson et al. 1971: 3-57). Whatever may be the intrinsic merit of this approach, which is derived from logical positivism, it is clear that in practice the identification of explanation and prediction works best in situations where causality is narrow and direct.

Causality and Integration

Underlying these principles were assumptions that were less clearly spelled out by the New Archaeologists. It was generally agreed that cultures were open systems interacting both positively and negatively with the natural environment and therefore parts of a larger ecosystem (Willey & Sabloff 1980: 191-92). Some archaeologists also paid lip service to the idea that neighboring cultures or societies influenced one another and might therefore be considered as parts of larger sociocultural networks (Binford 1965). Generally, however, these influences were analyzed rather mechanically in terms of processes of diffusion and adaptation as they had been during the culture-historical period (Binford 1972: 91-93; Clarke 1968: 321-55). For the most part, archaeologists studied sociocultural entities in isolation from one another, as if they were closed systems that constituted independent units of analysis. This trend reflected the general rejection of diffusion and migration as acceptable mechanisms for explaining change (W. Adams et al. 1978). It was reinforced when settlement archaeologists such as Gordon Willey (1953), Kwang-chih Chang (1963), Robert McC. Adams (1965), and myself (1965) began to treat the archaeological record as evidence of how the population of a region had modified its economic, social, and political institutions over long periods of time. In such an exercise, the traditional succession of archaeological cultures, defined on the basis of stylistic criteria, served primarily to provide chronological indices. Although the growing interest of archaeologists in explaining changes within sociocultural units or regions was a major step forward, it also represented the temporary abandonment of an earlier archaeological interest in relations among cultures. The tendency to analyze cultures as isolated units was sanctioned by Steward's dictum that every borrowing is an independent recurrence of cause and effect. By this he meant that a culture would only copy a trait from its neighbors if there were a need for it and the effect was the same as if it had been invented within the recipient culture (Steward 1955: 182; for an application see Chang 1962).

New Archaeologists also tended to assume that archaeological cultures were the material remains of tightly integrated cultural systems. They subscribed to the belief of social anthropologists that changes occurring in any part of the system will cause varying degrees of readjustment, and hence change, to occur throughout the entire system. Indeed, the systemic perspective of the New Archaeology stressed a higher degree of integration than did traditional social anthropology. Most New Archaeologists also espoused the deterministic view that changes in limited parts of a cultural system play a disproportionate role in bringing about changes in other sectors (Trigger 1982). A particularly narrow determinism was promoted in the 1960s by Meggers (1960) and Struever (1968: 134-35), who combined various ideas of White and Steward to argue that total cultural systems can be explained as a product of technology interacting with the environment. They maintained that similarities in these two sectors would produce basically similar total cultural systems. Strong determinism of this sort would be required to limit cultural variability to the point where unilinear (or even limited multilinear) evolutionism could adequately account for reality. Something approximating this view continues to be maintained as an ideal by Sanders, Parsons, and Santley (1979: 360), who argue that four or five major ecological variables should be able to account for 80 percent of cultural similarities and differences visible in the archaeological record. Yet these archaeologists honestly admit that they cannot identify these variables or demonstrate such a high degree of causality.

Superficially, a rigid determinism, especially one that is rooted in a materialist causality, would seem to augur well for archaeology. To judge from material appearing in annual surveys such as *Advances in Archaeological Method and Theory*, archaeologists continue to be most successful with reconstructing palaeo-environments and studying technology, subsistence, and long-distance trading networks. They have also made considerable progress in delineating prehistoric demographic trends and social organization, although there is still much circularity in discussions of relations between demographic and other forms of cultural change (Hassan 1981). Hodder (1979; 1982b), Bradley and Hodder (1979), and Wobst (1977) have proposed that stylistic and ritualistic elaboration can be interpreted as evidence of competition and tension within and between cultures. This may make it possible for archaeologists to investigate the class struggle that many social theorists regard as the primary cause of social change (McGuire 1983: 93) and, in particular, to test Marxist explanations of it (Wenke 1981: 97). If controlling for some or all of these factors allowed prediction of less tangible aspects of cultural systems and explanations of how whole systems change over time, archaeologists would be very little disadvantaged by their data by comparison with ethnologists.

Yet such a situation would also be extremely limiting for archaeology since, except for the Lower and Middle Palaeolithic cultures, for which no modern parallels may exist, archaeologists would have nothing novel to explain. All the variations in human societies would be represented by cultures at different levels of development found in the modern world, and these cultures can inevitably be studied more effectively and in greater detail ethnographically than archaeologically. If the only significant difference among societies is the stage of development they are at, archaeology has nothing new or valuable to offer anthropology. It can merely illustrate concretely the past history of specific regions and determine when they passed through different stages of development. At best, archaeology could help to shed light on a few stages of development, such as early civilizations, that are poorly represented in the ethnographic record. The realization of a similar limitation late in the nineteenth century played a significant role in the rejection of unilinear evolution by European archaeologists who were seeking a new and more important role for their discipline. Their realization that evolutionary stages alone could not account for the variations in the archaeological record led to the development of culture-historical archaeology (Trigger 1978a: 54-74; for modern parallels see Kohl 1981: 112). New Archaeologists have countered that archaeological data, because of their continuity and great time depth, are uniquely useful for studying change over long periods and for resolving major issues such as whether cultural change normally occurs gradually and continuously or suddenly in the form of punctuated equilibria (Plog 1973; 1974; Renfrew 1978b; Renfrew & Cooke 1979). I agree that this question is important, but it is not the only sort of important question that archaeologists can hope to address.

Most ethnologists have not found neoevolutionary formulations convincing. They have rejected Boasian historical particularism, which viewed cultures as collections of traits brought together by historical accidents, the result being constrained at most by the psychological compatibility of these traits, as argued by Ruth Benedict in *Patterns of Culture* (1934). Yet most anthropologists do not see evidence of the tight integration of cultures posited by the neoevolutionists. Too many neoevolutionist propositions when examined closely turn out to be special instances being treated as if they were universals. For example, the stage labeled tribal society is often delineated on the basis of New Guinea big-man societies, which have very different social and political structures from native societies in eastern North America that shared the same mode of production and are generally viewed as being at the same stage of development (Whallon 1982: 156). These objections are raised not only by idealists and eclecticists but also by many materialists. White argued that technology determines the general nature of social organization and these two together determine the general nature of ideology. He cautioned, however, that it was not possible to predict the specific content of social organization or belief systems from technology (White 1945: 346). For many materialists causality means that factors such as technology, demography, and the relations of production may restrict the range of possible variation in social organization and patterns of belief, not that they determine the specific content of these aspects of culture (Friedman & Rowlands 1978: 202-4). The observation that there is more variability in social organization and beliefs than in economic patterns provides a powerful theoretical basis for Hawkes' (1954) argument that prehistoric technology, economic behavior, social organization, and religious beliefs constitute a hierarchy of levels that archaeologists find increasingly difficult to infer. Despite the ridicule that the New Archaeology has heaped upon this hierarchy (Binford 1972: 93-94), Hawkes' scale of difficulty shows signs of surviving and even winning over its detractors (Binford 1983a: 16, 32; Haas 1982: 7-8).

During the 1970s, many archaeologists became disillusioned as a result of their efforts to use neoevolutionary formulations to interpret their data. Fried's (1975) argument that many of the more complex phenomena associated with tribal societies were products of acculturation resulting from contact with Western cultures rather than spontaneous internal developments has caused some archaeologists to regard this stage with great suspicion (Renfrew 1982b). Earle's (1977) demonstration that the economy of early historical Hawaii, and by implication those of other chiefdoms, were not based on the centralized redistribution of staples is now widely accepted and has begun to modify the views that archaeologists hold of this stage (Cordy 1981: 25-38; Peebles & Kus 1977). Less attention has been paid to his demonstration that in Hawaii physical coercion was used to extract economic surpluses for the benefit of the upper classes (Earle 1978: 18-19). This observation challenges the idea that institutionalized inequality preceded the development of coercion and the state. The latter position has been popular in American anthropology since it was made central to Steward's (1955: 178-209) trial formulation of the development of civilization. It is also closely related to popular views of American society. We are now beginning to see a growing emphasis on alternative evolutionary patterns with respect to the overall development of complex societies (Blanton et al. 1981; Flannery & Marcus 1983; F. Wiseman 1983) that in some respects represents a return to the multilinear views that were eclipsed among American anthropologists by Steward's work (Childe 1934; Frankfort 1956). There is also a growing emphasis on conceptualizing evolutionary changes in terms of processes rather than patterns (Flannery 1972; G. Johnson 1978; 1981; McGuire 1983; Van der Leeuw 1981b; H. Wright 1969).

Growing skepticism about neoevolutionism also encourages doubts about the assumptions of strong and focused causality on which neoevolutionism is based. This opposition first became evident in archaeology in the form of growing support for a systems theory approach that avoided preconceived ideas about the nature of causality and was conceptualized in a more inductive fashion as a method for searching for regularities. This approach has flourished despite the claim that it is neo-Boasian in its general orientation (Leone 1975). In particular, it has manifested itself in growing claims that political and social, as well as economic, factors play a dynamic role in bringing about social change (Brumfiel 1983; Conrad 1981; Parsons et al. 1982).

Opposition to neoevolutionism has also been manifested in the increasing support for an explicitly societal approach to the study of the past. The early formulations of the New Archaeology by Binford (1962) and Clarke (1968) were framed in terms of cultural systems. More recently there has been a tendency to emphasize social systems (Redman et al. 1978; Trigger 1968b), a position already favored by settlement archaeologists in North America and by Renfrew (1972; 1973b) in England, but with still earlier manifestations going back through the work of Childe (1946a; 1951; 1958) and Soviet archaeologists (Kruglov & Podgayetskiy 1935) to Durkheim and Marx. Gould (1980: 44) has argued that culture is a misleading concept for analyzing human behavior because it "posits an artificial separation between man and the natural world" (see also Dunnell

1981: 434). Other archaeologists have expressed doubts about whether individual cultures are universal or even appropriate units of study (Hodder 1982b: 2-8; Renfrew 1978a; Shennan 1978; Trigger 1968a: 14-15). In particular, it is queried whether, having been designed for the analysis of small-scale, sedentary societies, the concept of the archaeological culture has much value for studying more open hunter-gatherer ones or the complex political structures of the early civilizations (Trigger 1968a: 17-18).

Those who are influenced by Durkheimian sociology see the structured aspect of human behavior as being a network of social relations, with cultural traits, whether they have to do with technology, social organization, beliefs, or values, acquiring their functional significance from their relations to the social system (Harris 1968: 518-19). This view does not deny the importance of culture, or the human capacity for symbolic manipulation and communication, as a crucial emergent property of human behavior, the origins of which can be explained within the scope of a materialist perspective (Woolfson 1982). Yet it avoids the temptation to treat culture as an autonomous system by firmly insisting that its functioning must be understood in relation to the patterns of social interaction by which human life is sustained as human beings interact with each other and their environment. Within the longer perspective of primate development, social systems antedate the emergence of culture. The concept of society thus allows a much more specific view of integration, as well as a more human-centered one, than does the idea of a cultural system. The growing influence of a societal perspective therefore correlates with the abandonment of a narrow technological or ecological causality and of neoevolutionism.

The assumptions of Ian Hodder's structural or symbolic approach reinforce rather than contradict this view. If culture is structured, as the structuralists claim, it is on a cognitive level and hence the ordering is of a different type from the articulations posited by those who view societies or cultures as functionally integrated systems. Structural anthropologists cannot agree to what extent symbolic structuring is shaped by and therefore reflects the material basis of human life (Hodder 1982a: 10-14). Even most of those who claim that there is a causal connection (Deetz 1977; J. Fischer 1961; Lechtman 1977) tend to see it as a loose one that leaves much room for other factors to influence the resulting cognitive patterns. Extreme idealists would deny a direct connection between society and the general patterns underlying human thought, which they would attribute to universal properties of human psychology (Harris 1979: 165-215). Hodder argues that, whichever of these views more nearly describes reality, insofar as human thought and perception play a role in shaping the material basis of human life, the result is to increase random variation in human behavior and to make cultural patterns less predictable (Hodder 1982a: 1-14).

While a viable society can be analyzed as a structured network of human interaction, it is uncertain to what degree either a culture or a society can be accurately described as a system. For a society to survive, certain functional prerequisites must be maintained at an adequate level (Aberle et al. 1950). Beyond that, social scientists disagree whether its parts are interrelated to a considerable degree or there is much room for free variation. We have already noted that there may be more variation in some areas of culture than in others, and it is possible that the degree of constraint varies from one culture to another. The degree to which social or cultural units constitute formal systems is for archaeologists and anthropologists to determine. It is not something that can be assumed in advance, as has been done all too often in the past (W. Salmon 1982; Trigger 1982).

Boundaries

There is also a tendency to abandon the once-fashionable view that societies or cultures are closed or tightly bounded units of analysis that can be studied independently of one another (Kopytoff 1981; Wallerstein 1974: 348; Wolf 1982); the trend now is to pay more attention to the importance of external stimuli in bringing about cultural change. This was manifested in the development of the concept of an "interaction sphere" to explain how Hopewellian ritual patterns came to be shared by many different societies in the American Midwest (Binford 1972: 204; Caldwell 1964). Lamberg-Karlovsky (1975) and others also indicated the need to view Mesopotamian civilization as part of a much larger zone in which from early times many cultures shaped each other's development through various forms of interrelations (Alden 1982; Kohl 1978). There has also been discussion of "peer polity" interaction in prehistoric Europe (Renfrew 1982a) and "cluster interaction" in Mesoamerica (Price 1977). The intensive archaeological surveys of

Sanders and his coworkers in the Valley of Mexico have revealed marked diversities in local patterns of development within that region and the need to study the whole valley in order to understand what was happening in its various parts. For example, the massive increase in population and the growth of urbanism in the Teotihuacan Valley during the Early Classical period can be understood only when it is realized that similar population growth was not occurring elsewhere in the Valley of Mexico, but on the contrary the population was declining (Sanders et al. 1979). R. McC. Adams (1981; & Nissen 1972) has shown the same to be true in his studies of Mesopotamian settlement patterns. This work has severely challenged the belief that events in one area can be interpreted as representative of a whole region. The latter was the view that had guided ethnographic community studies in the 1940s and 1950s and which also pervaded the Viru Valley archaeological project (Schaedel & Shimada 1982: 360).

More recently, Blanton et al. (1981) have pointed out that, because of the high levels of interaction and economic interdependence throughout Mesoamerica in prehistoric times, the development of one region, such as the Valley of Mexico, cannot be understood independently of the rest. They propose to treat the whole of Mesoamerica as a single "macroregional unit." Such a view places prodigious demands upon the information gathering capacity of archaeology. It also raises important questions about how the boundaries of macroregional units are to be established, or if such boundaries can be defined. The core of what is recognized as Mesoamerica clearly was united by intensive and reciprocal economic, political, and religious interaction despite its diverse and often forbidding terrain. Economic and ritual influences of Mesoamerican origin also influenced the cultural development of the southwestern United States and eastern North America, although it is not often possible to determine the social context in which these contacts occurred (Bennett 1944; Ekholm & Willey 1966). Examining interactions of this sort brings archaeologists back to the type of problems that once were studied under the rubric of diffusion.

Recently some archaeologists have attempted to introduce more theoretical rigor into the study of interaction among societies by employing Wallerstein's concept of world systems (Blanton et al. 1981; Ekholm & Friedman 1979; Kohl 1978; 1979; 1987; Renfrew

& Shennan 1982: 58). World-systems theory involves the examination of large-scale spatial systems, assuming an interregional division of labor in which peripheral areas supply core ones with raw materials, the core areas are politically and economically dominant, and the social and economic development of all regions is constrained by the changing roles that they play in the system (Wallerstein 1974). Kohl (1987) has pointed out that the world systems of antiquity probably only superficially resembled those of modern times. In particular, he has suggested that the rankings of cores and peripheries were probably less stable than they are now and that political force may have played a more overt role in regulating these rankings. While this remains to be substantiated, what is important is the growing realization that societies are not closed systems with respect to their neighbors any more than they are with respect to their environment and that the development of a culture or society may be constrained or influenced by the broader social network of which it is a part. There is also increasing recognition that the general rules governing these processes are themselves worthy of scientific investigation. The challenge is to extend a systemic analysis to incorporate what used to be called diffusion.

It is also being acknowledged that not only goods, persons, and ideas but also whole institutions may be transferred from one society to another. The introduction of the Christian church as a hierarchical organization with its own trained personnel into Anglo-Saxon England and of Buddhism into Japan in the sixth century A.D. left a marked and lasting impact on the economic, social, and political organization of these countries that was arguably different from what would have happened had a purely indigenous state cult developed in either of them. In both cases an experienced clerical bureaucracy significantly strengthened the administration of nascent states (Trigger 1978a: 216-28). The fact that societies are open to their neighbors introduces complications that make their trajectories of development harder to predict than archaeologists had previously assumed.

These observations raise additional questions about the scientific validity of the concept of sociocultural systems. No one will deny that there are various boundaries marked by differing degrees of social interaction. Yet can a hierarchy of levels be distinguished in which individuals can be seen as members of families, families as parts of communities, communities as components of societies, and societies forming larger interaction spheres? Or do individuals participate differentially in patterned interaction at many different levels and as members of many different kinds of groups (McGuire 1983)? One must not minimize the importance of brokers and decision makers who, as chiefs, rulers, and government officials, mediate between different levels of society and effect varying degrees of closure. Yet a sober analysis of networks of social, political, and economic interaction calls into serious question the idea that whole societies or cultures are more significant units of analysis than are a series of other units. The entity to be studied is determined by the problem that is being investigated.

Archaeology, History, and Science

Ethnologists have long assumed that the earliest recorded descriptions of native cultures reveal what they were like prior to European contact and that such information can be used without serious question for cross-cultural studies of cultural variation. In North America, archaeology is now revealing that native cultures were vastly altered as a result of European contact before the earliest descriptions of these cultures were recorded by Europeans (Cordell & Plog 1979; Ramsden 1977; Wilcox & Masse 1981). It also seems possible that every hunter-gatherer or tribal society in the world was influenced to some degree by contact with technologically more advanced societies prior to ethnographic study (Brasser 1971; Fried 1975; Monks 1981: 228; Trigger 1981c; Wobst 1978). The San of Southern Africa have been treated as paradigmatic hunter-gatherers. Yet there is growing interest in the ways in which their life has been influenced in recent centuries by contacts with European settlers and with their agricultural and pastoral Bantu and Hottentot neighbors (Schrire 1980). The impact that these groups have had on the southern African environment may also have altered San life in many ways. Under these circumstances, it is dangerous for anthropologists to assume that the San or any other modern hunter-gatherer societies are necessarily equivalent to Palaeolithic ones.

The various economic ties that link modern hunter-gatherers to their non-hunter-gatherer neighbors also call into question whether modern and ancient hunter-gatherer or tribal societies share the same mode of production and can therefore be treated as societies at the same stage of development. Binford has used northern native groups that have engaged for generations in trapping and exchanging furs with the world economic system as a basis for suggesting certain universal generalizations about the nature of hunter-gatherer adaptations in high latitudes (Binford 1980). Some anthropologists believe that, because of their inherent flexibility, the economies of at least some of these groups have not been radically altered by the fur trade; others disagree (Francis & Morantz 1983: 14-15). Only detailed archaeological studies can objectively determine to what extent ethnographic descriptions of hunter-gatherer or tribal agricultural societies provide a representative picture of what these societies were like in prehistoric times (D. Thomas 1974).

Until more such archaeological studies have been made, the significance of major cross-cultural investigations based on ethnographic data must remain in doubt. For example, Driver and Massey's (1957) information about North American Indian cultures was drawn from descriptions of societies that had been altered in various ways as a result of European contact. Other studies have revealed that such data can give a misleading impression of the diversity in precontact cultural patterns (Eggan 1966: 15-44). It is therefore necessary to ascertain what native North American societies were like prior to European discovery before we can fully evaluate Driver and Massey's conclusion that diffusion played at least as important a role as did functional constraints in determining trait distributions among North American societies. Archaeology has an important role to play not only in unraveling the complex history of the past but also in evaluating anthropological problems of major theoretical importance.

It is becoming increasingly evident to archaeologists that ethnologists or social anthropologists, whether concerned with social structure or change, are investigating the results of acculturation, because their data concern small-scale societies that are in the process of being destroyed or incorporated more completely into the modern world system. History and archaeology alone can study the evolution of cultures in the past (Childe 1946b). It is also becoming clear that no society can be properly understood or even classified from a structural point of view without determining its relations to other societies (Wolf 1982). Every society must be understood as the structural transformation of its own previous state, the elements of which were manipulated as part of social and ecological strategies within a context that includes neighboring societies (Friedman & Rowlands

1978; Kohl 1981: 112). The latter not only provided competition but also were sources of new elements for manipulation.

Relations among contemporary societies, especially ones at different levels of development, are as important a stimulus for change and therefore as important an evolutionary force and as legitimate an object of anthropological understanding as are the changes affecting individual societies that have been studied by neoevolutionary anthropologists. Evolutionary theory should not only be concerned with endogenous change. It should also seek to understand how neighboring societies have influenced each other's development throughout history. In particular, archaeologists should be concerned with developing generalizations about how societies, especially those with different kinds of economies, influence each other. Social anthropologists interested in problems of development are already doing this for present day small-scale societies that are being drawn into the capitalist world system. Archaeologists are challenged by the more formidable task of developing similar generalizations for a vast array of precapitalist societies. Alexander and Mohammed (1982) have pioneered this sort of approach by elaborating a frontier model to explain the interaction of hunter-gatherer and early agricultural societies in the Sudan. Golson (1977) has stressed the need to consider competition among different types of hunter-gatherer societies as a major source of change.

By its very nature, a body of evolutionary theory that seeks to explain not only internally generated change but also change resulting from interaction between different societies must be exceedingly complex. It is probably unrealistic to think of such a theoretical structure ever being completely elaborated. It is something that will continue to be refined as long as the social sciences make progress in understanding human behavior. Such a body of evolutionary theory will also tend to be more eclectic and inductive in its origins than the traditional tenets of the New Archaeology would approve. It will, however, provide a more substantial and realistic basis for understanding cultural evolution than has neoevolutionary anthropology, with its almost exclusive preoccupation with endogenous explanations of change. It will also move archaeology closer to the general practices of the social sciences, both methodologically and theoretically.

At the same time that archaeologists perceive the need to broaden the range of their theoretical generalizations, they are also, as we have already seen, acknowledging that individual societies are so complex, their structures so loose, and the exogenous social and economic forces influencing them so eclectic that the precise course of their development can at best be predicted only partially and for the short term. For many archaeologists the complexity of early civilizations, or of any human society, renders the concept of causality meaningless for discussing their origins (Flannery 1972; Rowlands 1982). If historians, after generations of intensive research, continue to debate the reasons for the disintegration of the Roman Empire, it is surely unrealistic for archaeologists to imagine either that the processes they study can be definitively explained by simplistic formulations or that complexity necessarily precludes understanding (D. Fischer 1971). Above all, the prolonged and (by archaeological standards) sophisticated debate concerning the collapse of the Classic Maya civilization demonstrates that more data are needed to narrow the range of possible explanations and permit the formulation of more refined research problems (Culbert 1973). While increasing theoretical sophistication narrows the range of the unpredictable, it is no more possible for social scientists to retrodict the past than it is for them to predict the future with certainty. The explanation of the past is thus by its very nature idiographic, even though general principles must be invoked to support arguments in every possible instance. The complexity of social science data precludes the claim that prediction is the only legitimate form of explanation.

Historical knowledge, in the sense of an understanding of how and why specific societies developed as they did in the past, is essential for explaining their current social structure. As Childe pointed out long ago, the precise form of the British constitution, or of Protestantism in the nineteenth century, could not be deduced from the capitalist system alone (Childe 1936: 110). He was echoing Marx's more general observation that human beings make their history under circumstances inherited from the past (Kohl 1981: 112). Because only archaeology and documentary history can provide the evidence required to delineate cultural development in the past, they are essential for understanding the historical background of the data on which all of the other social sciences are based. The realization that this is so is slowly providing the basis for a new and complementary relation between archaeology and ethnology. It is a relation in which archaeology does not try to emulate ethnology, but by studying the evolution of concrete social systems provides an indispensable basis for producing reliable generalizations about structure and change for the social sciences. Far from being peripheral to these disciplines, archaeology and history become central for understanding them.

Explanations: Universal and Other

The New Archaeology has paid very little attention to studying the cosmology, religious beliefs, values, or even (with the notable exception of lithic reduction processes) the technological knowledge of prehistoric cultures (Bray 1982). Studies of archaeoastronomy (Aveni 1981) and prehistoric iconography (Donnan 1976; Gimbutas 1982; Nicholson 1976) have generally been carried out by archaeologists not closely associated with the New Archaeology. The lack of interest in religious beliefs is extraordinary, since the evidence for them is ubiquitous in the archaeological record from Middle Palaeolithic times onward. Such investigations appear to have been precluded by the strong emphasis on ecology and by the difficulties that seem to be encountered in applying a deductive strategy to the investigation of such problems. As Dunnell has observed, "the ecological and evolutionary approaches, borrowed from the biological sciences, were not designed to explain motivational and symbolic systems" (Dunnell 1982: 521). There has also been a tendency for the New Archaeology, with its narrow causality, to regard these aspects of culture as epiphenomena that are of little importance for explaining cultural change. Yet such interests are by no means excluded by a materialist orientation. Childe (1956a) argued long ago that the incorporation of cognitive aspects of culture into an overall explanation of human behavior was essential for the development of a successful materialist research strategy. Among the strong points of structural or symbolic archaeology is the fact that it is once again drawing attention to the potential importance of such cognitive factors for explaining cultural change (Hodder 1982a; 1982b).

The specific content of knowledge and beliefs is highly variable even among cultures that have similar modes of production. Generalizations seem to be possible about the broad types of knowledge and beliefs that correlate with societies that share a similar level of complexity or that have the same general type of economy, but these generalizations are at such a high level that they explain only a small portion of the variation that can be observed in the archaeological record (Childe 1949; J. Fischer 1961). As archaeologists once again take account of the complexity of human phenomena, they are beginning to realize that universal generalizations do not exhaust the regularities that characterize human behavior. Universal generalizations may vary from major assumptions about historical processes to regularities dealing with relatively trivial aspects of human behavior (M. Salmon 1982: 8-30). Yet in economics and economic anthropology, the substantivists argue that major generalizations about human behavior may apply only to a limited range of societies. They maintain that the body of theory developed by classical economists to explain market behavior is applicable only for explaining the economies of capitalist societies. Quite different corpuses of theory are needed to explain the economic structure of various types of noncapitalist societies (Dalton 1981). While economic formalists deny this distinction, the fact remains that many useful generalizations may apply only to societies at a particular level of development or occupying a specific type of environmental niche.

The third type of generalization is one specific to an individual culture or to a single group of historically related cultures. An example would be the definition of the canons of beauty that governed ancient Egyptian or Greek art (Childe 1947: 43-59; Montané 1980: 132-36). Generalizations about aesthetic standards can be derived from formal studies of archaeological evidence alone; however, when written records from early times are not available, more esoteric and culturally specific meanings can be recovered only by means of a direct historical approach. Many of the best pioneering studies of this sort in the field of cognitive studies have been done by historical archaeologists (Deetz 1977; Glassie 1975).

The importance of this sort of approach for prehistoric archaeology has been demonstrated by R.L. Hall (1979) and George Hamell (1980). Hall has drawn upon ethnographic and ethnohistorical material concerning native religious beliefs and symbolism in eastern North America to explain the structure of Adena burial mounds, as well as why certain classes of artifacts were included with Middle Woodland burials. Hamell has used regularities in historically recorded Iroquoian, Algonkian, and Siouan myths to explain the significance of the inclusion of crystals, objects made from marine shell and native copper, and various other materials in eastern North American burial contexts from late Archaic times into the historic period. Both of these anthropologists offer explanations of regularities in burial customs for which no cross-cultural generalization could account.

The main problem that is posed by this work, as by most interpretations offered by structural or symbolic archaeology, is that of verifiability. In the case of Hall and Hamell, proof rests upon the validity of analogies drawn between ethnographically and archaeologically known cultures that there is sound reason to believe are historically related. Hamell's evidence is particularly convincing because there is strong proof in the archaeological record of continuity in the use of these materials from their earliest occurrence into the historical period. The best verification is undoubtedly the establishment of a universal correlation between what is observed in the archaeological record and what is inferred from it; in other words, an exceptionless middle-range generalization. Yet it is increasingly recognized that, because of the complexity of human phenomena, most correlations are statistical rather than absolute, and most statistical correlations will be of a lower rather than a higher degree of magnitude. This is something that anthropologists engaged in cross-cultural studies have long recognized and had to contend with (Textor 1967). Under these circumstances, the problem of equifinality, or different causes producing the same effect, becomes increasingly troublesome, as archaeologists engaged in simulation studies have become aware (Hodder 1978; Sabloff 1981).

Because archaeology deals with complex phenomena and is not an experimental discipline, much of what is accepted as true tends to be what each generation of archaeologists finds reasonable. Archaeologists may establish sound correlations, weed out logical inconsistencies, and demonstrate that accepted interpretations do not accord with new data. Yet their interpretations are subtly influenced by social and personal preconceptions of reality that preclude an awareness of alternative explanations which might encourage formal testing of the actual limits within which a generalization holds true. In many instances, neither adequate data nor strong enough correlations are available to counteract such biases. Most historians have long realized that the interpretation of human affairs is itself a socially conditioned phenomenon (Carr 1962; Collingwood 1946). Under these circumstances, the difference between a nomothetic generalization and an argument by analogy is by no means clear-cut

(Charlton 1981). Finally, refusal to explain cultural regularities because they are not universal ignores and belittles large areas of human experience. It may also limit or preclude the ability of archaeologists to explain why change has taken place.

The growing awareness of the complexity of what archaeology has to explain not only is calling into question the claim that deductive modes of explanation are the only appropriate ones (G.A. Clark 1982), but also is leading more archaeologists to acknowledge that their experience of the present influences their interpretation of the past (Hodder 1983; Leone 1982). The milieu in which archaeologists live and work is seen as influencing both the questions they ask and the answers they are predisposed to regard as reasonable. Such factors not only play a major role in shaping national variations in archaeological practice but also change over time as social conditions change. The situation does not appear to be a reflection of the immaturity of archaeology, as some archaeologists have suggested (Clarke 1979: 154), but one of its permanent features (Trigger & Glover 1981b). The adoption in recent decades of the Boserup-based view that population increase is a major factor driving human beings from an easy, carefree life as hunter-gatherers to an existence characterized by increasing exploitation, oppression, and hard work has been interpreted as an archaeological reflection of growing political and economic insecurity in the United States, particularly as this insecurity is expressed in concerns with uncontrolled population growth, disastrous pollution, and the exhaustion of nonrenewable resources (Trigger 1981a). The widespread, largely implicit acceptance of a materialist perspective by American archaeologists (Kohl 1981: 91) also appears to reflect changing social conditions. Concern with social factors influencing the development of archaeology has led to a growing interest in the history of the discipline (Daniel 1981; Grayson 1983; Hudson 1981; Meltzer 1983; Schwartz 1967; Willey & Sabloff 1980). The relativist view does not deny that, as a result of archaeological research, it is possible to obtain a more complete and objective understanding of the past. Indeed, it can be argued that an understanding of the social factors that influence archaeological research should enhance the self-awareness of archaeologists and hence the objectivity of their interpretations. The results of such research seem to be of interest even to those archaeologists who reject it as "irrationalist" (Binford 1983a: 233, 241).

In recent years there has been much discussion of the goals of archaeological research. It would appear that the proposition is gradually being abandoned that archaeological data should be used in much the same way as ethnographic data to generalize about human behavior. The problems of processing archaeological data put such data at a disadvantage for this purpose. Some archaeologists have seen their discipline as the nucleus of a new science of material culture (Clarke 1968), although others would restrict this role to historical archaeology (Deagan 1982: 167). While archaeology is based on material culture, it can inform us about many other aspects of human behavior. Hence most archaeologists probably agree that to restrict the discipline in this manner would be to cultivate a new artifact-centered antiquarianism (Daniel 1975: 370-76). There is also agreement that one of the key strengths of archaeological data is their ability to document change over long periods of time. The growing awareness of the complexity of the forces that are responsible for bringing about cultural change is blunting the distinction between science and history that has dominated prehistoric archaeology since the 1950s (Binford 1983a: 26-30; Trigger 1981d; J. Wiseman 1983: 8). There is no agreement in the social sciences about high-level generalizations concerning human behavior. Even if such a body of theory existed, comparable to the synthetic theory of biological evolution, this would not provide automatic answers to a host of more specific problems concerning human behavior (Harris 1979: 77). Nor would it permit the prediction of specific developments in prehistoric times. The first responsibility of archaeologists therefore seems to be to recover evidence about the past and to use every analytical device and every scrap of knowledge about human behavior at their disposal to interpret this record as evidence of prehistoric human activity.

The understanding, within the limits that archaeological data will permit, of what has happened to specific groups of people in the past is a matter of great humanistic as well as scientific interest. Through archaeological studies, the idea that nonliterate peoples were primitive and unchanging savages has been refuted. Emergent nations in Africa and elsewhere look to archaeology for knowledge of their precolonial development (Posnansky 1982). In North America, Australia, and other parts of the world where native peoples have been overwhelmed by European settlement, the image of the "unchanging savage" has been demonstrated to have been a myth of colonialism (Mulvaney 1981). In spite of this, the historical synthesis of archaeological data, while reviving in American archaeology, has so far failed to produce any work of outstanding quality (Trigger 1983). The main weakness of such studies is their continuing domination by often ill-considered ecological approaches and the lack of attention being paid to nonuniversal generalizations. The notion that archaeological data should be used primarily to formulate and test a potpourri of universal theories about human behavior as an end in itself is increasingly being recognized as neocolonialist and insulting to the third world and to native peoples (Langford 1983; D. Miller 1980; Ucko 1983). By ignoring its social responsibilities, archaeology may be dooming itself to irrelevance, as well as encouraging needless hostility (J. Wiseman 1983). The patterns of human development as revealed through idiographic studies that employ archaeological or historical data, or a combination of both, are themselves a legitimate object of generalization. The duty of evolutionary theory is to explain what has really happened in the past, not to construct hypothetical schemes of development using ethnographic data, which are clearly insufficient for the task.

Conclusions

Between 1960 and 1984, archaeology experienced impressive institutional growth and received escalating financial support. Assisted by the development of radiocarbon and other physical dating techniques, it has also turned from a preoccupation with chronology to making considerable advances in interpreting its data in behavioral terms. All of this has enhanced the status of archaeology as a social science. Yet today there is growing uncertainty about what the goals of archaeology should be as well as about the validity of many of the assumptions that guided the development of archaeology in the 1960s. There is an increasing desire to define a role for archaeology that takes account of its specific data base and which, as far as possible, complements rather than duplicates those roles played by the other social sciences. This necessitates the development of a body of theory appropriate for the interpretation of archaeological data: Binford's middle-range theory.

The gradual rejection of the neoevolutionary views that played such an important role in the development of the New Archaeology is leading, not to a return to Boasian historical particularism, but to a more complex and less deterministic view of human behavior. Because of this, there are fewer aspects of human behavior that archaeologists can dismiss as epiphenomenal for understanding cultural change. The challenge is simultaneously to try by whatever means to infer more aspects of human behavior from archaeological data and to determine what kinds of problems archaeologists may and may not hope to address satisfactorily. It is also being recognized that societies and cultures are open with respect not only to the environment but also to each other. Any general explanation of cultural change must therefore take account of how neighboring societies influence one another as well as of changes that are of endogenous origin. This poses a formidable challenge for archaeologists to join in a long-term effort to understand human behavior better. All these developments negate the sharp distinctions that archaeologists have drawn between inductive and deductive approaches and between the explanation of specific historical sequences and the elaboration of general theories of human behavior and sociocultural process. The result should be that in the long run archaeology becomes increasingly historical in orientation while history is acknowledged to be scientific, in the sense that generalizations are both a means and an end of historical research. In the long run, archaeologists also may learn more fully that in historical investigations progress is measured as much by the questions that researchers learn to ask as by the answers that they offer at any given time (Collingwood 1939: 24-30).

6

Hyperrelativism, Responsibility, and the Social Sciences

In anthropology and the other social sciences there has been during the 1980s a renewed appreciation of the complexity of human behavior and an increasing interest in the idiosyncratic, the particular, and the contingent. This has been linked to a growing repudiation both of neoevolutionism and of a positivist epistemology that equates prediction and explanation. It has also made social scientists more aware of the subjective elements that influence their interpretations and of how fragile is the basis on which we can claim to know anything definite about the past or about human behavior. The result has been an increasingly vociferous confrontation in the social sciences between, on the one hand, an old-fashioned positivist certainty that, given enough data and an adherence to "scientific" canons of interpretation, something approximating an objective understanding of human behavior can be achieved (McCullagh 1984; Binford 1986; 1987; Spaulding 1988) and, on the other hand, a growing relativist skepticism that the understanding of human behavior can ever be disentangled from the interests, prejudices, and stereotypes of the researcher (Feyerabend 1975; Miller and Tilley 1984a; Spriggs 1984). This dispute addresses an issue that is crucial for determining the relevance of the social sciences and charting their future development. The aim of this paper is to assess, in the form of a case study, the positive impact that relativism has had on prehistoric archaeology as well as the problems raised by the relativist critique.

Relativism and the Social Sciences

The history of anthropology reveals that the interpretations favored by individual researchers and by various schools of anthropology have been strongly influenced by their social milieu. In the nineteenth century, American anthropologists and archaeologists (probably largely unselfconsciously) used an evolutionary paradigm to reinforce popular negative stereotypes of Indians as primitive people who were predestined to be annihilated by the spread of European civilization (Meltzer 1983). Historians, who were influenced by these anthropologists, portrayed native leaders, such as Pontiac and Tecumseh, as romantic figures, but they also emphasized that these men were exceptions, whose resistance to European domination was doomed to failure by the primitiveness and indiscipline of their followers (J. Walker 1971; Berkhofer 1978). Although Lewis Henry Morgan was fascinated by the Iroquois, he argued that no native inhabitants of the New World, including the Incas and Aztecs, had risen above the level of simple tribal societies. He also expressed the opinion that thousands of years of slow biological development would be required before any further cultural development would be possible (Bieder 1986: 194-246). Even John Wesley Powell, the first director of the Bureau of American Ethnology and a scholar who respected native people and sought to devise ways to alleviate their sufferings under white domination, sponsored the production of works that reinforced the belief of government officials and general readers that native people were unable to respond positively to European civilization (Hinsley 1981: 125-40). Long after anthropologists rejected such racist views, they continued to interpret the accumulating evidence of rapid changes in the archaeological record in prehistoric times as indicating the imitative rather than the creative talents of native Americans (Trigger 1980). The realization that the social sciences are not value-free disciplines shatters the widely held pretense of objectivity and challenges us to consider what factors are currently influencing our work and what role our findings play in the conflicts within our own society.

Yet social scientists do not agree on how far the influence of relativism extends. There is growing support for the idea that no objective understanding of human history or behavior may ever be possible. Instead it is claimed that each generation, social class, gender, and individual interprets such issues differently and that there may be no criteria that will allow scholars to evaluate differing interpretations objectively. Some social scientists accept this as a regrettable limitation on their work (Leone 1982). Others welcome it as the wholesome refutation of a dangerous view that surrounds social science research with a false aura of esoteric knowledge and encourages an uncritical acceptance of elitist views of society. They claim that all knowledge is contextually embedded in the discourse of groups engaged in political power relations and is primarily determined by that discourse. At its most neutral, scientific "truth" is a form of consensus produced by dialogue and shared within a scientific community (Kuhn 1962; Bernstein 1983). It follows from this that there is no way to distinguish scientific findings from any other sort of knowledge (Barnes 1974; 1977; Feyerabend 1975). A few would go so far as to maintain that there is no difference between social science reports, novels, and deliberately misleading political propaganda (Shanks & Tilley 1987a; 1987b). Extreme relativists deny that there can be any evidential grounds for assessing the relative merits of different interpretations of human behavior; these can be judged only on the basis of their internal consistency and the role they play in particular social contexts (Hindess & Hirst 1975: 1-5; Miller & Tilley 1984b: 151). The effect is to obliterate the distinction between "theory" and "ideology" by identifying all theory as a form of ideology. This raises the question of whether there can be any justification for public support of the social sciences if, by their own admission, they are incapable of providing even a limited objective understanding of society.

Recent developments in the study of history appear to support some of the more radical claims of the relativists. Most historians have long embraced a form of relativism. They acknowledge that their data consist of what literate individuals and groups in the past thought worth recording and that what they as historians select for study reflects their own interests. They further agree that different historians can interpret the same corpus of data in diverse ways (Collingwood 1946; Carr 1967; S. Cohen 1986). It is frequently observed that history is rewritten in every generation, not because the past has changed but because each generation asks different questions about it (J. Hill 1972: 15; Lowenthal 1985). It is further noted that individual historians interpret the past differently because of the personal views and class interests that they bring to their work (McLennan 1981).

Yet many of these same historians traditionally have insisted that their discipline has an objective, scientific aspect. If historical interpretation is merely an expression of informed personal opinion, historical data constitute a corpus of reliable factual evidence. It is this core of solid data, rather than historical interpretations, that is thought to constitute the basis of the discipline; progress is believed to be brought about by adding reliable new data to this core. Scientific history is produced by establishing the authenticity of documents and the degree to which data represent an objective record of the past as opposed to partisan claims and fantasies. This position, which was popularized by the followers of the distinguished German historian Leopold von Ranke in the late nineteenth century (Carr 1967: 5-7), continues to be defended by philosophers of history such as Maurice Mandelbaum (1977).

Yet, today, many historians and philosophers of science find this distinction between objective facts and subjective interpretations to be increasingly unconvincing. They insist that even what pass as facts are theory laden (Wylie 1985; S. Cohen 1986) and that as a result "historical descriptions are all interpretations" (McCullagh 1984: 232-3). No one would dispute the claim that Julius Caesar was assassinated in March of 44 B.C. Yet historians such as E.H. Carr (1967: 7-11) have long recognized that the facts they select as significant are determined by the assumptions about human behavior with which they approach their data. Thus, without denying that Caesar was killed in 44 B.C., it might be asked on what basis is this fact deemed more important for explaining the civil wars that followed than was a phenomenon to which classical historians have paid little attention—the need for the Roman government to secure an adequate food supply for the city (Garnsey 1988). The facts that are emphasized clearly alter with changing fashions of historical interpretation. This has been shown in a dramatic manner in the shift from political history and biography to economic, social, and intellectual history. The change has involved supplementing or replacing the study of administrative documents with the analysis of statistical data, legal archives, and the private records of ordinary people (T. Bender 1985; Berger 1986: 259-320). The significance of many historical data is also far from self-evident. What one historian will accept without question as a statement of fact will appear to another, working on the basis of different assumptions, as a self-serving fabrication or distortion of reality (cf. Campeau 1977; Pritchard 1987; Trigger 1987). These controversies illustrate that most historical facts are not self-evident but acquire meaning within the context of the stereotypes and beliefs about human behavior that are held by individual historians.

Finally, it is widely recognized that the complexity of factors that influence human behavior and bring about social change makes it very difficult to determine in a rigorous fashion why events happen. Because of this complexity and the abundant data that are available about some topics, it is easy for historians to marshal evidence to support many alternative interpretations. Traditionally, historians (at least the non-Marxist ones) have been less overtly concerned about the theoretical consistency of their explanations than social scientists have been (Axtell 1987). Carr (1967: 26) has argued that the plethora of historical data allows the historian to "get the kind of facts he wants" and hence also the answers. The wide variety of options that have been maintained in prolonged debates about topics such as the decline of the Roman Empire illustrate this situation. These debates do not prove, however, that a scientific understanding of human behavior is impossible. They reflect the complexity of the phenomena requiring explanation.

These observations suggest that historical facts and explanations cannot be clearly distinguished in the fashion that historians of the Ranke school maintained. They also call into question the notion that history has a clearly defined, slowly enlarging factual core, which constitutes the heart of the discipline. Ever more insistently, the case is being made that all aspects of historical research are permeated by theoretical considerations.

Archaeologists Confront the "Real" Past

Twenty-five years of changing fashions in archaeological interpretation provide dramatic evidence of the conflict between positivism and relativism. Archaeology aspires to be a social science that explains what has happened to human beings in the past. Yet, when archaeologists are restricted to using only archaeological data, they lack the ability to observe either human behavior or ideas. They must infer both from the material remains of what human beings have made and used (Clarke 1973; Schiffer 1976; Binford 1977a; 1981a). This sensory deprivation, compared to the other social sciences, has accentuated the dispute between positivists and relativists.

In the 1960s, many American archaeologists enthusiastically embraced a positivist epistemology. This development cannot be understood apart from broader intellectual, social, and economic trends that occurred in the United States in the early postwar decades (Trigger 1981a; 1989a; Patterson 1986a; 1986b). Leading ethnologists, such as Franz Boas, Robert Lowie, and Frank Speck, had traditionally stigmatized archaeology as a discipline that could study only a limited range of material culture and hence on its own was incapable of understanding human behavior in past times (Taylor 1948: 154). Even those anthropologists who granted that archaeologists were able to infer human behavior from their data believed that the range of such inferences would remain narrow and fragmented and that archaeologists would never be able to contribute significantly to an understanding of the development of social institutions (Hooton 1938: 218; Hoebel 1949: 436). By the 1950s increasing funding for American archaeological research by the National Science Foundation spurred archaeologists to emphasize the scientific aspects of their discipline (Patterson 1986a). As a result, a growing number of archaeologists, whose research opportunities now depended on asserting archaeology's scientific credentials, deeply resented these demeaning characterizations of their discipline and sought to disprove them (Willey 1953; Meggers 1955:129; Caldwell 1958; 1959).

To achieve this goal, the New Archaeologists of the 1960s drew upon two theoretical movements in anthropology, both of which had strong ties to the physical and biological sciences. The first was neoevolutionism, as represented in the writings of Leslie White (1949; 1959), Julian Steward (1955), Marshall Sahlins (1968), Elman Service (1962; 1975), and Morton Fried (1967), and later in a theoretically more sophisticated form by the cultural materialism of Marvin Harris (1979). Neoevolutionism posited a high degree of cross-cultural regularity in human behavior. This implied that, if archaeologists could determine what one aspect of a prehistoric cultural system had been like, it would be possible to infer with a high degree of probability the nature of other aspects of the system. New Archaeology also subscribed to a materialist view of the forces determining human behavior. Specifically, it embraced the ecological determinism of Julian Steward. Since archaeologists had already achieved some success in reconstructing prehistoric patterns of demography, subsistence, and settlement, it was reassuring to view ecological adaptation as the principal factor shaping cultural systems. Lewis Binford (1962; 1965), the undisputed leader of the New Archaeology, argued that if, by means of cross-cultural studies based on ethnographic data, archaeologists could establish firm correlations between material culture and specific aspects of human behavior relating to economics, social organization, and ideology, it would be possible for them to infer a broad range of human behavior from the archaeological record. His neoevolutionary belief in the uniformity of human behavior and in the relatively limited range of factors that influenced it to a significant degree led him to claim that most aspects of human behavior could be recovered in this fashion.

At the same time, Binford adopted a Hempelian logico-deductive approach as the only basis for creating a scientific archaeology. Science in general and archaeology in particular were seen as advancing by formulating and testing propositions that were logically related to broad theoretical frameworks. In Binford's case this framework was ecological adaptation, although many New Archaeologists were later to prefer Marvin Harris' (1979) more broadly based combination of economic and demographic determinism. Binford and his followers acknowledged that the formulation of the specific theories they were testing might be influenced by subjective factors that reflected the social milieu of the investigator. Yet they argued that the truth or falsehood of these claims could be established if archaeologists possessed a sufficient corpus of data and followed scientifically valid procedures of verification (Watson et al. 1971: 3-57). They did not doubt that prehistoric human behavior was objectively knowable, provided that universally valid correlations were established between material culture and human behavior (Binford 1967b). This belief in the regularity of human behavior was combined with an additional certainty that once such behavior had been inferred, it could be explained objectively regardless of the prejudices of the investigator.

It was frequently observed in the 1950s that the nature of the data that archaeologists had to work with forced them either to adopt a materialist strategy (Piggott 1965: 7) or to admit that they were largely limited to studying what was generically animal rather than what was specifically human about prehistoric behavior (Hawkes 1954). The desire to learn as much as possible about such behavior and to establish the scientific credentials of their discipline explains the eagerness with which New Archaeologists embraced neoevolutionism and ecological determinism. Yet, while both these approaches had been formulated by ethnologists, neither had won the support of a majority of American anthropologists (Harris 1979: 165-341). In their efforts to construct archaeology as a positivist science, the New Archaeologists chose to ignore evidence, that seemed self-evident to many ethnologists, of a high degree of variation in human behavior as well as indications that ecological factors limited rather than determined such behavior. For almost two decades neoevolutionism was to dominate American archaeology and to influence archaeology in many parts of the world (Willey & Sabloff 1980: 181-210).

Despite its sectarian approach, the New Archaeology achieved much that was positive during the 1960s and 1970s. It drew attention to undoubted regularities in human behavior that had been ignored by the previous Boasian culture-historical approach, which had emphasized the uniqueness and incomparability of individual cultures. It also pioneered new techniques for inferring human behavior from archaeological data and for recovering more comprehensive sets of data that expanded the range of what archaeologists could learn about the past. During these years archaeology also acquired its currently important role in discussions of theoretical issues relating to human behavior (Harris 1968: 683-7).

Yet at the same time that New Archaeology was enjoying these successes, archaeologists were becoming increasingly aware of the limitations of neoevolutionism and ecological determinism. If human behavior was less random than the historical particularists had maintained, it could not be demonstrated to be as regular as neoevolutionists had hoped. As a result, specific generalizations about relations between material culture and human behavior were more difficult to formulate and far more limited in their range of applicability than neoevolutionists had anticipated (Hodder 1986). Cross-cultural generalizations turned out to be statistical more often than absolute and far fewer statistical ones were at a high level of probability than at a low one (Textor 1967). Moreover, ethnological and historical research by Hodder (1982b) and other archaeologists (Pearson 1984; Leone 1984; D. Miller 1987) indicated that material culture often does not passively reflect social and political behavior, as the New Archaeologists had assumed it did. When two ethnic groups are competing for scarce resources, the weaker one sometimes finds it advantageous to suppress material evidence of their distinctiveness—a finding in accordance with Karl Marx's claim that all human productions are mediations of the objective world, not merely its reflection (Hodder 1981). Archaeologists also began again to believe that ecological adaptations limit the range rather than determine the nature of other cultural responses. At the same time, growing attention was paid to cultural traditions as a source of the material that is reworked in each generation (Hodder 1986; 1987a). All of this carried archaeology very far from the conviction of the New Archaeologists that everything that is important about a cultural system can be accounted for in terms of its adaptive significance (Meltzer et al. 1986).

In an effort to cope with the problems that are seen as inherent in New Archaeology, some archaeologists are relying increasingly on contextual analysis (Hodder 1986; 1987b). It is argued that each facet of archaeological data concerning a specific culture should be correlated with all other available data before conclusions are drawn concerning its significance. For example, by examining the full range of house types in a culture it can be determined more effectively whether simple burials indicate an egalitarian social organization or reflect an egalitarian ideal that was not realized in everyday life. Archaeologists also recognize that historical ties account for cultural regularities that are of no less interest than those produced convergently by cross-cultural uniformities. Yet they continue to encounter serious problems in tracing historical connections over long periods of time and in distinguishing similarities that result from parallel development from those produced by historical relations (von Gernet & Timmins 1987). Finally, they are once more recognizing that by utilizing other sources of information about the past, such as historical records, oral traditions, folklore, historical ethnology, historical linguistics, and physical anthropology, they may be able to resolve specific problems about the past that cannot be answered using archaeological data alone (Hodder 1986). In these ways, it is becoming possible for archaeologists to cope with problems that lie outside the narrow range of archaeological interpretation that is made possible by cross-cultural generalizations. While we are not witnessing a return to the culture-historical approach, we are seeing a situation in which some of the major concerns of that approach are once again being taken seriously (Trigger 1984b).

From the beginning, many American archaeologists were highly selective in their acceptance of the tenets of New Archaeology, while others rejected its entire program either tacitly or openly (Bayard 1969; R. Watson 1972; Dumond 1977; Trigger 1978a: 1-52). During the years when New Archaeology was dominant, this intellectual resistance made little impression on New Archaeology's role as the prevailing discourse in the discipline. Declining faith in New Archaeology resulted in part from growing perceptions of its inability to make good its promises to provide a comprehensive understanding of the past.

The rapid acceptance and equally rapid decline of the New Archaeology led many archaeologists to recognize for the first time that more than purely objective factors were involved in archaeological interpretation (Leone 1984; Wilk 1985; Patterson 1986a). This encouraged a growing interest in the history of archaeology (Trigger 1985b; 1989a). Studies revealed that all the social sciences had experienced rapid shifts in high-level theories that did not result primarily from the accumulation of new data. For example, biological explanations of variations in the behavior of different human groups ceased to be accepted in the 1940s, not as a result of accumulating anthropological evidence but because of their association with Nazi racial policies. This association also discouraged the serious investigation of the biological basis of any form of human behavior for almost a generation (Cartmill et al. 1986). Such events seemed to accord with Thomas Kuhn's (1962) subjectivist concept of scientific revolutions. Growing realization of the importance of such developments called into question the relevance of positivism for archaeology no less than for the other social sciences (Gibbon 1984).

The questioning of positivism has, however, taken varied forms in archaeology, as it has in the other social sciences. Most archaeologists now are probably prepared to admit that not only the questions they ask but also the answers that they are willing to accept as persuasive are influenced by the presuppositions they bring to their research (Saitta 1983). The testing of propositions concerning the meaning of archaeological data is no longer viewed as objective and clear-cut, but rather as a procedure in which a significant subjective element is involved (M. Salmon 1982; Wylie 1982; 1985). It is now generally acknowledged that archaeologists tend to require lower standards of proof for propositions that they hold to be reasonable or self-evident than they do for hypotheses of which they disapprove. Even the most strongly supported positivist theory, insofar as it claims predictive value, is based on faith that what applies in the cases that have been studied will apply to all other similar cases. In recent years, a growing number of archaeologists who are inclined to support a positivist approach have been laying renewed emphasis on the testing of multiple working hypotheses rather than using a deductive approach based on a single general theory (Gallay 1986). This is seen as a means of helping to overcome prejudices that affect the formulation of middle-range hypotheses as well as undue dependence on specific high-level theories of human behavior, none of which has won overwhelming support among social scientists.

Of growing importance to the relativist critique is the debate about how society influences the interpretation of archaeological data. Many now maintain that archaeologists, both collectively and as individuals, are influenced, largely unconsciously, by their social milieu (Trigger 1980; 1981a; Conkey & Spector 1984; Patterson 1986a). This is not a simplistic, normative interpretation which maintains that all archaeologists react in the same way to a particular set of social stimuli (Shanks & Tilley 1987a: 31). Even those explanations that see large numbers of archaeologists influenced in a particular fashion by a specific set of social circumstances specify that this happens because archaeologists generally belong to and receive patronage from the same social class. In Western Europe and America this has been, for the last 200 years, the middle class, and more particularly the administrative and intellectual fractions of that class (Kristiansen 1981; Trigger 1981a; 1989a). This approach also does not exclude individual variation resulting from idiosyncratic factors.

Two opposed positions have developed concerning the significance of this influence. Extreme relativists maintain that it indicates that it is impossible ever to eliminate subjective influences from archaeological interpretations to a significant degree. They argue that while it is possible, as a result of changing social perspectives, to recognize how subjective factors have influenced archaeological interpretations in the past, archaeologists cannot do this effectively for current work (Gathercole 1984). More moderate archaeologists maintain that, as a result of their heightened awareness of subjective influences on archaeological interpretation, archaeologists can take account of such influences in their own work and increase the objectivity of their interpretations (Leone 1982; 1984; 1986). They do not specify, however, what practical measures are required to achieve this goal.

Some extreme relativists, who often identify themselves as neo-Marxists, argue that the notion of social conditions unconsciously influencing archaeological interpretation objectifies human behavior to an unacceptable degree. They maintain that ideas always relate to domination and power and that every archaeologist employs data to construct a personal vision of the past which he or she uses to promote their own interests. The construction of the past is dominated by the preoccupations and goals of individual archaeologists to the degree that it is these interests rather than archaeological data that inevitably determine the nature of archaeological interpretations. Thus these interpretations are viewed as part of the struggle for political, economic, and sexual power that these archaeologists believe has dominated all societies throughout history (Miller & Tilley 1984a; Shanks & Tilley 1987a; 1987b). Within this network of conflicting and contending viewpoints, there is no privileged position from which the relative objectivity of different theories can be established or any techniques that would allow them to be objectively assessed.

Some neo-Marxists see the only valid measure of the relative worth of theories as being their ability to change society. This view has much in common with Plato's ancient "noble lie" and even more with Nietzsche's dictum that "the falseness of an opinion is not ... any objection to it. ... The question is how far it is life-furthering, life-preserving, species-preserving, perhaps species-creating" (Carr 1967: 31). These neo-Marxists also argue that interpretations can only be assessed in terms of their internal consistency or coherence, never in terms of their factual correspondence with empirical data (Miller & Tilley 1984b: 151). This viewpoint claims a venerable intellectual pedigree which is said to have its roots in the works of Hegel and Marx, although this claim is rejected by many orthodox Marxists. It certainly does not accord with Marx's distinction between true and false consciousness (Eyerman 1981). More recognizably, this viewpoint is grounded in an extreme interpretation of the relativist views of disillusioned German Marxists, such as Max Horkheimer, Theodor Adorno, and Herbert Marcuse, who felt betrayed by the working class during and after the First World War and were associated with the Institute of Social Research founded in Frankfurt in 1923 (Held 1980). It is also grounded in the critical theory of Jürgen Habermas (1971; 1975) and the efforts of Paul Feyerabend (1975) and Barry Barnes (1974; 1977) to demolish the distinction between scientific and non-scientific knowledge. These critiques claim to be seeking to free humanity from the "grip of all closed systems of thought" (Held 1980: 150) and to combat what their authors see as the social paralysis that is induced by a reified consciousness. They object that a positivist approach to the social sciences seeks to produce particularistic knowledge of human behavior that elites can use to control ordinary people. While the current divisions among the social sciences seriously impede a holistic knowledge of human behavior, the claim that positivism is inevitably in league with conservatism and political oppression (Tilley 1984: 138; Hodder 1986: 166) is historically untrue, as the Polish philosopher Leszek Kolakowski (1978: 400-2) has amply demonstrated. Many hyperrelativists also overestimate the power of ideological formulations to control and manipulate people and underrate the ability of the lower classes to see through the ideologies by which elites seek to dominate them (Trigger 1985c; Hodder 1986: 64-65). Finally, it is not clear on what grounds these relativists can claim any special significance for their own views. If their analysis is correct, neither archaeology nor any of the other social sciences can transcend its subjective political role or acquire any intellectual integrity. The latter requires some objective evaluation of a discipline's claims.

The advocacy of an "anything goes" approach to scientific methodology also creates major social and political problems. If the social sciences lack integrity, they are vulnerable to manipulation by any interest group, however reprehensible its goals and beliefs. Extreme relativists provide no basis except a political one for objecting to their discipline's manipulation by governments, elites, and totalitarian movements (Trigger 1985c; Hodder 1986: 168-9). By adopting such a position, Western social scientists play, in the manner of a self-fulfilling prophecy, into the hands of reactionary elements in their own societies, who are only too pleased to regard the social sciences as erroneous and irrelevant, except when they provide specialized knowledge that can be used to control the economy and manipulate ordinary people in their own interests. In the past, the political uses that have been made of archaeological findings have been harmful at least as often as they have been beneficial to humanity. Although he made important lasting contributions to techniques of archaeological analysis, Gustaf Kossinna's (1911) subjective glorification of the prehistoric Germans, at the expense of other peoples, helped to provide the intellectual basis for the rise of Naziism. While political or ideological commitments may offer sufficient justification to some archaeologists for their work, most archaeologists, and the general public, rightfully must ask if this is all that archaeology can ever hope to accomplish.

Potential and Responsibility of the Social Sciences

So far we have documented that strongly subjective factors pervade most, if not all, aspects of the study of human behavior. For many archaeologists and other social scientists, and perhaps increasingly for the general public, such observations cast doubt on the possibility that these disciplines can have anything objective to say about the human condition. Is there any answer to such doubts? Can it be argued that the social sciences have an autonomous role to play in understanding human behavior?

In the physical sciences, hyperrelativism takes the form of arguing that science cannot be objectively distinguished from magic and other forms of popular belief. Thomas Kuhn (1962) and Barry Barnes (1974; 1977) have demonstrated that in terms of their sense of problem, use of metaphors in the construction of theory, and modes of shaping consensus, the physical sciences do not differ substantially from any other system of belief. Barnes suggests, like many populists before him, that distinguishing between science and other forms of belief is a spurious attempt by scientists to claim a monopoly of significant knowledge rather than a defensible operation. To this extent, the objectivity of the physical sciences has been subjected to the same attacks as has that of the social sciences and has proved vulnerable to many of the same criticisms.

Yet the most important criterion that distinguishes the physical sciences (including all forms of technological knowledge) from other (religious, aesthetic) types of understanding natural phenomena is found in their application. This application is very different from that of social science theory to political conflict and real-world economic behavior. The physical sciences are able to predict transformations of matter and energy in a precise, quantified manner and have been able to construct increasingly elaborate theoretical structures that have the capacity to transform humanity's relations to the natural world to a substantial degree. The crucial features of the physical sciences are their quantifiability and their capacity to produce predictable and replicable results. Magic and other supernatural schemes may claim to produce similar results but they cannot do so (Childe 1950). At best, they provide vital psychological assurance to individuals or societies in situations with which existing technology cannot cope. At worst, they distract attention from the search for technological or political solutions to problems. Prayer or invoking the thoughts of Chairman Mao cannot make water run uphill, as the careful avoidance of such claims by charlatans and fanatics clearly acknowledges. While optimism may help to stimulate an individual's immunological system, the history of population growth demonstrates that inoculation and effective garbage disposal are more effective than prayers and sacrifice. Although it is impossible for a society to distinguish clearly between its own technological knowledge and other forms of belief, it is the former that has transformed humanity's relations with the natural world and, by doing so, the nature of human society and values (Childe 1949; 1956a).

In the social sciences, as we have already observed, the criterion of practical application provides far less convincing evidence of the objectivity of theoretical formulations. It is much more difficult to predict transformations of information than it is to predict transformations of matter and energy. Nor, in most instances, is it possible to conduct laboratory experiments in which the relations between variables can be rigorously examined in an artificially closed system. Yet we have around us abundant evidence of human behavior. Even if the basic recognition and classification of such evidence is influenced to a significant degree by subjective factors, the evidence is real, in the sense that what is observed ultimately exists independently of our imagination. Because of this, it exerts some degree of constraint on the freedom of social scientists to imagine anything they wish about human behavior or history (Wylie 1982; 1985). This does not mean that we do not select or seriously misinterpret facts, but it does mean that behind what we accept as evidence there is a reality that is independent of our will and which, together with our imagining, constitutes a significant part of our data base. In the case of archaeology, this involves acknowledging that there was a past which existed independently of the present and produced the archaeological evidence that we study. Our understanding of the past is clearly influenced by class privilege, ethnic stereotypes, and gender bias. Because most archaeologists have been male, interpretations of the past generally manifest male bias (Conkey & Spector 1984). Likewise, the agricultural basis of the societies that practice archaeology seems to have led archaeologists to undervalue the attractiveness and productive potential of hunting and gathering as a way of life (Price & Brown 1985). Yet these biases are not inherent in the archaeological record. Despite easily documentable trends to misinterpret that record, in the long run the concrete realities of the archaeological record counteract such biases. Moreover, as techniques for the recovery and analysis of data become more complex, the constraints imposed by the archaeological record increase.

Adopting this stand does not require support either for the more dogmatic and ultimately restrictive claims of positivism, or for those of its current rival, realism (Bhaskar 1978; Gibbon 1989), which in its more extravagant manifestations threatens to confer concrete existence on academic imaginings (Kelley & Hanen 1988: 368-73). What is needed is a limited, and carefully nuanced, commitment to empiricism. Seen from this perspective, the main role of relativism is to sensitize archaeologists to the subjective influences that have shaped the beliefs and actions of the people whose remains they study and that also influence their own interpretations, both as individuals and as members of a profession. Neither empiricism nor relativism ensures objectivity, but when utilized together they promote a more informed and self-reflective analysis of human behavior.

The constraints of archaeological evidence are not negligible. I have documented elsewhere the tremendous degree to which the interpretation of archaeological data in North America during the nineteenth century was influenced by the widely held belief that native people were biologically incapable of change (Trigger 1980). Yet this view of American Indians was refuted at least in part as a result of the slow accumulation of evidence of change in the archaeological record. It is also frequently pointed out by relativists that, from the time of Cecil Rhodes until the end of white rule in 1980, European settlers in Rhodesia sought to prove that the impressive prehistoric stone ruins found there had been constructed by fair-skinned colonists who had come from the Near East to mine gold in biblical times. What is less often noted is that this view was definitively refuted in 1929, when the British archaeologist Gertrude Caton Thompson discovered that Chinese porcelain of medieval date underlay the earliest stone construction levels at these sites. Since then, professional archaeologists have not doubted that these ruins were the work of Bantu-speaking people. By the 1920s the art of stratigraphy was sufficiently well developed to explode a racist fantasy. After that time, the dream of a Zimbabwe created by ancient Near Eastern colonists was limited to amateur archaeologists and racist white settlers (Garlake 1973).

Archaeology continues to expose erroneous interpretations of human history. Recent studies of the uppermost levels of archaeological sites have documented that the economic decline of Cyprus occurred in the early sixteenth century when Brazilian production undercut the Western European markets for its sugar (Silberman 1989: 68-86), while the impoverishment of Palestine resulted from the loss of its cotton market in the nineteenth century (Silberman 1989: 228-243). Both of these events were related to the evolution of a Western-dominated world market. This archaeological research calls into question interpretations based on traditional negative stereotypes of Turkish rule that have been promoted by European historians.

It is also clear that archaeological research has irreversibly changed many fundamental aspects of human beings' understanding of the past and of their relationship to the natural world. Two hundred years ago, the biblical account of human origins was competing with various philosophical schemes that postulated evolutionary, cyclical, and degenerationist views of human history, but none of these views had any significant scientific evidence to support it. Today it is clear that human beings and their cultures originated in the tropical regions of the Old World, almost certainly in Africa, and that they spread from there to all habitable parts of the globe. It is also evident that human beings long remained scavengers and hunter-gatherers and that the development of food-production and of increasingly complex societies occurred independently in many places, probably only during the last 10,000 years. At the same time that this was happening, many other human groups maintained low population densities and hunter-gatherer ways of life (Trigger 1986b).

Archaeologists are far from agreed about why these developments took place. In archaeology, as in history, definitive explanations may never be achieved. Yet archaeologists do agree about the general outline of human history. To reject this pattern, as some fundamentalist Christians do, it is necessary to propose a supernatural origin for the archaeological record and to treat it as a divine artifice created in 4004 B.C. in order to deceive those who do not believe in divine revelation. This requires rejecting not merely archaeology as a discipline but also the basis on which all scientific enquiry is carried out. While the proposition that there is objective evidence that can be studied by means of observation requires an act of faith, proof or disproof of this belief rests upon all scientific enquiry, not that of a single discipline.

Archaeologists can also distinguish interpretations of the past based on comprehensive data sets that are carefully analyzed and compared for the consistency of results from the claims of von Dänikenists and other cult groups that seize upon isolated fragments of archaeological evidence as proof that civilization has come from outer space and that "little green men" are waiting to save the fortunate among us from a nuclear holocaust (Cole 1980; Feder 1984; Eve and Harrold 1986; Harrold and Eve 1987). To place all of these interpretations on an equal footing is to reject the whole concept of scientific investigation, which means challenging a methodology based on patterns of behavior that for better or worse have played a central role in transforming human and proto-human life for at least three million years.

In providing evidence of this broad sweep of human development, archaeology is doing more than satisfying the curiosity of a small coterie of dilettantes. The views that human beings have of themselves and their relations to the universe have changed dramatically as technologies and social organization have grown more complex. The ancient Sumerian conception of the universe, with its shallow time frame, ethnocentrism, quarrelsome gods, and supernatural interventions for and against human interests, was appropriate for an early civilization. This is evidenced by the broad structural similarities that, along with striking differences in specific content, characterize religious beliefs in all societies at that stage of development (Trigger 1979; 1993). Yet these same beliefs would be wholly meaningless for a technologically evolved society. It has been argued that a more objective understanding of the nature of humanity and of humanity's relation to nature both results from, and helps to create, greater social complexity (McNeill 1986: 19). Archaeology, like the other social sciences, has an important role to play in helping to forge an understanding of humanity that is appropriate to our own time.

Marx saw one of the qualities of the arts as being their partial autonomy from immediate economic and political needs and hence their ability sometimes to define goals for human action in opposition to an alienating social milieu (Lunn 1982: 66). The social sciences clearly share this capacity. Archaeologists cannot hope to use their findings to resolve the bitter struggles among interest groups that are a conspicuous feature of modern life. Given the diversity of their personal loyalties, it is improbable that all of them would ever find themselves supporting the same side on any particular issue. Therefore little positive can be gained by advocating, as some neo-Marxists do, that archaeologists should engage their discipline in a partisan struggle with whichever political action group they wish to support. By revealing the nature of cultural change in prehistoric times, archaeologists may provide information about the consequences of human behavior that will help individuals, regardless of their nationality, occupation, gender, and class loyalties, to behave in a more informed way. I cannot claim that the social sciences are sufficiently objective and influential to save humanity or even to avoid making major errors in interpreting data. Yet, if they are to play a constructive role in helping to chart a future course for humanity at a time when our very survival as a species is in doubt, instead of engaging in partisan struggle they must seek as far as possible to provide objective insights into human behavior.

The history of the social sciences indicates that they are far from objective disciplines. Their findings sometimes have been used to support social and political movements that have inflicted great suffering on humanity. Yet, in the long run, they are also capable of providing more detailed and objective insights into human history and behavior than human beings have possessed hitherto. The hope that this modicum of objective understanding may slowly contribute to human welfare must inspire social scientists to continue their search for it. If we are to do that, we must strive to avoid the current trap of extreme relativism, which threatens to be more debilitating to the social sciences than the excesses of positivism ever have been. Social scientists must have not only the wisdom to doubt but also the courage to believe in themselves and what they do.

7

Archaeology and Epistemology: Dialoguing across the Darwinian Chasm

In his *Finding Philosophy in Social Science*, the distinguished philosopher of science Mario Bunge (1996: v, 12) argues that philosophy can help to bring clarity, depth, unity, and insight to the social sciences. He maintains that, by providing a more complete and systematic understanding of the nature of scientific reasoning, philosophy can expose inconsistencies between theory and practice and demonstrate that some conclusions researchers envisage are erroneous or irrelevant. Archaeology is the only discipline that seeks to study human behavior and thought without having any direct contact with either. Instead archaeologists must infer what they seek to study from the material remains of the past (Binford 1983a; Clarke 1968; Embree 1987; Schiffer 1976; 1995). The handicap of having to function under such a severe limitation makes it especially important that archaeologists understand how interpretation in the social sciences works.

In today's postmodern intellectual environment, archaeologists also find themselves increasingly challenged to pay attention to philosophical concepts such as subjectivism, conventionalism, fictionism, constructivism, relativism, and hermeneutics, which in the past they might have dismissed as inconsequential. Yet few archaeologists have the time or inclination to acquire a detailed understanding of these concepts, let alone to view them within the broader context of philosophical thought. One result of this is a tendency, recently described by Christopher Chippindale (1993), for archaeologists to treat such ideas as if they were novelty items in an intellectual hypermarket. Exotic concepts are picked up, toyed with, and soon discarded, with little serious effort being made to evaluate them or determine their long-term potential for archaeology. There is also the danger that archaeologists will fall under the influence of philosophies that do not match the needs or practice of their research, with a consequent wasting of valuable time and effort (Bunge 1996: 4). If archaeologists do not have some general understanding of philosophy, they may borrow inappropriate concepts, while dismissing useful ones prematurely. This problem is evident with the current vogue for idealist philosophy. The present chapter documents, as one of its arguments, how an idealist approach, if used judiciously, can enhance archaeological understanding and greatly assist the development of archaeological method and theory but, if employed uncritically, can encourage destructive and unwarranted forms of intellectual nihilism. Since most archaeologists have neither the time nor the specialized training to become professional philosophers, there is a need to develop a lingua franca that can help to bridge the serious divide in outlook between these two disciplines.

In this chapter, I examine the value to archaeology of one of the most important branches of philosophy, epistemology. Epistemology, or the theory of knowledge, is concerned with understanding the nature and validity of human knowledge. Epistemologists investigate how knowledge is acquired, the varying degrees of certainty and probability in knowledge, and the difference between knowledge (with some level of certainty) and belief (without being certain). For the last two millennia, the two competing epistemological orientations have been rationalism, which stresses the role of reasoning in providing certainty, and empiricism, which emphasizes the role of sense perception. Today epistemologies tend to be classified in terms of three alternative schools or approaches: positivism, idealism, and realism (Ayer 1956; Bunge 1996: 104-107; Chisholm 1966; Woozley 1949).

Because epistemological questions are a central concern of theoretical archaeology, sometimes called metaarchaeology, it is important to investigate the problems that archaeologists encounter in trying to apply these approaches in their work. It is also clear that the problems that archaeologists must deal with in interpreting their data are of no less interest to philosophers studying epistemology than epistemological findings are to archaeologists (Embree 1992). I limit this study, however, to examining the use that archaeologists make, or could make, of epistemological concepts. A more specific aim of this chapter is to consider why archaeologists have a difficult time trying to understand philosophical arguments and how they can overcome these problems and use epistemological concepts more critically and productively to interpret their data.

Historical Background

It is widely assumed that archaeologists did not make significant use of philosophical concepts prior to the new or processual archaeologists embracing the ideas of Carl Hempel in the 1960s (Gibbon 1989; M. Salmon 1982; W. Salmon 1992: 243-253; Spaulding 1968). In fact, a considerably more profound encounter took place three decades earlier in classical archaeology, a branch of the discipline that prehistoric or anthropological archaeologists often erroneously assume lacks intellectual profundity, and during a period when culture-historical archaeology, another form of archaeology currently believed to have been wholly atheoretical, was dominant. This encounter occurred under the most favorable circumstances in the person of the Oxford academic, Robin Collingwood, who was simultaneously a leading classical archaeologist and one of the most distinguished British philosophers of his time. Collingwood was perhaps the first philosopher who viewed efforts to understand the past as a testing ground for investigating the nature of thought in general and hence as a basis for philosophical enquiry. Beginning in 1911, he concentrated on archaeological studies that made him the leading authority on Roman Britain. This work culminated in his definitive study, *The Archaeology of Roman Britain*, published in 1930. After that time, he produced his most important philosophical work, *The Idea of History*, which was published posthumously in 1946. A briefer and more accessible exposition of his philosophical ideas is available in his *An Autobiography*, which appeared in 1939, at a time when, because of illness, he feared he might not live long enough to complete his major work.

Collingwood was an advocate of idealist philosophy in the Kantian tradition. He believed that even the simplest perceptions make sense only as the result of concepts, or categories, that already exist in the human mind. Individuals cannot perceive or make sense of the world independently of their existing understanding of the nature of things. Many of these concepts are learned, but others, such as basic notions of time, space, and causality, appear to be innate. Whatever the origin of such concepts, without them the observations that constitute the basis of a positivist epistemology would remain meaningless.

For Collingwood, the past that the archaeologist studies is not a dead past, but one that exists entirely in the present. All that we know about the past comes from texts and artifacts that exist in the modern world, together with knowledge that we believe is relevant to understanding the past when applied to this material (Collingwood 1939: 97-99). Collingwood's idealism also led him to deny that facts and theories are distinct from one another. Archaeologists, he argued, only perceive what they are conditioned to look for and nothing acquires meaning except in relation to clearly formulated questions that the archaeologist poses (Collingwood 1939: 24-25). As an idealist, Collingwood also maintained that, because what is real to people is only what exists in their minds, archaeologists must seek to understand the past by determining in their minds the intentions, goals, and knowledge that motivated the behavior of the people being studied. Archaeologists must attempt to replicate the ideas that caused people to make and do things in particular ways in the past. Archaeological interpretation therefore consists of the ideas that modern archaeologists have about the ideas that people once had, and is an activity in which a scholar seeks to relive the past in her or his own mind. Only by seeking to reconstruct the mental activities that shaped events, and by rethinking the past in terms of their own experiences, can archaeologists discern the significant patterns and dynamics of ancient cultures (Collingwood 1939: 110-115).

To do this adequately, however, archaeologists must try to expand their own consciousness by seeking to learn as much as possible about variations in human behavior and about specific ancient cultures from literary sources. There is no evidence that Collingwood viewed social anthropology as a useful source of information about variations in human behavior, although this would have been a productive way for him to expand his awareness of diversity. Instead, his classical bias led him to use the written records of ancient Greece and Rome to become more aware of the thoughts and practices of those civilizations that were distinct from those of modern ones and helped to place the past on a different plane from the present by contradicting the archaeologist's conventional beliefs (Collingwood 1939: 120-46; 1946: 302-15). Collingwood did not believe that such understanding would provide the basis for a definitive knowledge of the past. For him the most that was possible was an imagining of the past that the archaeologist might hope approximated the understanding held by the people who had lived in the past. Working within the confines of the classical tradition, Collingwood seems to have been unaware of the dangers of ethnocentrism involved in this process.

Many British archaeologists of the 1940s and 1950s read Collingwood, or at least became generally familiar with his ideas. Yet most of them knew little about philosophy and were culturally predisposed toward some form of naive positivism or empiricism. That led archaeologists such as Glyn Daniel (1975), Stuart Piggott (1950; 1959), and Christopher Hawkes (1954) to interpret Collingwood's ideas along lines that in some respects were very different from what Collingwood had intended (cf. Patrik 1985). Like Collingwood, they accorded ideas a major role in shaping human behavior, but, unlike him, they drew a clear distinction between facts and interpretations. They believed that archaeological data constituted the real and cumulative core of the discipline. Interpretations, on the other hand, were matters of opinion that had little lasting importance. It was argued that, since the past no longer exists, there was no possibility of comparing inferences about the past with the actual events to establish if the inferences were correct. Because of the complexity of human phenomena, varying interpretations were possible and these were influenced to a considerable degree by the various standpoints or beliefs of individual archaeologists. Moreover, because material culture reflects only a limited spectrum of human behavior and only a small amount of material culture survives in the archaeological record, interpretations are shaped as much by the assumptions of the archaeologist as by archaeological evidence.

Archaeological interpretation is therefore heavily influenced by intellectual fashions and all understandings of the past are eventually undermined by new data and new explanatory fads. This position, which had much in common with the views of contemporary historians who followed the example of the great nineteenth-century German empirical historian Leopold von Ranke, combined extreme skepticism regarding the objectivity and lasting value of interpretations with unquestioning faith in the objectivity of archaeological finds (Carr 1962: 5-6; Iggers & Powell 1990). Not being sufficiently familiar with contemporary philosophy, leading archaeologists understood Collingwood in some respects to mean the exact opposite from what he had intended. This discrepancy illustrates one of the problems that chronically troubles archaeologists' efforts to use philosophical concepts.

Use of Philosophical Concepts by Archaeologists

Any sort of interdisciplinary dialogue is difficult, especially if the analytical approaches of the disciplines involved are very different. For various historical reasons, it is considerably harder for archaeologists and philosophers to understand the general approach and underlying assumptions of each other's field than it is for archaeologists to understand palaeontology, historical geology, or cosmogony. The latter are all historical disciplines and to that extent share many basic assumptions and methods. Philosophy and archaeology lack a similar, extensive common ground. Making philosophy comprehensible to archaeologists, so that archaeologists can apply its findings critically in their work, requires a systematic understanding of the basic ways in which these disciplines differ from each other. In my opinion, an important key to such understanding lies in their respective attitude toward evolution.

Philosophy is an old discipline, long antedating any generally accepted concept of evolution. In the medieval university the term philosophy covered all fields of knowledge except theology and perhaps medicine. Since then the sciences have split off, leaving philosophy concerned with such matters as the nature of logic, reality, perceptions, and values. Each of these fields represents traditions of thought that can be traced back without interruption to classical Greece (Copleston 1953-74; Jones 1969). Much of philosophical scholarship appears, at least to outsiders, to consist of commentaries on, and updatings of, the work of earlier philosophers or the issues they raised.

The concept of sociocultural evolution was forged by the philosophers of the Enlightenment. Yet, while they believed in technological, social, and moral progress, they also thought that progress came about as a result, not of human nature changing, but of its less desirable features being subjected to greater public control and individual self-discipline (Toulmin & Goodfield 1966: 122-23). The still earlier social-contract philosophers may look like evolutionists, but their accounts of individuals agreeing to form societies were in reality seventeenth- and eighteenth-century secular myths (or revivals of classical speculations) that sought to reassess the relations between society and the individual. For Thomas Hobbes the state was required to curb the violence and brutality inherent in human nature. For Jean-Jacques Rousseau society was an expression of human sociability and goodness (albeit these were characteristics that he thought were easily corrupted as society became more complex). For John Locke authority was an expedient to create an orderly social environment in which individuals, who were innately neither especially good nor bad but highly susceptible to social conditioning, might seek to better themselves (Boucher & Kelly 1994; Gough 1957; Riley 1982).

Today the post-Enlightenment romantic philosopher Georg W. F. Hegel may look superficially like an evolutionist but, since the spiritual self-realization that was his end point of human development represented a return to the Absolute or All that had negated itself to constitute the particularity and determinateness of the finite world, what he was talking about more closely resembles late classical neo-Platonism. While Hegelian philosophy's holistic emphasis on viewing parts in relation to larger wholes constitutes a valuable challenge to examine issues from a contextual perspective, no clear-cut methodology has been created for implementing this approach. As a result, methodological holism has tended to encourage the dangerous belief that intuition alone can supply complete and final truths (Bunge 1996: 258-63; Taylor 1975).

If modern philosophers display at best only a lukewarm interest in sociocultural evolution, they appear to be even less concerned with biological evolution as it relates to human origins; an exception being S. Sayers (1996: 153-72). Their main interest remains, as in the past, to consider how people as they currently are known behave or ought to behave. For them it makes little difference whether human beings were created essentially as they are today or evolved from some behaviorally less complex primate ancestor. A similar disinterest pervades disciplines such as economics, political science, sociology, and history, which are concerned mainly with human behavior in the present and recent past. Most linguists see the need to relate the origins of language to biological evolution, but there are exceptions, such as Noam Chomsky (1988: 166-70), who views language in essentially creationist terms as a phenomenon that transcends biological evolution.

Most archaeologists, however, and especially prehistoric archaeologists, are trained to think about human origins in relation to biological evolution. As a result, they naturally incline to view different aspects of human behavior in terms of how these developed. This is very different from the philosophers' older tradition of trying to understand human beings as they are now. As a result, archaeologists and philosophers find themselves discussing the same issues in what often turn out to be mutually incomprehensible languages.

This incomprehensibility has an impact on epistemology. A positivist approach maintains that the task of science is to explain what is evident to the senses. The eighteenth-century philosopher David Hume, the first systematic exponent of positivism, by rejecting anything that could not be perceived by the senses as an object of discourse, sought to remove appeals to God and Providence from the realm of scientific discussion. The rules that he established also, however, compelled him to eliminate the concept of causality, which he nevertheless recognized was essential for the conduct of everyday life.

In positivist epistemology, explanation takes the form of establishing regularities between different classes of observable phenomena and trying to group these to form more general patterns. This has encouraged a behavioral approach in the social sciences, since it favors what can be directly witnessed at the expense of investigating more elusive thoughts and motives. It also privileges methodological individualism and calls into question the usefulness of concepts such as society on the same grounds as it does causality; people are real because they are entities that can be observed but society is only a construct. A positivist epistemology is also invoked as a reason for not studying macroeconomic processes (Brenner 1994). As a result of positivism's doubts about the epistemological validity of emergent qualities, it tends to be reductionist: its ideal is to explain social phenomena at the biological level and biological phenomena in turn at the physical level. It promotes a belief in "unified science," which maintains that the same scientific approach applies regardless of the nature of what is being studied. In practice that means that the methodology pioneered for studying physics is held to provide a model for the social sciences (Kolakowski 1968; 1972; von Mises 1951).

At the other extreme is idealism, which we have already encountered in the philosophy of Collingwood. Idealism, which traces its modern origins to the writings of the eighteenth-century German philosopher Immanuel Kant, maintains that perception is shaped by the concepts that each individual uses to interpret sensory data. In contrast to the positivists, who treat sensory data as givens, epistemological idealists maintain that perceptions only acquire meaning as a result of selection and classification that go on in the observer's mind. Some of the categories that interpret sensory data are learned, others are biologically innate. The latter may include the capacity for forming concepts, such as those of causality, time, and space, as well as the neural structures that facilitate the learning of languages. However differently such abilities are culturally elaborated, they appear to be based on biological substrates that are panhuman and essential for any individual to function normally. Idealists therefore maintain that concepts play an important role in determining perception. Human beings do not adjust to the world as it really is, but to the world as they imagine it to be. Because of this orientation, idealism encourages a cultural rather than a behavioral approach to the study of human activities. It also promotes an interest in relativism and subjectivism and, in extreme forms, claims that there is not only no way to know what reality is like but also no way to know how anyone else perceives or feels about anything. The current expression of this belief is the postmodern slogan that every decoding is another encoding (Ewing 1934; Hoernle 1924).

The third major epistemology and the most recent is realism. It identifies the object of scientific study as being not only what can be perceived with the senses or conceptualized in the brain, but all things that exist and are worth examining because they are capable of changing in some respect. Ideas, far from being autonomous, are viewed as processes that occur in the brains of some creatures and hence can be studied from a materialistic perspective. But realists also maintain that some imperceptible entities, such as processes or phenomena that are presently unobservable, are appropriate objects for scientific investigation even if they can be known only conceptually. Realists thus do not confine themselves to appearances, as positivists seek to do, but they also do not join with idealists in belittling the significance of appearances. Often they start from appearances and try to explain them in terms of imperceptible entities and processes. In studying the social sciences, realism seeks to embrace both the objective and the subjective. Because it accepts the scientific validity of studying structures as well as the entities that compose structures, realism is antireductionist and embraces a view of science that takes account of the need for employing different modes of inquiry to study different kinds of phenomena (Bhaskar 1978; Harré 1970; 1972; Harré & Madden 1975).

Over the past forty years archaeologists have invoked each of these three epistemologies as a basis, or a rationalization, for their interpretation and explanation of archaeological data. In the 1960s processual archaeologists adopted a positivist approach as the basis for what they called an explicitly scientific research program. Following the early work of Hempel (1965; Hempel & Oppenheim 1948), they insisted that interpretive hypotheses should be rigorously tested following a deductive-nomological model of confirmation. This involved a "covering law" approach that required every explanation to incorporate the statement of a universal law and to demonstrate that a specific event could be subsumed under that law (Binford 1972; Watson, LeBlanc & Redman 1971). Hempel insisted that explanations of human behavior and physical events were formally similar and hence both could be accounted for in this manner.

Alternative epistemologies were generally ignored, as were warnings that the Hempelian model had already been substantially undermined by philosophical critiques and by its failure to account for the progress being made in the physical and biological sciences, where models that could not initially be tested by direct evidence frequently turned out to be verifiable in the long run and much progress was made by the haphazard accumulation of separate generalizations. As a result of these experiences, it was concluded that a rigid adherence to positivist methodology would impede rather than enhance the development of scientific understanding (Rudner 1966: 47-53).

While some philosophers and archaeologists continue to defend a positivist approach, even many of these have sought to adapt it to the complexity and messiness of human behavior by advocating a statistical-relevance model of explanation in place of a deductive-nomological one (Bell 1994; Dray 1957; M. Salmon 1982; W. Salmon

1967; 1984; R. Watson 1991). Explanations are based on statistically significant correlations instead of only on those that are without exception. However, abandoning perfect correlations between specific forms of behavior and material culture in the modern world as a basis for inferring behavior from material culture in the archaeological record creates uncertainties that were not envisaged by the early processual archaeologists, who, as unilinear evolutionists, had assumed that there was much more uniformity in human behavior than has turned out to be the case.

Still other archaeologists, such as Guy Gibbon (1984; 1989), have advocated a realist approach to archaeological interpretation, while many others, as a result of the impact of postmodernism on the social sciences generally, once again have embraced various forms of idealist epistemology (Conrad & Demarest 1984; Hodder 1991; Miller & Tilley 1984a). Others seek to avoid epistemological commitments by championing a pragmatic approach, which maintains that explanations are simply answers to why-questions and that a theory should be evaluated on the basis of its relative explanatory power when tested against competing theories in specific situations (Kelley & Hanen 1988). Still others assume that a positivist and behaviorist approach is best suited for explaining ecological adaptation, while an idealist approach is more appropriate for the analysis of religious and other cognitive phenomena (Gould 1980). Bunge (1996: 355-58) maintains that all reasonable and productive scientists are scientific realists in practice, whatever epistemology they advocate.

Archaeologists find it challenging to sort out these epistemologies and establish their relevance for their work. A graduate student from East Asia who took my seminar on the philosophical foundations of archaeology a few years ago announced, following the section on epistemology, that until then he had regarded Westerners as sensible and pragmatic; now he was convinced that they were raving lunatics. It is obvious that each epistemology privileges a different aspect of reality: realism, the world as it exists, whether or not we can perceive it; positivism, the evidence of the senses; and idealism, the world as we conceive of it. For archaeologists the obvious question is whether there is some higher level at which these competing approaches to understanding fit together. Exploring that question requires either getting involved in ongoing, often highly convoluted, debates in philosophy or setting these concepts into a framework that archaeologists can relate to more easily. I follow the latter course by considering how these concepts relate to one another when viewed from the perspective of biological evolution. The following sketch, which is a simple exercise in trying to ground philosophy in the realities of primate life, is not intended as an espousal of sociobiology or an attempt at biological reductionism.

An Evolutionary Approach to Epistemology

To adopt a biological evolutionary perspective is to accept the proposition that selection is a process that enables individual organisms that are better adapted to their environment to reproduce more successfully than competitors and hence avoid the extinction of their lineages. Human behavior, however special it may be and however determined in its specificity by learning, is the outcome of natural selection acting upon a particular primate lineage. Among the products of natural selection is the biological basis for those conceptual and behavioral patterns that all modern humans share as members of the same species (Brown 1991). Since philosophy is rooted in human experience, philosophy and the study of human evolution must have a considerable amount in common, even if this correspondence is not recognized by philosophers. This overlap constitutes a solid justification for adopting an evolutionary approach to understanding epistemology.

Let us begin with a tree shrew-like ancestor of humanity living some 65 million years ago. This plesiadapid did not have the intelligence to be a philosopher or an archaeologist, but it did live in a real world and, like us, had to adapt to that world if its body and whatever passed for its mind were to survive. The requirement of having to live in a real world, whether we wish to or not, validates many of the perspectives offered by a realist epistemology. Early primates survived because they were adequately adapted to preying on insects from the tree branches of tropical forests. This adaptation required them to have excellent paw-eye coordination and to be expert jumpers, able to calculate whether it was possible to jump from one branch of a tree to another and how much energy had to be put into each jump for it to be successful. The price paid for a defective calculation was a high one and highly efficacious in terms of natural selection.

Natural selection clearly developed the primates' physical senses, especially that of sight, in order to adapt them to their environment, and the enduring importance of such developments for their human descendants is recognized in the important role that positivism accords to observation as a source of knowledge and well-being. But even the early primate had to have some mechanism built into its brain for using that sensory information (although probably not in any form that we could recognize empathetically) to decide what acrobatics were appropriate. This mechanism must have involved at least a rudimentary ability to conceptualize time, space, and cause and effect relations. In other words, primitive as the plesiadapid's brain may have been, some process was occurring inside it that was analogous to what in the case of human beings provides the point of departure for an idealist epistemology.

In the course of higher primate evolution there has been a tendency for instinctive behavior to be replaced by learned behavior. Learned behavior has numerous adaptive advantages, but requires the development of more elaborate forms for processing and communicating knowledge. All these characteristics grew increasingly prominent as social life became more complex and important for adaptation and as body size increased. At some undetermined phase in hominid development, the capacity for symbolic manipulation reached the level where individuals could begin to objectify themselves, build explicit models of what went on in the minds of others, and by imagining alternative scenarios, relate socially in ever more intricate and subtle ways. The likelihood that the major selective factor encouraging the development of brains able to perform such intricate adaptive tasks was a social one is suggested by the fact that modern humans are still better able to conduct relations within the context of small rather than large groups and better able to devise strategies for the short term than for the long one (Boyd & Richerson 1985: 168-71).

The uniformity of the early hominid world lay not in the natural environmental settings in which they lived, which would have become increasingly varied as they expanded geographically. It lay in their all living in small groups and employing simple technologies. These were the most important and pervasive conditions to which natural selection would have slowly adapted them. Although human beings are both cooperative and competitive, even within small groups, the enhancement of cooperative behavior played an important role in ensuring human survival (Carrithers 1992; Conroy 1990;

Mithen 1996). It is not by accident that the human cerebral cortex, which is associated with the capacity to reason, is anatomically linked to the limbic system, the seat of the emotions (Armstrong 1991). A close connection between affect and reason is essential if the capacity for reason is to serve social ends.

But symbolic capacities enhanced not only social relations. Human beings developed the means to perceive the biological and physical world in symbolic as well as sensory terms. As a result, human beings do not adapt to the real world but to the world as their society imagines it to be (Childe 1949: 6-8). As a consequence of biological evolution, the human mind has developed to the point that all relations, including those between humans and the natural world, are mediated by concepts that are transmitted by learning from one generation to the next, while at the same time these concepts are capable of rapid modification in ways that instinctive behavior is not. Human infants are born into the world with certain basic capacities wired into their brains, such as the ability to form concepts of time, space, and causality and to learn languages. Yet everything they need to know to adapt to society and the natural world must be slowly learned. This observation attests to the importance of the human mind, but is not an endorsement of idealism. While Childe noted that humans adapt to a symbolic world rather than to the real one, he cautioned that this symbolic world had to correspond to the real one to a very considerable degree if a society was to survive (Childe 1956a: 58-60). Since individuals and cultures do tend to survive, and human beings, for better or for worse, have been able to penetrate every portion of the earth and dominate the planetary ecosystem, it is evident that cultural systems possess considerable capacity for promoting realist behavior.

The speed with which cultural change can occur renders humans capable of adapting to quickly changing situations, but also enhances the possibility for the rapid spread of maladaptive patterns of behavior. As societies become more complex and the tempo of sociocultural change increases, there is growing danger that ideas that have been inadequately tested, and therefore are more likely to be counterproductive or to promote individual interests at the expense of the group, will have deleterious effects on society and the natural environment. What began as a more efficient general mode of adaptation could, as it becomes more successful, also become increasingly dangerous (Boyd & Richerson 1985: 278-79). Yet, to the extent that individuals can observe the erroneous, dysfunctional, or counterproductive nature of what they believe, they may be able to modify their ideas. Such discrepancies can be noted when other people are observed to behave differently from how an individual expected them to act. Similarly, the natural world does not always behave the way people believe it does and plans may not work out as those who formulated them hoped they would. In these cases, sensory perception plays an important role in helping to adjust understandings to reality.

It is therefore obvious that positivist, idealist, and realist epistemologies are not alternative explanations, but account for various aspects of human behavior in ways that complement one another. An idealist epistemology generalizes the everyday processes by which human beings deal with each other; a positivist one generalizes the way in which humans cope with the natural world; and a realist one takes account of the selective processes acting on all forms of human behavior.

This view is very different from the widely held opinion that idealism and positivism constitute opposed and mutually irreconcilable epistemologies that are naturally linked to radically different political options. Idealism is often portrayed by its detractors as the preferred worldview of romantic reactionaries and by its supporters as the chief bulwark protecting individual dignity and cultural diversity (Bunge 1996: 283; Marcuse 1964). Positivism is construed by its enemies as the preferred epistemology of technocrats and the middle-class establishment, who are anxious to dehumanize the people they exploit (D. Miller 1984: 38; Miller & Tilley 1984a: 2; Wax 1997). There may be some superficial truth to all these caricatures, but such associations are not inherent in the epistemologies. The Polish philosopher Leszek Kolakowski (1978: 400-402) specifically has refuted the charge made by Herbert Marcuse and others that positivism, with its emphasis on observations rather than on values, has played a special role in rationalizing economic exploitation and political oppression. He also demonstrated that, far from developing as a reflection of capitalist values, British positivism, which he associates with the beginnings of modern science, democratic legislation, and universal human rights, can be traced as far back as Roger Bacon in the thirteenth century.

Neither idealism nor positivism can be held responsible for the political wrongdoings of modern times. A far more important and intrinsic difference between positivist and idealist approaches is that subjective data, relating to individual feelings, perceptions, and desires, which are the special concern of an idealist epistemology, are inadmissible objects of study in the natural sciences, whereas they are not only admissible but indispensable in psychology and the social sciences. In these disciplines they complement data derived from the objective observation of behavior (Bunge 1996: 85-86). Traditional philosophers might have avoided much needless and misleading debate about how human behavior can be studied and understood had they taken more account of what has been learned over the past 140 years about primate evolution, human psychology, and the process of socialization.

Different aspects of human behavior have to be studied in different ways. Other people's beliefs, motivations, and feelings must be inferred, as they are constantly in the course of daily life, by a process of sympathetic understanding that, already in the nineteenth century, German social scientists referred to as *verstehen* (Dilthey 1883; Preucel 1991: 21-23). Verstehen involves trying to construct in our own minds how other people view things based on how we ourselves do, and constantly comparing our own and other people's reactions to specific situations in order to adjust, update, and refine our understandings. Even in the most familiar social settings, most people encounter a considerable range of behavior and attitudes that reflect differences in age, gender, social position, occupation, and individual personality. For dealing with other cultures, a still broader range of knowledge is required. It is evident that sympathetic understanding does not constitute certain evidence of how others perceive and feel about specific matters, but only hypotheses. These hypotheses may be checked in living societies by detailed discussions with people about their beliefs or observing to what extent people behave as we imagine they should. The utility of such tests is limited, however, by people not always expressing or acting upon some of their most deeply held beliefs. In some situations they go to great lengths to conceal these beliefs.

When it comes to some of the more obvious adaptations to the material world, such as hunting strategies or the management of irrigation systems, archaeologists, lacking any direct ways to investigate beliefs and motivations, frequently decide to ignore beliefs and model people's behavior in relation to the environment in rational ecological terms (Mithen 1990). This decision may cause archaeologists to overlook interesting sorts of information, such as whether hunters in a particular culture regarded killing animals as proof of their personal resourcefulness and courage or interpreted it as evidence of their effective spiritual relations with animals, which led some of these animals to sacrifice their lives to help humans (Feit 1978; Tanner 1979). It has also long been recognized that metallurgy has been influenced by ritual, magical, and aesthetic as well as by purely technological considerations (Budd & Taylor 1995; Hosler 1995a; 1995b). When no reliable information concerning beliefs is available, a rationalist behavioral approach may be all that is possible.

While, in order to survive, all societies must possess an understanding that permits people to cope with the environment, that understanding, as I have already suggested, can be encoded in many different ways, and may change as the nature of society changes. An industrial society is likely to encode its understanding of how the environment works in terms of an ecosystemic model, while hunter-gatherers are more likely to encode such knowledge in religious terms (Godelier 1986; Trigger 1993: 102-103). To dismiss these differences as epiphenomenal not only underestimates the extent of cultural variation, but also may fail to recognize systemic differences between various types of societies. Archaeologists must therefore resist the temptation to claim that whatever they cannot study using archaeological data alone, or any ideas about adaptation that do not conform to modern Western ideas about ecological adaptation, are not of scientific interest.

Something resembling an idealist perspective is necessary to understand why people perceived the need to behave as they did, while a behaviorist or ecological approach will shed light on the physical constraints that encouraged, or even required, people to behave in a particular way. Yet, because human behavior cannot exist apart from belief, the study of one is complementary to the study of the other. A complete explanation of human behavior must take account of what human beings believe about their social and natural environment, what that environment actually is like, how people's ideas are modified by sensory observations, especially as they seek to act upon the environment, and finally how actions modify the environment. This sort of project draws upon, curbs, and unifies the insights derived from applying idealist, positivist, and realist epistemologies, but in its totality it most closely approximates a realist position.

I have not yet mentioned materialism because it is not an epistemological term, referring to how we know things, but an ontological one, relating to an understanding of the actual nature of things. Its opposite, ontological idealism, in its most extreme form denies the existence of the material world, holding only ideas to be real. A less extreme version of ontological idealism that is prevalent in the social sciences accepts the existence of the material world but asserts the autonomous existence and primacy of ideas (Bunge 1996: 282-304). I find it difficult to imagine that anyone who acknowledges a biological evolutionary origin for the human species, and therefore accepts that the human body, including the human brain, has evolved as a particular form of adaptation to the material world, could be anything but a materialist.

Yet, because of the strongly symbolic component in the ways that human beings adapt to the environment, there is considerable disagreement about the relative importance of the role played by ideas and material factors in shaping human behavior. In this debate materialists treat ecological, economic, and demographic factors as primary in determining relations between groups of people and the natural environment. For them, culture is merely an epiphenomenon or a kind of computational device that reflects this adaptation and plays a relatively passive, facilitating role. A classic expression of this view is Leslie White's (1949: 391) dictum that "social systems are ... determined by technological systems, and philosophies and the arts express experience as it is defined by technology and refracted by social systems." In other words, if we understand the material aspects of adaptation, we can predict the general nature of society and culture.

On the other hand, many people believe that ideas play a major role in shaping the operation and evolution of cultures. For the most part, these ideas are transmitted from one generation to the next in the form of cultural traditions. This view does not rule out a materialist understanding of change, if it is also accepted that symbolic manipulation has evolved, and functions, as a means of adapting individuals and groups to their natural and social environment. Indeed, Boyd and Richerson (1985: 116-117) have demonstrated that ideas that have been tested for their social efficacy over long periods generally are less disruptive and serve the interests of society better than do recent innovations, which tend to promote individual interests. More strongly committed idealists tend to ignore the adaptive nature of ideas and view them alone as constituting the reality that shapes human behavior. They attribute relatively little significance to external constraints as factors shaping human behavior. Hodder (1991: 4,6) has claimed that "cultural relationships are not caused by anything else outside themselves" and that because meanings are dependent on the context "we cannot generalize from one culture to another." Carried to an extreme, idealism results in a cultural determinism that is as unrealistic as ecological determinism and, in addition, is wholly incapable of explaining sociocultural change (Laudan 1990: 115; Bloch 1983: 31).

The understanding of symbols as an independent adaptive force was greatly enhanced when, in the early 1980s, on the basis of a series of brief ethnoarchaeological studies carried out in various parts of Africa, Ian Hodder (1982b) was able to demonstrate that, in addition to its technological role, material culture could be used to disguise and invert social relations, as well as to reflect and reinforce them. This discovery definitively killed the notion that symbolic aspects of culture merely reflect economic and social relations. Yet it did not call into question the proposition that culture had evolved as an adaptive strategy. It merely indicated that the flexibility of culture results in spears and calabashes of different designs reflecting the tensions and struggles, as well as the integrative tendencies, of human societies.

As an emergent property, culture has transformed human behavior to the point that the symbolic representations human societies create mediate all forms of human behavior. Because the primary purpose of symbolic representation is adaptive, its capacity to generate an almost infinite variety of ideas must be curbed if culture is to be meaningful, and hence useful, to those whose behavior is guided by it. The self-ordering structural properties of culture are, as Ernest Gellner (1982) pointed out, very different from humanity's relation to the natural world, which is ordered by the scarcity of material resources and of the energy needed to utilize them. Structural properties are most spectacularly evident in the realm of language. Despite the totally arbitrary relations between phonemes, morphemes, and grammatical principles, on the one hand, and meaning, on the other, historical linguists have demonstrated remarkable internal consistency in the manner in which these features of language change, to the extent that "a good etymology depends not on phonetic similarity, but on phonetically regular patterns of correspondence"(Jasanoff & Nussbaum 1996: 182).

It appears that in other cultural realms, to the extent that external factors play a less important role in constraining human behavior, this ordering must be provided by structures that are inherent in culture itself. The aesthetic principles underlying Classical Greek sculpture constitute no less an example of regularity in human behavior than does the most solidly established cross-cultural generalization (Montané 1980: 135). Mediating between the real world and the human understanding of that world is the realm of perception. While perception is influenced by beliefs and expectations, it has sufficient independence to convince people that reality does not always behave as they expect and permits them to adjust their understandings to make them more congruent with reality. If this could not happen, culture would not be adaptive. Without successful adaptation, which in the case of humans is simultaneously symbolic and material, there would be no human bodies, and without human bodies there would be no human minds. This, I submit, is the essence of an understanding that is materialist and takes account of cognitive phenomena. The archaeological record is a product of human behavior that was shaped with varying degrees of directness by material constraints, as these were comprehended in terms of culturally conditioned understandings of reality.

Conclusion

Philosophy has a 2,500-year tradition of studying how to construct arguments that promote clarity, depth, unity, and insight in the interpretation of data. It also has a long and distinguished tradition of investigating how human beings understand the world around them and each other. This knowledge, which is highly elaborated in very complex, and sometimes arcane, language, is recognized by many social scientists to be of value for their work. Often, however, because philosophical treatments of issues are only partially understood by social scientists, what is known about them generates much confusion. This is not a reason to abandon contact between philosophy and the social sciences, but it is a challenge for social scientists to apply philosophical insights more knowledgeably and critically.

Where archaeologists and the other social scientists have a clear advantage over philosophy is in the realm of ontology: defining the nature of what there is to study as this applies to their own disciplines. Archaeologists and social scientists share with philosophers a common-sense understanding of how human beings behave, but they also possess more specialized knowledge of the nature of human behavior based on research in the physical, biological, and social sciences. Many aspects of this understanding are highly controversial and keenly contested. Archaeologists and physical anthropologists, because of their subject matter, tend to be more aware than are most other social scientists and philosophers that human beings, like all other animals, are a product of biological evolution and that their physiology, which includes the biological basis of their behavior, has evolved as a result of natural selection working on available material. Hominid evolution has resulted in increasing dependence on learning, communication, and symbolic mediation, rather than on instinct and individual trial and error, as means to adapt to natural and social environments. By making their behavior increasingly flexible and self-reflective it has endowed human beings with an enormous selective advantage over other species. Provided that an evolutionary perspective does not become biologically reductionist or ecologically determinist, it supplies a basis for evaluating and integrating explanations of human behavior that is more focused and unified than are approaches that do not take account of how such behavior developed.

The development of a cultural mode of adaptation means that while, as physical entities, each of us has the capacity to understand the emotions and feelings of all reasonably functional human beings, we are not anatomically equipped to understand the values, beliefs, and more symbolically influenced behavior of people who belong to other cultures. Since the Enlightenment, scholars, especially social anthropologists, have believed that the variation among existing cultures represented either the total range that was possible or an adequate sample of that variation. Today, as a result of the work of Eric Wolf (1982) and others (Schrire 1984), it is recognized that most cultures were modified as a consequence of European contact long before Europeans studied them. Hence, social anthropology, despite its claim to be a general study of humanity, is starting to look more as if it were a science of acculturation. Only through history and archaeology is there a possibility of ascertaining the kinds of societies that existed in many parts of the world prior to the industrial revolution and everywhere prior to the beginnings of literacy. Archaeology is challenging social anthropology's long-standing claim to be the integrative core of the social sciences. At the same time, the social sciences are becoming increasingly dependent on archaeology's ability to infer ever more forms of behavior from the archaeological record and to reconstruct prehistoric societies for which there are not necessarily any living analogues.

Any full explanation of human adaptation must consider not only human behavior but what goes on inside the human mind. Since humans do not adapt to reality directly, but only through each individual's conceptions of reality, any complete understanding of human behavior must take account of mental phenomena, which cannot be treated as a black box. The material expression of religious beliefs that bulks so large in the archaeological record is no less important for understanding human adaptation than are stone and metal tools. It is also impossible from an evolutionary perspective to treat the cognitive realm as autonomous from the material world. On the contrary, it has evolved, both as a biological potential and in its culturally specific expressions, as the means by which people adapt to their social and natural environments. The development of a capacity for culture, which facilitates humanity's ability to learn and to modify learned behavior, has greatly benefited humans by switching the main locus of selection from the whole organism to individual beliefs and concepts. This does not, however, guarantee an idyllic world for individuals or societies. Many ideas are maladaptive and those who, for whatever reason, persist in holding them must pay a price for doing so. The real world passes its own judgments on human actions and on the ideas that underlie them.

8

The Real, the Perceived, and the Imagined

Neoevolutionism and Processual Archaeology

The processual archaeologists of the 1960s and 1970s chose to utilize a very narrow spectrum of epistemological options, which accorded with a view of human behavior that has not withstood the test of trying to explain the full range of archaeological data. Processual archaeology was based on a joint commitment to neoevolutionism and ecological determinism. For several decades the anthropologists Leslie White and Julian Steward had interpreted the idea that cultures were adaptive systems to mean that individual sociocultural systems, either in their entirety or at least in terms of their most significant features, were shaped by the material requirements of their adaptation, which could be measured in terms of energy flows within cultural systems and between those systems and the natural environment. They further maintained that human consciousness, in the form of beliefs and values, was shaped by adaptive requirements, thereby minimizing, or even ignoring, the role that existing beliefs and human agency played in bringing about sociocultural change (White 1949; Steward 1955).

Central to the new project was the idea that cultural variation was limited and that its essential features could be summarized in terms of a unilinear series of stages of development, most commonly composed of bands, tribes, chiefdoms, and states. While neoevolutionary anthropologists, such as Elman Service (1962), Marshall Sahlins (1968), and Morton Fried (1967), did not rule out variations arising as a result of cultures having to adapt to specific environments, they firmly believed that significant sociocultural variation could be understood in terms of a limited number of types (for Sahlins' later repudiation of neoevolutionism, see Sahlins 1976).

The ideas of White and Steward were applied to prehistoric archaeology by Lewis Binford and his followers in the 1960s (for accounts and critiques of the development of processual archaeology, see Gibbon 1989: 61-117; Trigger 1989a: 294-328; Willey & Sabloff 1993: 214-311). They assumed that, if human behavior were highly regular, it would be relatively easy, by establishing correlations between material culture and behavior in living societies, to discover a series of regularities that would permit them to interpret the archaeological record in behavioral terms. They further argued that, since material culture was influenced by all aspects of human behavior and all aspects of sociocultural systems were adaptive, it should be as easy to infer past behavior relating to the ideological and social subsystems as it was to infer that relating to the economy. Thus Binford advocated a massive program of ethnoarchaeological research that it was hoped, by establishing invariant relations between behavior and material culture in living societies, soon would produce the generalizations that were required to read all sorts of behavioral meaning into the archaeological record (Binford 1962). His own research among the Nunamiut Eskimos of northern Alaska was intended to provide information about regularities in the spatial behavior of big-game hunting peoples (Binford 1978).

Processual archaeology accorded closely with the philosophical and social concerns of the 1960s. It was grounded in a very specific ontology, which maintained that sociocultural systems were shaped directly and rationally as the means for adapting populations to their environmental settings. This position accorded with the non-Marxist materialism that was popular in the United States during this period of unparalleled economic prosperity. Second, the approach adopted by Binford and his followers was, like most of the social science of the 1960s, strongly behaviorist in orientation (J. Watson 1929). Beliefs, and culture generally, were treated as by-products of human activity, the main function of which was to facilitate adaptation. Binford maintained that any attempt to infer the psychology and beliefs of prehistoric humans using archaeological evidence alone was doomed to failure and, for this reason as well, dismissed efforts to understand archaeological data from a culturally specific viewpoint (Binford 1972: 198).

Processual archaeologists strongly privileged the study of human behavior over the study of beliefs; this position must be kept in mind when assessing Binford's claim that, if archaeologists only tried, they could learn as much about the ideological subsystems of cultures, which include religion, as they had about their economies (Binford 1962). This behavioral bias naturally predisposed processual archaeologists, like most social scientists of that period, to favor a positivist epistemology. It was believed that, if archaeologists could establish generalizations about human behavior, like other social scientists they could provide governments and the private sector with information that would be useful for public control and manipulation (Martin & Plog 1973: 364-368). This would ensure archaeology an honored position in a society in which "technological efficiency is regarded as the highest value" and justify continued public support for archaeological research (Gibbon 1989: 118-141; Kolakowski 1972: 235). A positivist approach also enhanced the scientific credentials of archaeological findings by endowing them with an aura of ethical neutrality, which was highly valued at that time.

Above all, in embracing a Hempelian nomological-deductive approach, Binford was seeking an epistemological rationalization for his assumptions about the nature of sociocultural systems. It is evidence of the continuing philosophical naiveté of most archaeologists in the 1960s that no effort was made to assess Hempel's position in relation to the philosophical debates of the period. Nor was much attention paid to the problems with Hempel's position that were drawn to archaeologists' attention in the few critiques of Binford's ideas that were published (Bayard 1969; C. Morgan 1973; 1974). Both friends and foes of the New Archaeology seemed prepared to treat Hempel's views as philosophy's last word on epistemology. Archaeologists generally accepted what they were told philosophers believed.

It also went unnoticed by archaeologists at the time, or, if noted, was dismissed as nothing more than an indication of social anthropology's backwardness, that, while a number of social anthropologists were vociferously promoting neoevolutionism, they never constituted more than a minority movement within that branch of anthropology. It was also a minority movement that peaked in the 1960s and then quickly declined in relative importance. Neoevolutionism flourished at a time when cultural studies were in disarray in anthropology (Harris 1968: 393-463). The culture and personality approach, which had dominated Boasian anthropology in the 1940s and 1950s, no longer attracted anthropologists and it was not until the 1970s that structuralism, and later poststructuralism, revived an interest in beliefs rather than behavior.

That neoevolution did not fare better among social anthropologists in the 1960s was the result, not of their lack of theoretical sophistication, but of their realization that cultural variation was much greater than would be the case if a neoevolutionary ontology applied. It is unfortunate that at this time cultural anthropologists did not criticize the neoevolutionist position more vigorously, preferring, it seems, to let it burn itself out. Nor were most archaeologists, despite protestations to the contrary, sufficiently interested in social anthropology to compare the claims of neoevolutionists and processual archaeologists with the ethnographic evidence of cultural variation. Neoevolutionary models of tribes and chiefdoms were based mainly on ethnographic evidence from the Pacific region, without any systematic effort being made to determine how similar or dissimilar societies at analogous levels were in other parts of the world (Sahlins 1958; Service 1962). Instead, archaeologists and neoevolutionary social anthropologists utilized each other's ideas, producing the same kind of self-contained and uncritical intellectual feedback that characterized relations between processual archaeology and Hempelian philosophy.

Despite these weaknesses, and contrary to the views of some archaeologists such as Paul Courbin (1988), processual archaeology made important and lasting contributions to the development of archaeology. By compelling archaeologists to become more self-conscious, explicit, and critical about their methodologies, it challenged complacency, and encouraged more sophisticated and productive research, which eventually resulted in archaeologists gaining deeper and more informed insights into what had happened in the past. Speculation was replaced by efforts to test and verify interpretations. The development of middle-range theory, which sought systematically to infer human behavior from archaeological remains, gave archaeologists new confidence in their ability to contribute to the development of the social sciences (Binford 1977a; 1981a). It is for these reasons that processual archaeology has influenced, in varying ways and to varying degrees, subsequent work done in all branches of archaeology (Morris 1987; Shanks 1996: 132-144; Snodgrass 1987).

Postprocessual Counterpoint

Beginning in the late 1970s, there was a growing awareness among processual archaeologists of ontological weaknesses in their approach. Ethnoarchaeological research continued to produce generalizations that were useful for the behavioral interpretation of prehistoric technology, subsistence patterns, and other aspects of adaptation, but these were the same areas that archaeologists had addressed most successfully prior to processual archaeology (Hawkes 1954). There was a greater awareness of diversity in the archaeological record, which suggested that, if ecological adaptation had played a more important role in shaping the archaeological record than Boasian-inspired culture-historical archaeologists had acknowledged, cultural traditions, which might be no less adaptive, had played a more important role than processual archaeologists had imagined. Furthermore, Hodder's (1982b) ethnoarchaeological observations that material culture could disguise, distort, and invert, as well as reflect, social relations called into question processual archaeology's assumption that the ideological sphere was of only epiphenomenal significance.

It was also observed increasingly frequently that the material remains of religious activities and belief systems bulked large in the archaeological record in the form of temples, tombs, and iconography (W. Walker 1995). Over time interest grew in the symbolic as well as the social meaning of such remains. A tomb might (but did not necessarily) reflect the status of a dead person, or that person's family, and thus yield information about social organization that had cross-cultural and evolutionary significance, as the early processual archaeologists had maintained (J. Brown 1971; O'Shea 1984). But the layout of a tomb and the material evidence of rituals carried out at the time of the burial might provide insights into culturally specific beliefs that many archaeologists were beginning to find no less interesting (Chapman et al. 1981; Lenoble 1991; Lustig 1993).

Some processual archaeologists attempted to adapt their approach to a growing awareness of behavioral diversity by assigning beliefs a more significant role in the regulation of social relations (Flannery & Marcus 1976). Other archaeologists concluded that, while processual archaeology had contributed significantly to a better understanding of ecological issues, it had erred in its ecological determinism and its denial of agency to human beings. Some began, along Marxist lines, to assign social conflict over material resources a greater role in bringing about social change (McGuire 1992; Spriggs 1984), while others once again ascribed a major role to ideas (Hodder 1982a; Miller & Tilley 1984a).

These changes were not taking place in a vacuum, but in a broader intellectual climate in which behaviorism was giving way to a growing interest in cultural studies. For over thirty years, I have taught an undergraduate course at McGill University on early civilizations in which students are each required to write an essay on a topic of their own choosing. Throughout this period, I have tried to cover all aspects of early civilizations. Yet, in the 1970s, most papers were concerned with ecological, economic, and political issues. In recent years, more than 80 percent of the papers have dealt with religion and symbolism. This trend, I believe, reflects a broader shift in interest that has occurred, both in society in general and in archaeology and anthropology in particular, over the past thirty years. In the practice of archaeology, this transformation has taken the form of a rebellion against the taboos and restrictions of processual archaeology that has been no less strident, confrontational, and fueled by career building than was processual archaeology's rebellion against culture-historical archaeology in the 1960s. The principal emphasis of the innovators has been on studying religion, cultural agency, and the human mind (Hodder 1991; Preucel 1991). What is strikingly different is that postprocessualism is theoretically considerably less unified than processual archaeology was in its early days and does not have a single leader.

This transformation has also affected relations between archaeology and philosophy. Because these relations have become part of a broader set of interdisciplinary connections linking philosophy, the social sciences, and cultural studies, they are far more developed and sophisticated than were the limited, bilateral ties between archaeology and philosophy in the 1960s. They also have acquired more vociferous social and political dimensions.

The repudiation of processual archaeology has become part of a more extensive, postmodern revolt against positivism and what is seen as the production of objective knowledge to serve the interests of the rich and powerful. The supporters of a postmodern position maintain that there is no single true version of human affairs, but multiple truths that are constructed from the varied standpoints of rich and poor, winners and losers, males and females, and different ethnic groups. Radicals seek, by encouraging the development of multiple views of the past, to decenter and disempower what they characterize as hegemonic archaeology, which they maintain serves the interests of the most privileged and conservative groups in society (Bapty & Yates 1990; Hodder 1984; Shanks 1992; Tilley 1991; Ucko 1990: ix-xxi).

This perspective has been inspired by the classical Marxist view that knowledge is not neutral and objective, but reflects the particular understandings and vested interests of the people who create it, as well as those of their public and private patrons. Such an interpretation initially reflected the materialist belief that knowledge is created to help realize specific political and economic goals. It was maintained that to understand why people propagate particular ideas, it is necessary to ascertain the goals that they are pursuing and the way in which their ideas relate to these goals. That requires deconstruction: taking ideas apart and critically analyzing them to learn how, why, and by whom they were put together. This approach was further developed and propagated, beginning in the 1920s, by the Frankfurt School within the general context of what is now called neo-Marxism. The members of this school attributed increasing importance to ideas themselves and less importance to material conditions as determinants of what people believe (Held 1980). The ideas of the Italian Marxist philosopher Antonio Gramsci (1992), who stressed the role of ideologies as support for resistance as well as hegemony, also have contributed to the development of critical analysis.

Critical analysis provides an intellectual structure and rationalization for an interest-driven examination of archaeological interpretation. At the same time, the realization that archaeological interpretations are subjective and influenced by the social milieus in which archaeology is practiced has become much more widely accepted as a result of the study of the history of archaeology. That process began with Robert Silverberg's (1968) *Mound Builders of Ancient America*, which demonstrated how ideas about the so-called Mound Builders both reflected the nineteenth-century racism that was directed against aboriginal Americans and reinforced that racism. By the early 1980s, as the result of increasing knowledge of the history of American archaeology, more archaeologists were becoming aware that archaeological interpretations had been deeply influenced by ethnic prejudice (Trigger 1980). Nineteenth-century interpretations of archaeological data reflected European and Euro-American ethnocentrism and the belief that these people had in their own racial superiority. The assumption that indigenous peoples were primitive and unchanging had encouraged serious misreadings of the archaeological record. Cultural change generally had been attributed to migration or diffusion rather than to indigenous development, and evidence of change often had been totally ignored.

Slightly later in the 1980s, feminists began to examine gender biases, both in the practice of archaeology and in the interpretation of archaeological data. These two issues were connected, since the small number of women who in the past had managed to become archaeologists and the subordinate roles their male colleagues had tried to assign them ensured that female viewpoints were rarely considered. In the 1980s, androcentric views of the past were critically examined, including the shortcomings of the "man the hunter" version of hominid evolution. It became obvious, as a result of these critiques, that archaeologists had viewed the history of humanity almost exclusively from the perspective of the male half of the world's population (Conkey & Spector 1984; Conkey & Tringham 1995; Hanen & Kelley 1992).

Last of all, class biases began to be exposed. Especially in historical archaeology, the main emphasis long had been directed toward studying the material culture of elites and interpretations were characterized by projecting modern power relations and social values into the past in a way that made these relations appear natural and unproblematical rather than as results of specific historical circumstances. Archaeologists began to pay special attention to evidence relating to the daily lives of peasants, slaves, and industrial workers, on the grounds that these are the groups least well represented in written records and hence the ones to whose understanding archaeologists potentially can contribute the most (M. Johnson 1996; Leone & Potter 1988; McGuire & Paynter 1991).

While some archaeologists grumble about fanaticism and protest that radical ideas are becoming too influential, most accept the essential validity of these criticisms. Many hope that greater awareness of these problems will help the interpretation of archaeological evidence to become more rounded and objective. At the same time, however, revealing subjectivity and biases in archaeological interpretations also has encouraged the revival of extreme versions of epistemological idealism. Many archaeologists once again accept the proposition that belief determines action and explains human behavior. Many have also been influenced by the subjectivism that has developed in comparative literature under the influence of postmodernism. This subjectivism has as its central tenet that there is no way to ascertain how anyone else perceives or feels about anything. Every decoding of a message is another encoding, largely determined by the presuppositions, experiences, and associations that each person brings to the message. This view is represented as empowering the individual by making each human being's understanding unique. The individual is further thought to be empowered when relativism as well as subjectivism is taken into account. Relativism maintains that there are no objective standards by which any person's or group's beliefs may be judged or compared with any other's (Bhaskar 1989a; 1989b; Feyerabend 1987; Hollis & Lukes 1982; Lyotard 1984; Rose 1991).

Ironically, archaeologists who espouse idealism and the notion that the world can be whatever an individual imagines must now deal with a reality in which the resources available for archaeological research are becoming increasingly limited as public sources of research funding are curtailed. Like many idealists in other fields, they deal with this problem, not by addressing the political and economic sources of their difficulties, but by denying the significance of material constraints and stressing the power of ideas. One must inquire if this response is a functional one or resembles the proverbial ostrich with its head buried in the sand.

Inferring the Symbolic

These developments have led many archaeologists to acknowledge the first part of Childe's argument: that the world people adapt to is not the real world but the world as they imagine it to be. In order to understand why people behaved as they did, archaeologists must ascertain what they believed. It therefore follows that the past must be understood culturally before it can be studied socially or ecologically. It is argued, for example, that animal bones in middens cannot automatically be used to infer prehistoric diet and subsistence patterns. Some of the animals whose bones are present may have been killed for their hides or feathers alone, while taboos may have required the bones of other animals that were eaten to be disposed of in ways that leave no trace in the archaeological record (Hodder 1990: 262-64). Even a carefully butchered carcass may have been an offering that was not consumed by humans. This position marks a return to the viewpoint of Collingwood.

Materialists can counter with Childe's second proposition: that, while people may indeed adapt to the environment as they perceive it to be rather than as it is, the perceived and the real environments must be reasonably congruent if society is to survive. Richard Gould has argued that archaeologists should explain what they can ecologically and interpret only residuals symbolically. Thus preferences for different types of chert should be studied initially in terms of their relative utility for making specific types of tools. Only if the preferred type turns out to perform less well or to be much harder to work than other equally available varieties should symbolic explanations be considered (Gould 1978b). This proposal, which privileges a behavioral approach, does not take into account that all relations are symbolically mediated. Archaeologists come closer to reality when they maintain that there is no way to distinguish the ecological and the symbolic in the archaeological record, even though it is often possible to demonstrate that some forms of behavior that are recorded archaeologically were ecologically or economically adaptive.

The obvious answer lies in archaeologists doing what they can to infer both the behavioral patterns and the belief systems of the past, so that the two may be compared with each other. Both processual and culture-historical archaeologists have had considerable success in inferring technological processes and trading patterns from archaeological data. The strictly limited number of workable solutions to any technological problem and the utility of trace element analysis for determining the source locations of various kinds of stone, pottery clay, and metal ores permit these processes to be inferred with a high degree of accuracy. On the other hand, variations in the detailed religious beliefs that might have been associated with metallurgy or flintknapping are so great that the archaeologist has no hope of inferring the specific content of these beliefs from artifacts alone (Childe 1956b: 39-56).

Similarly, processual archaeology has made considerable progress in discovering cross-cultural correlations between material culture and behavior in living societies that permit general hunting strategies, social hierarchies, and lineage structures to be inferred from archaeological remains (Binford 1983a). Once again, however, the archaeologist cannot emulate the social anthropologist in ascertaining the specific beliefs associated with such behavior.

Yet the situation is not hopeless with respect to cognitive phenomena. While ecological determinists often assume that middle-range theory applies only to the more practical aspects of human behavior, similar beliefs recur in historically unrelated situations. The idea of the king as a stranger, or as being in some other way of a different nature from his subjects, has been identified in many cultures around the world that lack any obvious historical connections (Feeley-Harnik 1985; Gillespie 1989: 215-56). My comparative study of seven early civilizations has revealed that in each of these societies the cosmos was believed to function as a series of energy flows by means of which supernatural forces sustained the natural world, while human beings in turn sustained the gods by means of offerings that were channeled into the supernatural sphere, with the upper classes acting as the principal intermediaries. These surprising regularities in terms of the general structure of religious beliefs can be interpreted as a projection into the cosmic realm of the tributary relations that bound commoners and rulers together in each of these societies (Trigger 1993: 86-108).

The constraints shaping these particular beliefs were not calculations of efficiency or security, such as deciding which animal species were the most energy-efficient to hunt. Instead they were the products of cross-culturally similar reflections on crucial aspects of the social order. If such concepts prove to be universal in all historically documented early civilizations, they will provide useful hypotheses that can be tested archaeologically by looking for archaeological evidence of the sort of ritual behavior associated with such beliefs in those early civilizations for which textual evidence is not available. By contrast, ethnographic and historical evidence demonstrates that it is sheer nonsense to interpret all female figurines as representing mother goddesses (Ucko 1968; Hamilton et al. 1996). Yet, at best, even valid generalizations can suggest only general patterns of belief, not their specific content (Lewis-Williams &

Dowson 1988). For knowing the latter, a single Egyptian or Mesopotamian religious text counts for far more than any cross-cultural generalization or any amount of nontextual archaeological evidence.

Hodder (1987b) has proposed that a contextual approach can be used to distinguish between beliefs and practices in the archaeological record. This approach involves playing off the information provided by one aspect of the archaeological record against information provided by other aspects for the same culture or community. For example, in modern Saudi Arabia kings and commoners are buried in the same fashion, as an expression of Islamic belief in the equality of all Muslims before God and of Wahabi emphasis on the community of believers (Huntington & Metcalf 1979: 122). Future archaeologists might conclude from a study of Saudi burials that they were dealing with an egalitarian society. Yet an investigation of Saudi settlement patterns would reveal quite the opposite, making it clear that the burial practices were a reflection of ideology rather than of social reality. Even so, without written texts or oral traditions, it would be impossible for archaeologists to infer the specific content of such beliefs.

I reluctantly conclude that specific beliefs cannot be inferred from material culture alone. To infer the meaning of symbols, it is necessary to have verbal information in the form of written records or oral traditions either from the same culture or from cultures that are historically related to the one being studied (Hays 1993). Insofar as texts normally are understood to be recordings of the spoken word, nothing could be less appropriate than the ubiquitous postprocessual claim that the archaeological record is a text that archaeologists can learn to read (Hodder 1988; 1991: 126-128; Shanks & Tilley 1987b: 95-117; 1989a: 4-5; Tilley 1990). Verbal information is most evidently applicable for interpreting archaeological data when both the archaeological and the textual information date from the same period and come from the same culture. That is why historical archaeology is proving so useful for studying relations between beliefs and material culture (Cannon 1989; Deetz 1977; Glassie 1975; R. Isaac 1982; M. Johnson 1996; Lissarrague 1990; McGuire & Paynter 1991). Unfortunately, processual archaeology's hostility toward the investigation of the culturally specific, as opposed to what is cross-culturally recurrent, has left this a very undeveloped, and until recently an almost abandoned, field.

Archaeologists have long assumed that, where there is significant continuity in the archaeological record, it is possible to project historically documented uses or meanings of material culture back into progressively earlier time periods. This is often called the direct historical approach (Wedel 1938). This approach was castigated by Binford, along with all other analogical efforts to attribute behavioral or symbolic meaning to archaeological data, on the grounds that it merely suggested hypotheses rather than demonstrated relations (Binford 1967; 1968a: 8-12). In many well-documented cases, however, the concept of continuity appears to be sound. Historical evidence from ancient Egypt demonstrates that a specific set of religious beliefs was expressed using the same general iconographic system for over 3,000 years, before both gave way to Christianity in the fourth century A.D. (Kemp 1989). Similar examples of continuities can be found in Christian Europe, China, India, Islamic countries, and many other parts of the world.

On the other hand, there are contrary examples of continuity in symbols being accompanied by radical transformations in their meaning, while concepts that endure for long periods may, for various political and social reasons, express themselves iconographically in different ways at different times (Goff 1963: xxxv; Goodenough 1953-1968; Panofsky 1939; 1960). It has also been demonstrated that the intensity with which particular beliefs manifest themselves in material culture can vary considerably from one period to another; hence continuity in beliefs is not necessarily matched by continuity in their expression in the archaeological record (von Gernet & Timmins 1987). Clearly much remains to be learned about relations between beliefs and their symbolic expression before the direct historical approach can be used with confidence to infer the meanings that practices had in prehistoric times.

Skeptics maintain that, in the absence of accompanying textual information, the direct historical approach does not allow beliefs to be inferred very far into the past. Yet, in northeastern North America, marine shells, native copper, and rock crystals, as well as objects made from these materials, were buried with the dead beginning in the Archaic period, some 6,000 years ago. Historical and ethnographic evidence indicates that in historical times these substances, which were thought to come from the underworld and were associated with the primal life forces of that region, were believed to confer beneficial powers on both the living and the dead. It therefore seems likely that analogous, though not necessarily identical, beliefs were held in this part of the world as early as the Archaic period (Hamell 1980; 1987). A growing corpus of comparative ethnographic studies suggests that many aspects of aboriginal American religions are derived from a set of shamanistic beliefs that may have been brought from Siberia into the New World by Palaeo-Indian colonists and were transformed to varying degrees as big-game hunting bands became increasingly sedentary (Furst 1977; Seaman & Day 1994). This historical continuity might provide a basis for attributing fairly specific meanings to religious paraphernalia spread over an entire hemisphere and spanning more than 12,000 years.

While the direct historical approach may not prove useful for inferring the precise meanings of Upper Palaeolithic cave art in Europe, it does appear to be capable of shedding light on beliefs over much longer periods than most archaeologists have believed. To be really useful, however, as much energy needs to be expended on developing this culturally specific approach as processual archaeologists have devoted to elaborating Binford's middle-range theory. That requires establishing a better understanding of the nature of cultural transmission to complement the adaptationist concerns of processual archaeology. It also requires ascertaining what kinds of archaeological evidence may serve as useful indicators of cognitive and behavioral continuity.

On the other hand, the direct historical approach does not work well, even in the short term, in the absence of both associated textual or verbal evidence and significant cultural continuity. I am not certain what arguments could be used to justify Nanno Marinatos's use of textually attested Late Bronze Age Egyptian and Middle Eastern religious beliefs and practices as analogues for inferring those of Minoan Crete. Despite evidence of vigorous trade and cultural exchanges linking these three cultures, there do not appear to be enough contextual similarities among their religious practices and iconography to justify this operation. Moreover, the belief systems and cultural practices of Egypt and the Middle East, which are documented both textually and iconographically, appear to be very different from each another. Finally, there is no reason to believe that, even if Minoans had been intimately familiar with the religious beliefs of their trading partners (which is by no means certain), they would have been significantly influenced by them. The historical reasons that Marinatos gives for not wanting to project well-attested later Greek beliefs back into the apparently ethnically distinct Minoan culture seem methodologically sound. Yet the fact that some sites display, in her words, "remarkable cult continuity" suggests that in this case the direct historical approach might be stronger if applied temporally within Crete itself, rather than by trying to link Crete with neighboring cultures, as she proposes (Marinatos 1993: 123).

Over the past fifteen years, archaeologists appear to have moved beyond the stage where they treat culture, or the ideas that facilitate human understanding, as something that is ecologically determined and epiphenomenal in nature. An approach that is simply ecological or behaviorist cannot account for the totality either of human activities or of the archaeological record. That realization does not, however, justify going to the opposite extreme and adopting a purely idealist approach, which would constitute an equally limiting form of cultural determinism.

Human beings simultaneously inhabit a conceptual environment that exists in their minds and a social and natural environment that exists independently of their wills. A challenge that is faced by archaeologists, other social scientists, and philosophers is to define more precisely the relations between this inner and outer environment. That is, as I see it, primarily an ontological question that can be answered only on the basis of more detailed evidence. If archaeologists were limited to studying only behavior, as processual archaeologists seem originally to have believed was the case, archaeology would be unsuited to participate in this project. On the other hand, if archaeologists can forge the tools to study ideas and behavior independently of one another, they will be equipped to participate in the study of this key issue.

The Dangers of Extreme Relativism

At the same time that postmodern encouragement of an interest in subjective phenomena has been a source of significant theoretical and methodological progress in archaeology, an exaggerated emphasis on subjectivism and relativism has been calling the mission, and perhaps the very reasons for the existence, of archaeology and other social science disciplines into question. While even most positivist archaeologists are prepared to admit that the social environment in which they live influences the questions they ask, they believe that by employing proper scientific methods it is possible to distinguish true propositions from false ones (Binford 1987). All relativists are agreed, however, that not only the questions archaeologists ask but also the answers they are prepared to accept as true are determined to a considerable degree by what they believe. This is so to the extent that all humans are predisposed to accept what they think is likely to be true on the basis of minimal supporting evidence, but demand next to impossible levels of proof for propositions that they regard as being extremely distasteful or unreasonable. Contrary to positivist assertions, there is no wholly objective measure of truth. Even positivists accept a general law if it is not contradicted in any, or in the case of statistical generalizations in numerous, observed instances. Yet, in terms of the formal positivist definition of laws as generalizations based on observations, all relevant cases, past, present, and future, would have to be observed before a proposition would qualify as a fully confirmed universal generalization. In the real world this is never possible and proof always involves some element of faith (Barnes 1974; 1977; Feyerabend 1975; Kuhn 1962).

In archaeology, strong relativists, such as Christopher Tilley, Michael Shanks, and Peter Ucko, have maintained (although not always consistently) that there is no empirical basis on which archaeologists can demonstrate that one interpretation is right and another wrong. They argue that scholars are so blinded by their prejudices and their culture, that archaeological findings exert little, if any, influence over what they believe. The only way in which an archaeological theory or interpretation can be refuted is to demonstrate that it is illogical (Hindess & Hirst 1975: 1-5; Miller & Tilley 1984b: 151; Shanks & Tilley 1987b: 195; cf. 1987a: 114-15; Tilley 1990: 338, 340-341; Ucko 1990). In other words, they accept the validity of coherence truth, that arguments must make sense logically, but deny, or minimize, the efficacy of correspondence truth, the requirement that claims must accord with available evidence (Lowther 1962). Rarely if ever, to my knowledge, have archaeologists claimed that logic itself is culturally relative and hence that what is illogical in one culture might be logical in another (Damerow 1996; Hallpike 1979; Hamill 1990; Lloyd 1990). I am surprised that some of the more extreme archaeological relativists have not taken this final step. Even without it, the effect of strong relativism is to turn all archaeological interpretation, or at least that which is logically coherent, into a form of mythmaking.

It is further argued by strong relativists that it cannot be maintained that one person's or group's interpretation of archaeological evidence is better than another's. Professional archaeologists' claims to have special qualifications are grandiloquently branded as forms of elitist pretension and hegemonic obfuscation and as attempts to control the past in the interest of dominant groups. It is asserted that any individual or group has the right to use archaeological data to create the past that they want and that there is no valid basis for challenging the validity of such interpretations. Such a position is hailed by its proponents as democratizing archaeology and purging it of its elitist pretensions (Hodder 1984; Shanks & Tilley 1987b: 195; Tilley 1990: 338; Ucko 1990: xix-xx).

Moderate relativists stress problems of objectivity and admit that no one can be certain that interpretations are free from bias. Yet, like the philosopher Alison Wylie, they maintain that archaeological evidence was produced independently of archaeologists and therefore offers resistance to the totally free exercise of their imagination and to erroneous interpretations. Archaeologists' beliefs and biases influence which sites are recognized and selected for excavation, which artifacts are noted and how they are classified, and how data are interpreted. Nevertheless, in the long run, erroneous interpretations are countered and eventually falsified by contrary new data (Leone 1982; Trigger 1989a: 407-11; R. Watson 1990: 683; Wylie 1982).

Many of the more extreme, and frequently cited, misinterpretations of archaeological data, such as the Mound Builder myth in America and the idea of the non-African origin of Great Zimbabwe, were perpetrated at a time when the archaeological record was far less well understood than it is at present. It could be argued that these errors and the colonial mentality that produced them are now obvious only because they are temporally and socially far removed from us, and that equally biased interpretations of the archaeological record still are being produced. There is no way to prove that this is not the case. Yet both these interpretations were rejected, not as a result of arguments that were advanced by propagandists who were strongly opposed to the racist and colonialist mentalities that had encouraged them, but because of archaeological discoveries that were incompatible with them. Both Caton Thompson, who definitively established the Bantu origins of Great Zimbabwe, and Cyrus Thomas, who demonstrated that the Mound Builders were not a separate race from the North American Indians, tried to make their finds more acceptable to the racists of their time by arguing that the cultures they had shown to be of indigenous origin were not as evolved as previous researchers had claimed (Kuklick 1991:152-56; Thomas 1894: 659-87).

While the archaeological record undoubtedly still is being interpreted in ways that are biased and erroneous, it appears that as it becomes better known, as a result of the collection of more data and the development of better techniques for interpreting these data, it is more able to constrain the imagination of archaeologists. Hence today's erroneous interpretations tend not to be so long-lived, and are more contested and less socially persuasive than they were in the past. While an unbiased interpretation of archaeological data may never be possible and archaeologists may never be able to establish the truth of any specific interpretation, it has proved possible over the years to construct a more comprehensive and accurate picture of what happened in the past and to gain a better understanding of how and why change has occurred.

There is also evidence that ingrained prejudices may be countered by archaeological evidence. Because most North American archaeologists in the nineteenth century believed that Indians were primitive and incapable of learning to do things differently, they did not expect to find evidence of change in the archaeological record and did not bother to look for it. When such evidence was found, most of these archaeologists maintained that aboriginal cultures were static and tried to explain cultural change in specific regions in terms of unchanging cultures shifting about and replacing each other in specific locales. By the early twentieth century, it was clear that changes had occurred within cultures that could not be explained in this fashion. These changes were attributed to a form of cultural diffusion in which most of the important new ideas came from Mexico and Siberia. The implication was that North American Indians were intelligent enough to adopt ideas from elsewhere but not creative enough to produce new ideas themselves. A still more detailed understanding of the archaeological record slowly revealed that postulating the exogenous origin of new ideas failed to explain a growing corpus of evidence. As a result of such observations, archaeologists finally had to admit that aboriginal Americans were as innovative as any other peoples (Trigger 1980).

There is a temptation to read the history of North American archaeology as an indication of the extent to which all archaeological interpretations are influenced by the prejudices that archaeologists bring to their work. There is, however, strong evidence that more favorable interpretations of aboriginal behavior did not result so much from archaeologists being influenced by improving social attitudes toward aboriginal people as from their realizing the incompatibility between existing archaeological interpretations and their underlying assumptions about Indians, on the one hand, and the evidence that they were collecting, on the other. Such developments bear witness to the erroneousness of a strong relativist position and to the capacity of evidence to alter even deeply entrenched understandings.

Strong relativism and its associated idealist ontology emerge as philosophies of despair and, like most such philosophies, turn out to be unduly pessimistic. Archaeological interpretation is not merely, as extreme relativists would persuade us, a matter of politics and propaganda, or, as Glyn Daniel and Stuart Piggott more modestly suggested, of personal opinion. This is so, at least in large part, because real life is not whatever we want it to be. Humans almost certainly, as Childe realized long ago, adapt to the world not as it is but as they imagine it to be. Yet, if the world as groups collectively imagine it is not fairly congruent with the world as it really is, such groups may starve to death and have no ideas at all. By acknowledging physical constraints and trying to understand how human beings conceptualized the world, archaeologists can provide useful insights into the forces that have shaped human history and will continue to do so.

Realism as a Framing Epistemology

Archaeologists can never be sure that a particular interpretation is correct, still less that it can never be improved. Yet today they are asking more questions than ever before, have more techniques to analyze data than ever before, and are increasingly aware of their biases and trying to compensate for them. A growing awareness of the role that such biases play in the interpretation of archaeological data, and in the practice of archaeology, is a development that all archaeologists should welcome. But multiple standpoints do not simply create multiple, incompatible archaeologies. They challenge all archaeologists, wherever possible, to use this multiplicity to create more holistic and objective syntheses. Their goal should be an archaeology that is more complete and less biased because it is informed by an ever-increasing number of viewpoints and constrained by more data.

The only way to achieve this goal that is compatible with a biological evolutionary view of human origins is to adopt a materialist ontology and a realist epistemology. Human beings exist by drawing energy from the physical world, and the mind, as a property of the brain, is as material as anything else. Archaeologists must study the human mind in terms of both the innate cognitive abilities of the brain and the acquired knowledge that together allow the brain to interpret sensory observations. The resulting understanding constitutes the conceptualized world to which human beings adapt. Culture in turn must be viewed as a highly flexible mechanism that serves to adapt human beings to the external environment and has enabled them to transform that environment to an ever greater extent. Archaeologists finally must acknowledge the role that the senses play as mediators between the external real world and the inner world of the mind, and the ability of sensory observations to alter conceptions relating to the real world. Because the conceptualized world is linked to the real world through our senses, all humans (including extreme idealists—both epistemological and ontological) must pragmatically acknowledge that they do not exist independently of external constraints. Without the ability to respond to sensory stimuli, the mind would be unable to play an adaptive role.

Realism is a messy and eclectic epistemology, embracing the study of processes and emergent properties as well as of what can be observed directly; interested in causality as well as correlation; and trying to incorporate mind into a system of knowing that also involves sensory experience and entities that are external to the observer. Its principal and overwhelmingly important virtue is that it treats mind, senses, and external reality in an interrelated fashion. This view corresponds more closely with reality as archaeologists experience it in their daily lives than does positivism's efforts to privilege sensory experience or idealism's efforts to privilege the mind as an exclusive means of knowing.

The questions that archaeologists must address in order to understand the past bear a close resemblance to those that all humans must confront in their personal and professional lives. This correspondence is no accident. The processes that shaped life in the past must have resembled, at least in a general fashion, those that shape it today. Unfortunately, this observation does not take us very far in actually understanding the past since, ironically, one of the most striking uniformities in human behavior is humanity's biologically conditioned capacity for cultural diversity. In the next chapter, I consider some of the conceptual problems that are involved in trying to understand this diversity.

9

Imagination and Scientific Curiosity

In popular belief and the mythology concerning scientific practice, science and imagination have nothing in common. Science is assumed to employ the most rigorous criteria of logic to draw conclusions from observations made under stringent and ideally replicable conditions. Imagination, by contrast, appears to belong to the realm of art and creative literature. Yet even brief reflection indicates that this dichotomy is untenable. Imagination is essential if scientific progress is to be made.

Imagining the Unimagined

Richard Bradley (1993) has reminded us that, without creativity, archaeologists would be left without anything new to say. He stresses the value of imagination as a source of ideas that will promote the growth of archaeology and maintains that, unless archaeology nurtures the creative imagination, it will cease to flourish as a scientific pursuit. More specifically, progress in archaeology depends on the archaeologist's ability to imagine pasts that are radically different from the present and from the ways that the past is currently imagined. Very little attention has been paid, however, to the role of imagination in archaeology or any other social science.

The development of science largely consists of the once unthought of becoming commonplace. In classical times, among astronomers and geographers, the flat earth of common sense gave way to a spherical planet as efforts were made to explain numerous observations, both terrestrial and celestial, for which a flat earth could not account. In a similar manner, an earth-centered universe yielded to a heliocentric one, that more recently has been expanded by the vision of a cosmos composed of a vast number of galaxies. These successive views were not products of simple induction, but resulted from individuals being able to conceptualize radical alternatives to received opinions and eventually to persuade others that their views accounted for reality better than did previous concepts.

A spectacular example of such a transformation in recent times is provided by the phenomenon of continental drift. In the nineteenth century, uniformitarian geologists assumed that continents did not move. This assumption, however, created problems for biologists and palaeontologists who were trying to account for distributions of plants and animals. They postulated the appearances and disappearances of land bridges, which Darwin protested were invoked so often and erratically that they violated the principles of uniformitarian geology. Others, including Darwin, tried to account for distributions of plants and animals by postulating forms of marine and aerial transport that even their proponents found unconvincing.

In 1915, the German meteorologist Alfred Wegener (1915), drawing on earlier observations, proposed that a single great land mass, Pangaea, had begun to separate into the present continents in the Mesozoic era. Although much of his theory was based on the apparent fit of the bulge of eastern South America into the west coast of Africa, subsequent researchers, especially those working in the southern hemisphere, noted numerous geological and palaeontological resemblances that suggested that currently separated landmasses had once been joined together. Yet, even when I took an undergraduate geology course at the University of Toronto in the late 1950s, continental drift was still being dismissed as improbable speculation. The idea was not considered seriously until the 1960s, when evidence of seafloor spreading from oceanic ridges proved that ocean basins were not permanent global features. Today continental drift is being measured on a yearly basis and mechanisms have been proposed that explain both it and many other geological features in uniformitarian terms. The challenge in this case was to imagine a process that was too slow to be apparent to human observers (Marvin 1973).

Nowhere has the problem of imagining the unimagined been harder for archaeologists than in dealing with the early development of hominids and cultural behavior. In the eighteenth century, Enlightenment philosophers had believed that, by arranging cultures existing in the modern world from simplest to most complex, they could replicate the various stages through which European civilization had evolved. Once it became apparent, however, that human beings had not been created in essentially their modern form only a few thousand years ago, but had evolved over a much longer period from some apelike ancestor, the problems posed by the origins of culture became more complex and ethnographic evidence insufficient to answer them. In 1872, Charles Lyell (1872: 470-71) had argued that early humans had lived by gathering vegetable food in a tropical environment and had only begun to hunt after they had expanded into the temperate zone. In 1913, the British physician Harry Campbell (1913: 1260) suggested that, while the ancestors of the human species had abandoned the trees in search of meat, they were at first limited to eating "vermin," and only later became able to hunt larger game. These proposals were formulated long before any archaeological evidence was available to test them.

Donald Grayson (1986: 77) has demonstrated that middle-range research, and in particular research directed toward the extraction of evidence that is diagnostic of formation processes, is not a new phenomenon but has been "routinely spawned by situations in which archaeologists recognize perplexing ambiguity in the patterning presented to them by archaeological data." Nowhere is such ambiguity more omnipresent than in the archaeology of the Lower Palaeolithic era. By the 1860s, European evolutionists postulated that Late Tertiary artifacts might be found but they would be so crude that they could be distinguished only with difficulty from naturally broken rocks. In 1867, the Abbé Louis Bourgeois claimed to have found such crude artifacts in Thenay, east of Tours. The leading French Palaeolithic archaeologist, Gabriel de Mortillet, accepted these and other Late Tertiary finds as artifacts, which he called eoliths, or dawn stones, and introduced into the earliest stages of his classification of European prehistory. Some other archaeologists, however, failed to see traces of human workmanship in such specimens and Adrien Arcelin demonstrated that similar material occurred in lower Eocene deposits and hence could not have been produced by early humans. Supporters of eoliths tried to establish diagnostic signatures of a human role in their production, while opponents sought to prove that they could have been shaped by natural forces. The issue was finally resolved in the late 1930s, when the British archaeologist A.S. Barnes (1939) found that 75 percent of the numerous stone flake tools he measured had "angle platform-scars" of less than 90°, while this angle exceeded 90° in 75 percent of the naturally broken specimens he studied. These edge angles were formed by the intersection of the surface on which pressure had been applied and of the scar left by the flake removed. Barnes argued that acute angles were necessary for effective flake removal and tool use. Collections of eoliths from different sites clearly fell into the natural category. European eoliths ceased to be regarded as artifacts and, given the absence of other conclusive evidence, it was generally accepted that hominids had not lived in Europe prior to the Acheulean epoch.

Claims of early Palaeolithic discoveries in the United States were countered even more quickly. In 1860, an amateur archaeologist, Charles Abbott, became convinced that crude artifacts being turned up on his ancestral farm near Trenton, New Jersey, had been produced by the precursors of modern Native American groups. In 1876, he attributed them to a different, probably Palaeolithic, race and two years later proclaimed that these finds dated from the glacial period. Abbott's claims were supported by Frederick Putnam, the curator of the Peabody Museum of Archaeology and Ethnology at Harvard University, and by various geologists. The Smithsonian Institution countered by sending William H. Holmes to investigate an Indian lithic quarry site. Holmes's work indicated that the so-called turtlebacks, which were hallmarks of Abbott's Palaeolithic age, were in reality rejects marking a stage in the manufacturing of stone tools rather than finished implements. The relative crudeness of an implement could not be interpreted as evidence of its antiquity. Holmes continued after 1890 to examine all known quarries and alleged Palaeolithic sites in eastern North America, including those of the Trenton gravels. While his findings did not completely silence the proponents of an early hominid presence, his work introduced a strong element of caution into their previously unrestrained speculations. It was left to Aleš Hrdlička's refutation of supposedly early human skeletal finds and the failure of later archaeologists to discover archaeological remains in North America dating from Lower Palaeolithic times to refute Abbott's claims (Meltzer 1983).

As earlier forms of hominids were discovered in southern and eastern Africa during the twentieth century, new interpretive problems arose. The evidence that the earliest hominids had brains that were little bigger than those of modern great apes suggested that a human hunter-gatherer model might not by itself supply appropriate analogues for interpreting the behavior of these creatures. Apes lack the symbolic and linguistic skills that are shared by all human groups and their sexual physiology is quite different from that of humans. By the 1950s, it had been concluded that the behavior of nonhuman primates as well as that of modern hunter-gatherers would have to be taken into account in modeling the behavior of early hominids.

But which nonhuman primates? Some looked to chimpanzees and gorillas, who were the surviving species most closely related to humans. Others drew analogies with baboons, who were less closely related to humans but lived on the savannas, as the early hominids appear to have done. Still others sought to utilize a combination of features from both groups. These analogies drew upon the more social primates, while generally ignoring the solitary or pair-bonding orangutans and gibbons. Males, who are physically larger than females, were seen as playing a major role in defending females, and hence the reproductive capacity of the group, and their hierarchical male bonding was interpreted as a central feature of early hominid social organization.

Comparisons of such behavior with that believed to be common to all modern hunter-gatherer societies suggested that the main changes that had taken place in social organization in the course of hominid evolution had been the development of male-female pair bonding and the emergence of the nuclear family within the context of small societies that continued to be dominated by rivalrous and hierarchically organized males. It was argued that greater dependence on meat-eating favored greater intelligence, slower maturation, and a sexual division of labor in which males risked their lives hunting for game while females cared for children and collected vegetable food and small game near base camps (Washburn & Howell 1960; Washburn 1960; Woolfson 1982; for primate models, Kinzey 1987). The main conclusion of this research was that early hominids had soon come to behave much like modern hunter-gatherers.

More recently, feminist critiques have called traditional interpretations of hunter-gatherer societies into question and studies of bonobos, or pygmy chimpanzees, have provided examples of highly social great apes whose females play an active role in selecting mates and maintaining social cohesion. Among bonobos cooperation is more important and competition less so than among other chimpanzees and gorillas (Fedigan 1986). This research provides a wider range of options for modeling early hominid social behavior.

Hypotheses about early hominid social behavior proved very difficult to confirm or refute using archaeological data. Many disputes remain unresolved. Did crude stone tools, such as those associated with the Early Oldowan industry, which changed slowly if at all over long periods, indicate a lack of cognitive ability, the absence of challenge to perform better, or a dearth of cultural capital on which significant innovations could be based? Opinions still differ widely, with some archaeologists treating symbolic and linguistic ability as developing very early in hominid history and making pre-*Homo erectus* forms only quantitatively different from ourselves. Others, noting the lack of symbolic representations or other evidence of symbolic behavior in Lower or perhaps even Middle Palaeolithic times, have concluded that modern forms of linguistic and symbolic behavior do not antedate modern forms of *Homo sapiens* (Mellars 1996; Noble & Davidson 1996; R. White 1982).

Once again, however, the development of middle-range theory has allowed significant progress to be made. The first major debate concerned the status of Australopithecine remains found amid innumerable fractured animal bones in the limestone caves at Makapansgat and Sterkfontein in South Africa. Raymond Dart (1949) interpreted the Australopithecine bones as those of hominids who had frequented those caves and had killed and eaten many other species of animals and used their teeth and bones as tools and weapons. Dart's dramatic view of modern human beings being descended from "killer apes" was popularized by Robert Ardrey in his book *African Genesis* (1961). Others, however, believed that all these bones, including those of the Australopithecines, represented the meals of hyenas and other scavengers. Taphonomic studies suggested that at least some of the Australopithecines had been killed by large carnivores and that their bones, like those of the other animals, had been washed into the caves (Brain 1981).

Mary and Louis Leakey interpreted their early hominid sites in East Africa as the remains of encampments of big-game hunters (Leakey 1971). The evidence that Jane Goodall had collected of the important role played by small-game hunting among male chimpanzees suggested that early hominids might have confronted and killed the larger animals whose bones were found in these sites. While this model received considerable support (G. Isaac 1971; Washburn & Lancaster 1968), Binford (1977b; 1985), who had long expressed considerable doubts about early hominid cognitive abilities, remained skeptical. He proposed that early hominids might not have been big-game hunters, but scavengers along the lines of hyenas and jackals. Binford's proposal stimulated important taphonomic research. He argued that, before animal bones found in Lower Palaeolithic sites are interpreted as having been brought there by early hominid hunters, it is necessary to determine what types and numbers of bones would have occurred in particular sorts of terrain in the absence of any hominids. Binford in this way called into question the interpretation of various Lower Palaeolithic finds as kill sites or hunting camps (Binford 1981a; 1989: 282-481).

Subsequent study of bone remains has revealed breakage patterns that strongly support scavenging rather than big-game hunting. During the Oldowan period, hominids may have hunted small game as chimpanzees do, but most of the meat they consumed was obtained from carcasses already much picked over by feline predators or other scavengers. Evidence of big-game hunting does not appear until later Lower Palaeolithic times (Blumenschine 1987; Schick & Toth 1993). By questioning received opinions, Binford and earlier researchers stimulated research that has altered our understanding of early hominid behavior in significant ways.

Some of the ideas we have been considering relating to life in Palaeolithic times were confirmed by subsequent research and others were refuted. What is important in each case is that, by contradicting accepted interpretations of the past, these ideas stimulated research that tested both old and new ideas. The result in each case was to advance archaeology both methodologically and in terms of its understanding of the past. The greatest obstacle to making progress in archaeology is intellectual complacency. Without the ability to imagine alternative explanations, archaeology languishes. On the other hand, without the opportunity and determination to test ideas, imagination is of little value.

Controlling Imagination

Bradley (1993: 132) sees talent and imagination in archaeology today as being curtailed, and even crushed, by moral earnestness and acute critical self-consciousness. What he calls moral earnestness embraces political correctness and a related desire that archaeological findings should support what are deemed to be, and in many instances undeniably are, progressive causes. It is true that archaeologists, like all other social scientists, have a moral duty to defend freedom of inquiry and that they are now, perhaps even more than in the past, being consciously manipulated by people with political agendas. Yet there is nothing fundamentally new about this sort of behavior; only the issues have changed. One even has some reason to hope that an ever-growing database renders the negative impacts of political correctness on research less virulent.

A more serious problem, which appears to be encouraged by the vogue for idealist epistemology, is an overabundance of imagination without adequate concern for archaeological testing. Hodder's (1990) *The Domestication of Europe* is the most sustained application of a structural approach to archaeological data yet attempted. In it Hodder examines the distribution of iconographic, or what are assumed to be iconographic, elements in relation to various examples of houses, tombs, settlements, and landscapes in Europe from Neolithic times into the Iron Age, with evidence from the Middle East being considered as it relates to the beginning of this sequence. On the basis of these examples, Hodder postulates a series of changes in beliefs that took the form of structural adjustments in relations among a set of binary oppositions that include nature and culture, male and female, wild and domestic, field and house (*agrios* and *domus*), outer and inner, front and back, light and dark, east and west, life and death. He also makes considerable use of the concept of boundary (*foris*).

As a structuralist, Hodder assumes that human thought is constrained by conceptual dichotomies that can undergo significant permutations in their mutual relations, while the system to which they belong remains unchanged. He assumes that underlying culture is a deep structure, or essence, governed by its own laws, that is hidden from view but ensures regularities in the phenomena that emanate from it. Within this structure, concepts acquire their meaning by the position they occupy vis-à-vis other concepts. In other words, culture as a whole is assumed to have many of the same properties as language (Barthes 1972; Lévi-Strauss 1963; 1966). Hodder then imputes meanings to these patterns and suggests how alterations in their meanings over time relate to social change.

It is by no means clear, however, how Hodder has gone about interpreting the patternings he has observed in the archaeological record. Sometimes he appears to have assumed universal meanings, a procedure that runs contrary to his insistence on the incomparability of cultures, but which he also uses elsewhere, as, for example, in his argument that trash is used symbolically in many cultures to demarcate boundaries (Hodder 1982b: 125-84; 1982c: 60-65; 1990: 127; 1991: 4,6). Yet, despite his inclusion of material relating to the Middle East, Hodder also suggests that, from perhaps as long ago as the Upper Palaeolithic period to the present, there has been sufficient continuity in various concepts that are unique to Europe that someone nurtured in modern Europe could, as a result of sharing these ideas, have privileged intuitive insights into the thought patterns of prehistoric times (Hodder 1990: 2-3; 282-300). Those insights presumably would not be shared by an archaeologist who had been born and grew up in China but had studied European prehistory, while analogous ones concerning China would be inaccessible to European archaeologists who were trained as Sinologists.

Hodder does not specify whether these continuities correlate with a biological population, a cultural tradition, a language family, or perhaps all three, although his use of Indo-European terms to label some of his oppositions suggests that they might be tied to the Indo-European language family. This aspect of Hodder's analysis represents an extension of the direct historical approach to embrace intuitive and even mystical notions resembling those once associated with the more chauvinistic interpretations of European archaeology. The nature of his proposed continuities is never clearly defined and continuity is assumed rather than demonstrated archaeologically.

Many of Hodder's oppositions also appear to be highly ethnocentric and of questionable antiquity. I doubt, for example, that the distinction between nature and culture that is central not only to Hodder's analysis but also to much of Lévi-Strauss's, meant anything to Europeans prior to about 500 B.C. Historical and ethnographic evidence suggests that, prior to that time, Europeans would have conceptualized what we view as the natural world as being animated by spiritual powers that possessed minds and wills similar to those of humans. This understanding made no use of the distinctions that Europeans and others later would draw between nature, society, and the supernatural. It was only after the desacralization of nature that took place in Greece, parts of the Near East, India, and China around the middle of the first millennium B.C. that a distinction between nature and culture probably had meaning anywhere in the world (Childe 1949; 1956a; Eisenstadt 1986; Frankfort 1948; Hallpike 1979; MacCormack & Strathern 1980).

Similarly, ethnographic evidence suggests that many peoples, especially hunter-gatherers, do not view the wild as being dangerous and the home as being protective, however natural this dichotomy appears to ourselves and perhaps most other sedentary peoples. Instead the wild is viewed as a nurturing sphere controlled by powers on whose friendship and benevolence humans must rely (Bird-David 1990; Ingold 1996). Hodder's delineation of patterning in the archaeological record, while far from systematic, offers empirical generalizations that invite study and interpretation. Yet his own interpretations, while often very clever and thought-provoking, are frequently unprovable and in many cases may be highly misleading.

Archaeological interpretation along these lines is nevertheless currently very popular. Archaeologists search the archaeological record for patterning that may have symbolic meaning. Distributions of different types of human bones or broken pottery are established in relation to different parts of European megalithic tombs. Or the orientations of burials and cult centers are correlated with various astronomical phenomena and with natural features of the landscape. The archaeologist then proceeds to suggest symbolic meanings that these remains might have had in the cultures that produced or used them (Bender 1993; Tilley 1984; 1993; 1996). This research often has the merit of drawing attention to hitherto unobserved patterning in archaeological data. For example, landscape archaeology systematically is identifying features that can and cannot be observed from other points in various regions. Although religious beliefs and ideas such as geomancy have long been recognized as playing a role in shaping the distribution of human structures across the landscape and influencing how the landscape was conceptualized (Trigger 1968c: 59-60, 66, 69-70), prehistoric archaeologists had paid little attention to this issue until recently. Processual archaeology encouraged the belief that such meanings were imposed in an epiphenomenal fashion on a landscape that already had been shaped by material considerations, which implied that meanings would be both archaeologically inaccessible and of trivial importance. Yet the problem remains of how the inferences concerning meaning that archaeologists have attached to these patterns can be tested.

When more solid arguments cannot be offered, in the form of universal generalizations or the direct historical approach, these archaeologists often will represent their interpretations as suggestions that future research may support or refute. In principle, such "anarchic subjectivity" is harmless, but it encourages the accumulation of increasing amounts of unverified and often mutually reinforcing speculation. Those who are attracted by extreme idealist epistemologies or postmodern sophistry may go further and attempt to justify their inconclusive interpretations as valid end points of archaeological research. Archaeologists are held invariably to be biased by contemporary beliefs and concerns; hence any interpretation of the past is bound to reveal more about the prevailing ideology of their own culture than about prehistoric beliefs or actions (Bintliff 1988b: 18-19; 1993; Kristiansen 1988).

It has been further argued that material objects as symbols are "irreducibly polysemous," which means they signify different things to different people and even different things to the same person at different times (Olsen 1990: 195; Shanks & Tilley 1987b: 115-117; Shanks 1996: 121). This not only implies that the symbolic meanings that artifacts might have had in prehistoric cultures are frequently inaccessible, but also denies that there ever was an "original meaning to be textually recreated in an analysis of a set of artifacts" (Tilley 1990: 338). Under these conditions, the only meanings that artifacts can have today are those that archaeologists and others assign them. Shanks and Tilley (1987b: 195) have asserted that "there is no way of choosing between alternative pasts except on essentially political grounds." That conclusion has such nihilistic implications for archaeology that in recent years even its more vocal advocates have begun to distance themselves from the extreme subjectivism that underlies it (Shanks & Tilley 1989a: 4; 1989b: 48; Shanks 1996: 4-5; Tilley 1995).

The solution is not to curb the archaeological imagination, which as a source of new ideas contributes to the health and vigor of the discipline. But, like genetic mutations in living organisms, novel ideas must be subject to some form of rigorous selection if they are to contribute to the well-being of a discipline rather than destabilize and trivialize it. In the sciences, selection takes the form of testing, refutation, and verification. An archaeologist can produce any number of ideas about the past or the nature of cultural change, but unless these ideas can be tested, they will do little to advance archaeology. On the contrary, they will have a negative impact by wasting time and resources and sowing unnecessary confusion. The greatest contribution that processual archaeology has made to the general development of archaeology is its insistence that interpretations must be subjected to explicit forms of verification. The aim of such testing is not simply to refute hypotheses, as Karl Popper (1957) advocated, or to establish absolute truth, which is not humanly possible. It is to achieve a deeper and more accurate understanding of the past. All testing does not have to be conducted in terms of universal generalizations, which do not account for culturally specific regularities (Bell 1994; Renfrew 1989; Renfrew & Zubrow 1994).

A productive discipline of archaeology requires both the flourishing of creative imagination and a determination to subject the products of that imagination to rigorous testing. Deprived of either of these ingredients, archaeology will fall short of its creative potential. We must recognize that some ideas cannot be tested, although they may become testable in the future as new data or new analytical procedures become available. We must also acknowledge the truth of Bunge's observation that "we shall never attain an exhaustive knowledge of the past or even of the present, because most facts are never recorded [and] some documents are destroyed or lost" (Bunge 1996: 105).

Cultivating Imagination

The greater problem for many archaeologists, including myself, is not that of controlling a hyperactive imagination but of not having enough imagination. What recourse is there for the imaginatively challenged? Collingwood, as a classical archaeologist, advocated immersing oneself in the nonarchaeological data relating directly to the culture being studied—which may amount to a great deal or very little. Provided that the distinctive nature of the textual and oral sources is taken into account, this approach provides insights into the meaning of archaeological data, at the same time that archaeological finds stimulate a better understanding of the meaning of textual sources and oral traditions.

Such a synergistic approach has tended to be the preferred form of interpretation in classical studies, Egyptology, Assyriology, and Sinology, and, as a consequence of recent advances in the translation of Mayan texts, it is struggling against processual archaeology to establish itself in Maya studies (Coe 1992; Sabloff 1990). One of the main weaknesses of this approach is the tendency for textual sources to dominate the interpretation of archaeological evidence. Another is that, while this approach is very efficient at drawing archaeologists' attention to culturally specific meanings, it leaves them unaware of broader, cross-cultural parallels that facilitate valuable and often quite different insights into the behavioral significance of archaeological data. This suggests the importance of supplementing what is known from textual or ethnographic sources about the culture that is being studied archaeologically with a greater awareness of more general cross-cultural variation.

While such knowledge is often stressed as the principal strength of an anthropological approach to archaeology, social anthropologists, especially those who espouse unilinear evolution, have been curiously negligent about studying cross-cultural variability. Neoevolutionists, with rare exceptions such as R. Carneiro (1970), showed little interest in cross-cultural research utilizing extensive databases such as the Human Relations Area Files. Nor have other anthropologists made significant use of such resources for delineating cultural similarities and differences since the 1960s (Murdock 1981; Textor 1967). By failing to compare societies at similar levels of development in different regions of the world, and basing their ideas about what such societies are like largely on examples from the area best known to them, they have greatly underestimated the variation in human behavior. Archaeologists who rely on such studies frequently forfeit the advantages to be gained from learning, on the one hand, about societies worldwide and, on the other, about those that are linked most closely, geographically and historically, to the ones they are studying. Archaeological interpretation is a challenging task to which no one ever can bring enough comparative knowledge.

Imagination can also be stimulated by the manner in which theories are constructed and tested. Binford's advocacy of a nomological-deductive method, combined with his support for an ecologically determinist approach to explaining human behavior, encouraged a premature commitment to a theory that in the long run has turned out not to account for as many aspects of human behavior, or of the archaeological record, as was anticipated. Supporters can argue that much has been learned along the way and that archaeology is the better for having adopted this approach. Yet, it equally could be maintained that archaeology would have progressed further, both in the interpretation of data and in theory building, had it stayed with the method of multiple or alternative working hypotheses that was being advocated by many archaeologists in the 1950s. As expounded by T.C. Chamberlin (1944), this approach proposed that, where a single explanation of data is inconclusive, it is best to formulate a series of alternative explanations, each with its own test implications. The discovery of new data may eliminate specific alternatives and permit surviving ones to be elaborated (Knapp 1996; Rouse 1972). The advantage of this approach, which has much in common with ideas advocated by Kelley and Hanen (1988), is that it does not commit archaeologists to a particular high-level theory. On the contrary, it encourages the empirical testing of how various general theories accord with specific explanations that prove viable in the long run.

This approach is especially important given the ambiguous and controversial nature of what passes for high-level theories in the social sciences. They still cover a spectrum that runs from ecological determinism at one extreme to cultural determinism at the other. If there is broad agreement that the more plausible explanations of human behavior are to be found somewhere in the middle, there is no consensus concerning the precise nature of these explanations (Trigger 1982; 1989a: 19-25). A second advantage is that the method of multiple working hypotheses encourages social scientists to search for alternative patterning and significance in their data. As a result, imagination is promoted rather than stifled by this approach to formulating and testing explanations of archaeological data. Science cannot operate without having general propositions to apply and test, but to try to structure decades of archaeological research exclusively around a single, highly specific, high-level theory at this stage in the development of the social sciences is to waste resources and invite disappointment.

Finally, I would suggest that processual archaeology limited the development of a more profound understanding of human behavior by advocating that the principal goal of archaeology, as well as social anthropology, should be to create general laws concerning human behavior and cultural change. This view overlooked the fact, repeatedly emphasized by Alfred Kroeber, that the physical and biological sciences embrace both generalizing and historical disciplines. Cosmogony, historical geology, and palaeontology are all historical, but they are not, for that reason, regarded as any less scientific than physics, chemistry, astronomy, geology, botany, and zoology (Kroeber 1952: 66-78).

Moreover, while the currently accepted synthetic theory of biological evolution explains in a satisfactory manner how change occurs, it cannot predict the specific lines that change will follow or what its consequences may be. This is because the factors involved in any specific example of change, such as the nature of the particular species that is evolving, the changes that are occurring in the environment, and the specific characteristics of competitors, are extremely complex and frequently vary independently of one another. As a consequence, each instance of biological evolutionary change can be explained in retrospect, but cannot be specified, or predicted, in advance (Bunge 1996: 160-163).

Because processual archaeologists, as neoevolutionists, assumed that human behavior was highly regular, they thought that it would not be difficult to formulate general laws that would explain the most salient aspects of human behavior as well as account for the histories of specific societies. In general, sociocultural change appears to display more unilinearity than does biological evolution. That is because, at least in the long term, more complex societies are able to dominate, encapsulate, and even absorb smaller societies when the two compete for the same territories and resources. As some societies have grown more complex and expanded the scope of their operations at the expense of neighboring groups, the range of intersocietal variation has declined, although at the same time intrasocietal variation has increased as surviving societies have grown larger and more complex. Moreover, because cultural behavior is learned, it is possible for humans to abandon uncompetitive behavior patterns and lifestyles and emulate those of more successful groups, although this process may take a long time and be very difficult if the gap in complexity between two groups is very great.

An additional constraint on social variation arises from there being only a limited range of economic, political, and ideological patterns that can fit together to form viable systems. It seems certain that no society will ever be found that has both a big-game hunting subsistence base and a divine monarchy. Sociocultural variation may be considerably greater than processual archaeologists once imagined, but the need for functional integration limits what is possible within viable systems. For these reasons, there tends to be less diversity among human societies than among reproductively isolated biological species that can adapt to many ecological niches and whose existence is terminated as a result of natural selection bringing about the replacement of one species by another. This produces the dendritic pattern that has characterized biological evolution (Trigger 1998a).

In spite of this, there is much specific variation between one society and another even when they are at the same general stage of development, and still more variation in the processes by which social change comes about (Childe 1951; 1958; Flannery 1972; Goldenweiser 1913; Hallpike 1986; Murdock 1949; Trigger 1993). It may be, and I believe it is, a valid task to try to identify and understand the general patterns and processes that characterize human history. But understanding the linear patterns that characterize sociocultural evolution is different from accounting for how specific societies have changed, which is a highly contingent process. The decline of the Roman Empire and the collapse of the lowland Classic Maya states may have features in common, but these shared features cannot be understood until the development and decline of both societies have been accounted for in their specific detail. Only in this way is it possible to delineate and try to understand the reasons for both the similarities and the differences between the two processes. Imposing general evolutionary patterns on particular cases is usually done, inadvisedly, only in situations where little is known about what specifically happened. At best it results in nothing new being learned, but more often it produces a pseudo-understanding that is detrimental to scientific advancement.

Unfortunately, the latter was the case with Steward's (1949) celebrated "Cultural Causality and Law: A Trial Formulation of the Development of Early Civilizations" and with most of the neoevolutionary schemes of the 1960s. Contrary to much sociocultural evolutionary practice, if the specific cannot be predicted on the basis of a generalized understanding, it is necessary to understand the particular in specific terms before using it as a basis for elaborating and testing any evolutionary or behavioral generalizations. Far from belittling generalization, such a procedure seeks to establish it on a scientifically credible foundation.

This perspective justifies adopting a historical approach to understanding cultural change, either as an end in itself or as a necessary prelude to attempting to formulate evolutionary generalizations about the processes of sociocultural change and the general shape of human history. In *The Logic of Historical Explanation*, Clayton Roberts (1996) argues that historical explanations are attempts to use facts to establish why events occurred. The goal of historians is thus to establish causes rather than merely correlations. Because human beings actively pursue goals, a search for causes is legitimate in terms of a realist, if not a doctrinaire positivist, epistemology. Roberts is particularly concerned with detailing the many different ways in which historians seek to trace and integrate sequences of causation in order to explain specific events. He provides an understanding of the nature of historical explanation that is far removed from the grossly simplistic caricatures that processual archaeologists produced of it in the 1960s (Binford 1968b; Spaulding 1968).

Karl Marx never drew a clear distinction between what I am here calling sociocultural evolution and history. On the one hand, he proposed grand schemes of evolution that seem to be materialist counterparts of Hegelian cosmic mysticism. On the other hand, in a work such as "The Eighteenth Brumaire of Louis Bonaparte," Marx applied his far-reaching understanding of economic and social behavior to provide a detailed analysis of specific events in which individual personalities, curious conjunctures, and sheer miscalculations played significant roles (Marx & Engels 1962, I: 243-344). His studies of the transition from feudalism to capitalism in Europe are also deeply grounded in empirical data and closely argued. One cannot help thinking that Marx's macroevolutionary schemes would have been of greater scientific value had they been derived more from his empirical research. Historical explanation of cultural change constitutes an essential and irreducible aspect of archaeological interpretation. Yet the detailed insights that it provides into the complex processes that have produced specific aspects of the archaeological record may draw attention to hitherto unrecognized processes that occur more generally. This too is a way of expanding the archaeological imagination in a fashion that permits archaeologists to move beyond superficial generalizations about the processes of cultural change.

10

The 1990s: North American Archaeology with a Human Face?

Canada is one of many countries whose indigenous populations have suffered from colonization and where archaeology has been developed by the colonizers. It is now recognized that archaeologists, both in these countries and in Europe, have played a significant role in denigrating native peoples and making possible their displacement and subjugation. Such behavior has been important in shaping the theory and practice of archaeology (Trigger 1980; Gathercole & Lowenthal 1989; Robertshaw 1990). In recent years, native peoples have vigorously objected to what archaeologists have done. Their protests have been one factor persuading some archaeologists to rethink their discipline. Today archaeology is changing in various important ways. It is therefore necessary to consider whether or not these changes will help to overcome the alienation that continues to separate archaeologists from native people.

Recent Trends

Three important new developments can be identified.

There is a growing fascination with religious beliefs, art, myths, and other features of specific cultural traditions. These are the "unique, exotic, and nonrecurrent particulars" that Julian Steward (1955: 209) saw as historical accidents deserving no place in a scientific concern with generalization. While this new fascination does not rule out rational explanations of adaptive behavior (Binford 1962), it causes cultural ecology to be viewed once again as an investigation of constraints on human behavior rather than of the determination of behavior. The revival of a historical approach complements evolutionary attempts to understand archaeological data (Hodder 1987a; 1987b; Bintliff 1988a).

Second, there is growing awareness of the inherently subjective nature of archaeological interpretation. Through more systematic study of the history of archaeology, this understanding has become more comprehensive and politically explicit. Interpretations of archaeological data are now viewed as expressions of the national, ethnic, class, and personal interests of archaeologists, sometimes to the exclusion of all else (Shanks & Tilley 1987b).

Finally, there are growing and closely related doubts about the ability of archaeology to provide objective knowledge about human behavior. Processual archaeologists searched for general laws of behavior that would be useful in modern life. Paul Martin and Fred Plog (1973: 364-8), for example, hoped that generalizations based on studies of ecological stress in prehistoric Arizona might help social workers to understand the behavior of visible minorities in modern urban ghettos. It is now argued that these claims were advanced, consciously or unconsciously, to provide archaeology with an attractive technocratic allure and a modern utility (Patterson 1986a), and many archaeologists no longer regard such goals as scientifically or morally acceptable. But what is an appropriate social role for archaeology? And what will be the relationship between archaeology and its social setting?

Archaeology and Public Curiosity

The perennial social function of archaeology has been to satisfy curiosity about what happened in the past. The most curious individuals are archaeologists themselves, but the general public has long appreciated archaeological revelations, especially spectacular discoveries, and found archaeology as a whole interesting both to do and to read about. It was in part to dispel this image, of a study both amiable and useless, and to win the respect of scientific funding agencies that the New Archaeologists unfurled the banners of science and utility in the 1960s (Kolakowski 1976: 229). For the most part, their postprocessual antagonists have maintained this high-minded tone, at the same time that they condemn "scientism."

In recent years, public interest in prehistoric North American archaeology has been growing rapidly. It is evident that the increasingly historical orientation of archaeological research is of considerably greater appeal than was processual archaeology. Many nonspecialists, fascinated by the religious beliefs and intellectual culture of prehistoric North Americans, did not find that processual archaeologists were providing them with a comprehensive understanding of human behavior.

Archaeology and Native People

The most striking social feature of North American prehistoric archaeology remains its alienation from native people. Only a few native persons, such as the Seneca Indian Arthur C. Parker (1881-1955), have become professional archaeologists. Until recently, native people were rarely employed in archaeological excavations, and in the past archaeologists sought permission to excavate on Indian reserves from Indian agents rather than from native people (Fox 1989).

Personal contacts between archaeologists and native people were somewhat more common in the nineteenth century, when North American archaeologists were primarily interested in how artifacts had been made and what they had been used for. Culture-historical interests in the first half of the twentieth century terminated even these limited contacts, as archaeologists turned to formal artifact classifications as a means of defining and seriating archaeological assemblages (Trigger 1980).

During this same period, native people were overcoming intertribal divisiveness with a growing sense of pan-Indian identity and fighting against the injustices that Euro-Americans and Euro-Canadians were inflicting on them (Richardson 1987). This struggle has produced a renewed sense of dignity and power. An increasing number of native people now champion a better way of life for all humanity by urging respect for all living creatures. These ideas have deep roots in their traditional belief systems, even if they are now being expressed in new ways for modern Euro-American and European cultures (Sioui 1989).

Many native people deeply resent archaeologists, whom they accuse of denigrating the native past and trying to appropriate their cultural heritage. Many native traditionalists and their Indian supporters oppose all forms of archaeological research as interfering with the sacred sites of their ancestors. There is still more widespread opposition to the excavation of native burial places and the keeping and exhibition of the physical remains of native people (McGhee 1989). In many areas native people have demanded, and won, the right to approve and license the excavation of all prehistoric sites and that all human skeletons be returned to them for reburial. This has produced widespread tension between native people and archaeologists, and legal conflicts in some jurisdictions (Rosen 1980; Bard 1984; Meighan 1984; Day 1990). Archaeologists often find governments and ordinary Euro-Americans much more willing to support native claims than the freedom of archaeologists to do research. It is far easier, cheaper, and apparently equally soothing of tender consciences for non-native North Americans to support native rights in the cultural sphere than to render economic and political justice to native people.

Archaeologists would do well to admit candidly that much of this criticism is fair. Although they study the material remains of native people, most archaeologists have shown little interest in the living descendants of these people and even less concern with relating their research to them.

Relativism

Does anything distinguish archaeological interpretations from pure fantasies or deliberately misleading works of propaganda? Extreme relativists in the discipline now appear to think nothing does (Shanks & Tilley 1987b:195; 1989a), agreeing with the historian Michel Foucault that it is misleading and potentially dangerous to believe that what we now affirm is necessarily better or more true than what was believed in the past or is believed by others (Goldie 1989: 7).

Subjective influences on archaeological interpretation are real and powerful, as any detailed case study of archaeological interpretation clearly demonstrates (Silverberg 1968; Silberman 1982; 1989; Wilk 1985). Almost all archaeologists admit that the biases of individual archaeologists play a major role in influencing what they study. All but the ultrapositivists further acknowledge that biases strongly influence the amount and kind of evidence that individual archaeologists believe is necessary to establish a particular point; the more implicitly people believe that something is true, the less evidence they demand to confirm it. These observations constitute a powerful statement regarding the subjectivity of archaeological interpretation. Even in the experimental sciences, all generalizations are based to some degree upon faith.

Yet, as I have argued elsewhere (Trigger 1989a), underlying all archaeological interpretation is evidence that was created independently of the observer's will, by people who lived in the past, and which has survived in some form. The philosopher Alison Wylie (1982; 1985) has argued persuasively that this independent evidence constrains the archaeologist's imagination. Donald Grayson (1986) has likewise demonstrated that throughout the history of archaeology disagreement about the meaning of archaeological data has initiated a trial-like, adversarial search for additional archaeological information and for novel techniques of analyzing data. The goal is to persuade opponents and parties neutral to the dispute that a particular position is correct (Rudwick 1989). That the aim is to convince skeptics refutes the claim that the primary aim of archaeological research is merely to confirm individual researchers' beliefs.

While every archaeological interpretation is certainly influenced by subjective factors, in the long run archaeologists can hope to acquire some objective knowledge of the past. In the shorter run, every archaeologist may discover something that is new, unexpected, and challenges what he or she believes. As the discipline's database and analytical skills expand, so does the ability of archaeologists to produce evidence that contradicts their own stereotypes.

This observation accounts for a recurring pattern in the history of archaeology. While nineteenth-century American archaeologists did not look for evidence of cultural change in prehistoric times, nevertheless they found it. Today, not only archaeologists but also historians, the Euro-American public, and native people themselves are increasingly aware that throughout the millennia prior to the arrival of the first Europeans, native cultures were changing, often developing, rather than remaining static. As evidence for the creativity of native people permeates textbooks and popular literature, it is doing much to combat traditional Euro-American stereotypes of native Americans. Archaeological evidence has slowly forced revisions in the way that archaeologists view native people. In particular, it has led them to abandon the negative, static image held by older generations of Euro-Americans.

This development strikingly demonstrates that archaeological interpretation can be something more than a reflection of political and social prejudices. This is true even though professional archaeologists do not always rise to the challenge of evidence, and sometimes ignore its significance. Very often, as American archaeologists did prior to the 1960s, they prefer to make only the smallest adjustments to keep their interpretations in reasonable accord with new evidence. Yet the cumulative effect of grudging accommodations can push archaeological interpretations in significant new directions.

The End of Colonialist Archaeology

Today, a growing appreciation by archaeologists of the complexity of human behavior and of the contingent nature of cultural change is promoting a rapprochement between archaeologists and native people. Archaeologists increasingly treat native cultures as worth studying for their intrinsic interest, not simply as sources of data for cross-cultural generalizations. They are again interested in prehistoric religions, art, mythology, and other culturally specific beliefs and values. These themes have a more immediate interest to native people than did processual archaeology's preoccupation with ecological adaptation—even though native people who maintain traditional subsistence strategies, especially in the arctic and subarctic, know far more about specific adaptive behavior than does any archaeologist. Archaeologists who seek to understand the culturally specific meanings of art and rituals must use oral traditions, ethnohistory, comparative ethnology, historical linguistics, and other direct historical approaches that alone can bring subjective meaning to the archaeological record. This involves them in an increasingly holistic engagement with native cultures and with modern native peoples who are direct heirs to the traditions they are studying. Intellectual engagement, which often concerns matters of intense interest to modern native people, can make them partners and guides in intellectual pursuits, rather than merely objects of study, as they frequently have been for ecologically oriented ethnoarchaeologists. As archaeologists become involved as expert witnesses in land-claims cases, native people have evidence not only of a growing concern among archaeologists for their welfare but also of the practical value of archaeological research.

While some native traditionalists oppose all forms of archaeological research, a growing number of native people are viewing archaeology as yet another way to understand their own past and their cultural heritage better. Recently more native people have begun to work for archaeologists, both as members of survey and excavation crews and as consultants, providing essential specialized knowledge. The participation of native students in excavations increases their awareness of their cultural heritage, and this in turn helps to enrich the cultural life of some native communities. Consultations with native authorities and securing their permission for proposed research are now routine in much archaeological survey and excavation, and native authorities often require reports to be written in a style that the non-specialist can understand (Fox 1989).

In addition, a growing number of native groups employ archaeologists to research problems that are of special interest to them (E. Adams 1984; Ferguson 1984). These relate not only to practical issues of land claims and tourism, but also to the better understanding of cultural patrimony, particularly by bringing local archaeological findings into native school curricula. In addition, native people are acquiring archaeological research skills, and some research programs are now being directed by them. These developments make for an awareness of the positive value of archaeology among an increasing number of native people. Archaeologists and native groups have also begun to work together to save threatened archaeological sites and, if that is not possible, to ensure that they are properly studied before they are lost (Fox 1989).

Efforts to reach an accommodation about the excavation and study of native burials largely have shifted from confrontation and purely tactical responses by frustrated and perplexed archaeologists to a growing understanding of the various native points of view (Cheek & Keel 1984). Less understanding has been achieved of pan-Indianism; many archaeologists are puzzled and even indignant when modern Indians express concern about human remains that are thousands of years old or when they protest the excavation of skeletons belonging to groups known to have been their enemies in the historic past. It is widely suspected that agitation about such issues is mainly intended to cause trouble for archaeologists.

These reactions overlook changing views about ethnicity, and the historical forces which over the past 200 years have given Amerindians a new sense of common ethnic identity, alongside a continuing pride in their specific "tribal" affiliations (Hertzberg 1971). Archaeology helps in the intellectual underpinning of this pan-Indian identity, which is essential if native people are to pursue their collective destiny in the modern world. It is flattering when Joe Crowshoe, Sr., a highly respected Blackfoot Nation elder, states that nowadays archaeology has "done more for the betterment of Native people than all of the missionaries and government agents had ever done" (Fox 1989: 31). Archaeologists should feel challenged as well as encouraged to earn and to keep the respect of native people.

Not yet adequately achieved is professional training and employment for native people as archaeologists in universities, museums, and government services. The willingness of Euro-Canadian and Euro-American archaeologists to promote this will test their view of the role that native people should play in their discipline and their willingness to rescue North American archaeology from the last shackles of its colonialist origins.

This is not a test that archaeologists yet show signs of passing. It is argued that native people are not interested in becoming archaeologists and that educated ones have more attractive career prospects (Ames 1988). The growing interest of native people of all ages in archaeological findings and what archaeologists are doing, the participation of native people in archaeological research and the efforts of some native people to acquire archaeological expertise, as well as their general desire to win greater control over their cultural heritage, convincingly refute these suggestions (Doxtator 1988; Hill 1988; Webster 1988; McGhee 1989).

It has also been suggested that prehistoric archaeology, like the larger anthropology of which North American archaeology is a part, is essentially the study of the exotic, and hence of little concern to native people. The interest of European archaeologists in their own cultural heritage and the growing involvement of North American archaeologists with their continent's colonial past belie this claim. Archaeology is not always the study of the "other," except perhaps in the general sense that the past is always a foreign country (Lowenthal 1985). Native archaeologists can bring a new perspective, based on cultural participation and commitment, to North American prehistory, which may influence the kind of problems they wish to research, just as they will bring special background knowledge.

At least in the short run, native archaeologists would likely strengthen an interest in the culturally specific aspects of the archaeological record. This would increase the scientific rigor of North American archaeology, and play a significant role in completing its transformation from a male Anglo-Saxon hobby into a genuinely scientific enterprise. The recruitment of native people into archaeology is itself an important step forward in the development of the discipline.

At the present time a program, or more realistically a series of programs, of affirmative action is needed. The opportunities for the increasing numbers of native students who are graduating from high schools to attend universities must be expanded, not cut back. Archaeologists must convince native students that they will be welcomed into the ranks of professional archaeologists, and positions must be found, or created, for the native people who complete graduate archaeology programs.

Archaeology and Humanity

In the long run prehistoric archaeology has had a liberating influence. It has helped to free North Americans who are not of native origin from the racist myths that earlier generations of colonists constructed in an effort to naturalize and excuse their subjugation of native people and the seizure of their lands. It also provides native people with a fuller history of North America in which they and all other North Americans can take pride, at the continental, national, and local levels. Those Euro-Canadians and Euro-Americans who still view native people as "savages" incapable of change are exposed as being ignorant and prejudiced, as more North Americans become aware that archaeological and anthropological evidence indicates otherwise.

Yet, important as these accomplishments are, the full potential of archaeology is only partially realized when all of its attention is focused on specific peoples. The negative consequences of nationalistic archaeology have greatly outweighed the positive ones. The misuse of archaeology by German prehistorians, such as Gustaf Kossinna, who selectively interpreted archaeological evidence in order to glorify prehistoric Germans and denigrate neighboring peoples, is well known. Those archaeologists must bear a heavy share of responsibility for the criminal folly that overwhelmed most of Europe after 1933 (Fowler 1987; Arnold 1990). Yet archaeology continues to be used by the intelligentsia of many modern states to justify aggression against neighboring peoples, to condone the exploitation and suppression of ethnic minorities, and to deflect attention from injustice by seeming to honor the very groups who are being economically exploited (Silberman 1989; Trigger 1989a: 174-86). To offset the dangers of parochial vision, archaeologists need broader interests that relate to humanity as a whole. It is in pursuit of these interests that the generalizing abilities of archaeologists achieve their fullest scope.

In the long run archaeology has irreversibly influenced the views that most people in western countries have of themselves as human beings, knowing that humanity was not created in 4004 B.C., that most small-scale cultures are not the result of cultural degeneration, that human beings are descended from ape-like ancestors, that hunting and gathering preceded the development of food-production, and that food-production preceded the rise of civilization. Christian fundamentalists and native American traditionalists, in rejecting this view of human origins, reject not only the specific findings of archaeologists but also the whole of scientific methodology. Accompanying this broadly evolutionary view of human origins, for better or for worse, has been the growing conviction that technological and intellectual progress precludes any final or definitive understanding about how human beings should conduct themselves or about their place in the universe (Crone 1989: 190).

As societies change, their members require new views about human nature and the place of human beings in the universe in order to give meaning to their lives. In recent centuries the universal certainties of religion and the older philosophies have given way to what the American historian William McNeill (1986) calls "mythistory," and which he sees as providing a substitute for human beings' atrophied instincts. Mythistory is not mythology in the traditional sense, but provisional explanations based on current knowledge that provide human groups with a collective guide to action. Each explanation is an imperfect effort to make sense out of past social experiences that will help to avoid dangerous mistakes and steer human endeavors in a positive direction. Mythistory cannot simply justify the present and the parochial; it must distil what each individual and group believes to be true about the human condition as a whole. Some of these myths, such as the pseudoscientific racial philosophy of the Nazis (Stein 1988), quickly lead to disaster. Others enjoy great longevity and may genuinely promote human well-being.

Mythistory also challenges the existing social order and can help to create a new and better one. Grahame Clark (1989: 433) has noted that prehistoric archaeology has played a major role over the past 200 years in helping to formulate guiding "myths." In the nineteenth century archaeologists used the ideas of evolutionary biology to interpret the past in a fashion that justified free enterprise and colonialism as sources of human progress (Lubbock 1870). At the same time, archaeologists who shared these ideas unwittingly were collecting evidence that challenged the racist beliefs embedded in this evolutionary perspective.

In recent decades archaeologists have responded very quickly to growing concerns about ecosystemic pollution, the depletion of nonrenewable resources, and unrestrained population growth. While early efforts to treat population increase as an independent variable bringing about cultural change (P. Smith 1976; M. Cohen 1977) have foundered, archaeologists have noted much evidence in the archaeological record of overexploitation of the environment and of the collapse of political systems when they cannot maintain adequate levels of productivity (Renfrew & Cooke 1979; Tainter 1988; Yoffee & Cowgill 1988). These studies have encouraged archaeologists to come to grips with the abundant evidence of rapid shifts and social disintegration that has been uncovered by their excavations. It is hard now to understand how nineteenth-century cultural evolutionists and more recent neoevolutionary archaeologists, surrounded by so much evidence of "vanished civilizations," concentrated so single-mindedly on explaining progress. Archaeological findings have become significant for documenting long-term human impact on the environment. They emphasize large-scale social planning, respect for regional variation, and the encouragement of local decision making as behavioral patterns that are essential if modern societies are to cope with ever more powerful technologies. This challenges people to envisage a political order in which neither laissez-faire nor state control is viable. Human beings are also coming to consider a new social ethic in which technological innovation and sustained economic growth may no longer be desirable for their own sakes (Trigger 1986a, 1998a; Richardson 1990). By providing a long-term historical perspective, archaeology is helping scholars to think more clearly about issues that many people believe are quickly becoming matters of life and death for humanity and the entire planetary ecosystem. The archaeological documentation of the disastrous effects of deforestation, relentless ploughing, and overgrazing on the Mediterranean region is of practical value for assessing modern policies of land use (Attenborough 1989: 95-101). These developments make archaeology an important player in the interdisciplinary study of environmental issues; an approach that has the support of an increasingly concerned public.

The generalizing concerns of modern archaeology transcend, but do not in any way negate, the historically specific interests of an ethnically or nationally oriented archaeology. Many people no longer accept the argument that human beings have a mandate to exploit the resources of the planet in an unrestrained fashion. The challenge to an anthropocentric view of the universe and the concern to achieve more balanced and sustainable relations with nature have shifted both archaeology and popular western views about the place of human beings in the natural world much closer to those that have long been expressed by native Americans (Vecsey 1980; Sioui 1989). Professionally trained native archaeologists may have an important role to play not only in the study of their own past but also in the generalizing activities of their discipline.

Conclusion

The social role that I foresee for North American archaeology in the future is not the austere generalizing one that processual archaeology sought for itself in the 1960s and 1970s, as the relativist critique renews awareness among archaeologists of the social significance of their work. Archaeologists, among other duties, serve a public that is eager to know more about the past and which, in a general fashion, understands that this knowledge is significant also for the future.

Some totalitarian regimes have regarded the interpretation of archaeological data as so sensitive politically that this process has been carefully monitored by those in power. Some archaeologists have been more influenced by social prejudices than by archaeological evidence in their interpretations. Yet, as archaeological data accumulate and methods for interpreting these data are elaborated, archaeological findings increasingly resist subjective manipulation. A growing core of objective knowledge makes archaeology essential to understanding better the nature of human beings and their place in the world. Archaeological interpretations reflect the ideals of their societies, but they also contradict those ideals and play a significant role in the formulation of new ones. Archaeologists can only do this effectively by grounding their interpretations in facts, by a willingness to abandon theories that their data do not sustain, and by cultivating an awareness of the subjective elements that influence their thinking.

To do all of this more effectively, archaeology's hard-won insights into its own social context must be applied to changing archaeology itself. Archaeologists must increasingly involve native people in the planning of research programs and as assistants, with or without special training. They must also feed archaeological information back to native communities so that native people can derive from it a deeper sense of pride in their culture and what it has to offer the broader world. Above all, archaeologists must strive to transcend their own colonial heritage by sponsoring a vigorous program of affirmative action to train and recruit native people as professional archaeologists. Success in this endeavor will enrich the perspectives that archaeologists can bring to the study of the past in culturally specific and more general terms. If archaeologists fail in this task, regardless of how hard they strive to interpret their data objectively, serious doubts must remain concerning the intellectual and moral legitimacy of the enterprise in which they are engaged.

References

Aberle, D.F. et al. 1950. The Functional Prerequisites of a Society. *Ethics* 60: 100-111.
Adams, E.C. 1984. Archaeology and the Native American: a Case at Hopi. In E.L.Green (ed.). *Ethics and Values in Archaeology.* New York: Free Press, 236-42.
Adams, R. McC. 1965. *Land Behind Baghdad.* Chicago: University of Chicago Press.
—. 1981. *Heartland of Cities.* Chicago: University of Chicago Press
Adams, R. McC.& H.J. Nissen. 1972. *The Uruk Countryside.* Chicago: University of Chicago Press.
Adams, W.Y., D.P. Van Gerven & R.S. Levy. 1978. The Retreat from Migrationism. *Annual Review of Anthropology* 7: 483-532.
Alden, J.R. 1982. Trade and Politics in Proto-Elamite Iran. *Current Anthropology* 23: 613-40.
Alexander, J. & A. Mohammed. 1982. Frontier Theory and the Neolithic Period in Nubia. In J. M. Plumley (ed.). *Nubian Studies.* Warminster: Aris & Phillips, 34-40.
Ames, M. 1988. The Liberation of Anthropology. *Culture* 8(1): 81-5.
Ardrey, R. 1961. *African Genesis: A Personal Investigation into the Animal Origins and Nature of Man.* New York: Atheneum.
Armstrong, E. 1991. The Limbic System and Culture. *Human Nature* 2: 117-36.
Arnold, B. 1990. The Past as Propaganda: Totalitarian Archaeology in Nazi Germany. *Antiquity* 64: 464-78.
Attenborough, D. 1989. *The First Eden: The Mediterranean World and Man.* London: Fontana.
Aveni, A.F. 1981. Archaeoastronomy. *Advances in Archaeological Method and Theory* 4: 1-77.
Axtell, J. 1987. History as Imagination. *The Historian* 49: 451-62.
Ayer, A.J. 1956. *The Problem of Knowledge.* London: Macmillan.
Bapty, I. & T. Yates (eds.). 1990. *Archaeology after Structuralism: Post-Structuralism and the Practice of Archaeology.* London: Routledge.
Bard, K. 1984. Reburial as an Issue in California Again. *Early Man* 4(4): 1-2.
Barnes, A.S. 1939. The Differences between Natural and Human Flaking on Prehistoric Flint Implements. *American Anthropologist* 41: 99-112.
Barnes, B. 1974. *Scientific Knowledge and Sociological Theory.* London: Routledge and Kegan Paul.
—. 1977. *Interests and the Growth of Knowledge.* London: Routledge and Kegan Paul.
Barthes, R. 1972. *Mythologies.* New York: Hill and Wong.
Barton, C.M. & G.A. Clark (eds.). 1997. *Rediscovering Darwin: Evolutionary Theory and Archaeological Explanation.* Washington, DC: Archeological Papers of the American Anthropological Association, 7.
Bar-Yosef, O. & A. Mazar. 1982. Israeli Archaeology. *World Archaeology* 13: 310-25.
Bayard, D.T. 1969. Science, Theory, and Reality in the "New Archaeology." *American Antiquity* 34: 376-84.
Beauchamp, W.M. 1900. *Aboriginal Occupation of New York.* Albany: Bulletin of the New York State Museum, 7(32).

Bell, J.A. 1994. *Reconstructing Prehistory: Scientific Method in Archaeology.* Philadelphia: Temple University Press.
Bender, B. (ed.). 1993. *Landscape: Politics and Perspectives.* Oxford: Berg.
—. 1998. *Stonehenge: Making Space.* Oxford: Berg.
Bender, T. 1985. Making History Whole Again. *New York Times Book Review*, 6 October: 1, 42-3.
Benedict, R. 1934. *Patterns of Culture.* Boston: Houghton Mifflin.
Bennett, J.W. 1944. Middle American Influences on Cultures of the Southeastern United States. *Acta Americana* 2: 25-50.
Berger, C. 1986. *The Writing of Canadian History: Aspects of English-Canadian Historical Writing Since 1900.* Toronto: University of Toronto Press.
Berkhofer, R.F., Jr. 1978. *The White Man's Indian: Images of the American Indian from Columbus to the Present.* New York: Alfred A. Knopf.
Bernal, I. 1980. *A History of Mexican Archaeology.* London: Thames & Hudson.
Bernstein, R.J. 1983. *Beyond Objectivism and Relativism: Science, Hermeneutics, and Praxis.* Philadelphia: University of Pennsylvania Press.
Bhaskar, R. 1978. *A Realist Theory of Science* (2nd ed.). Atlantic Highlands, NJ: Humanities Press.
—. 1989a. *The Possibility of Naturalism: A Philosophical Critique of the Contemporary Human Sciences* (2nd ed.). New York: Harvester Wheatsheaf.
—. 1989b. *Reclaiming Reality: A Critical Introduction to Contemporary Philosophy.* London: Verso.
Bieder, R.E. 1986. *Science Encounters the Indian, 1820-1880: The Early Years of American Ethnology.* Norman: University of Oklahoma Press.
Binford, L.R. 1962. Archaeology as Anthropology. *American Antiquity* 28: 217-25.
—. 1965. Archaeological Systematics and the Study of Culture Process. *American Antiquity* 31: 203-10.
—. 1967a. Comment. *Current Anthropology* 8: 234-35.
—. 1967b. Smudge Pits and Hide Smoking: The Use of Analogy in Archaeological Reasoning. *American Antiquity* 32: 1-12.
—. 1968a. Archeological Perspectives. In S.R. Binford & L.R. Binford (eds.). *New Perspectives in Archeology.* Chicago: Aldine, 5-32.
—. 1968b. Some Comments on Historical versus Processual Archaeology. *Southwestern Journal of Anthropology* 24: 267-75.
—. 1972. *An Archaeological Perspective.* New York: Seminar Press.
—. (ed.). 1977a. *For Theory Building in Archaeology.* New York: Academic Press.
—. 1977b. Olorgesailie Deserves More than the Usual Book Review. *Journal of Anthropological Research* 33: 493-502.
—. 1978. *Nunamiut Ethnoarchaeology.* New York: Academic Press.
—. 1980. "Willow Smoke and Dogs' Tails": Hunter-Gatherer Settlement Systems and Archaeological Site Formation. *American Antiquity* 45: 4-20.
—. 1981a. *Bones: Ancient Men and Modern Myths.* New York: Academic Press.
—. 1981b. Behavioral Archaeology and the "Pompeii Premise." *Journal of Anthropological Research* 37: 195-208.
—. 1983a. *In Pursuit of the Past.* London: Thames & Hudson.
—. 1983b. *Working at Archaeology.* New York: Academic Press.
—. 1985. Human Ancestors: Changing Views of their Behavior. *Journal of Anthropological Archaeology* 4: 292-322.
—. 1986. In Pursuit of the Future. In D.J. Meltzer, D.D. Fowler & J.A. Sabloff (eds.). *American Archaeology Past and Future.* Washington, DC: Smithsonian Institution Press, 459-79.

—. 1987. Data, Relativism and Archaeological Science. *Man* 22: 391-404.
—. 1989. *Debating Archaeology.* San Diego: Academic Press.
Bintliff, J.L. (ed.). 1988a. *Extracting Meaning from the Past.* Oxford: Oxbow Books.
—.1988b. A Review of Contemporary Perspectives on the "Meaning" of the Past. In J. Bintliff (ed.). *Extracting Meaning from the Past.* Oxford: Oxbow Books, 3-36.
—. 1993. Why Indiana Jones is Smarter than the Post-Processualists. *Norwegian Archaeological Review* 26: 91-100.
Bird-David, N. 1990. The Giving Environment: Another Perspective on the Economic System of Gatherer-Hunters. *Current Anthropology* 31: 189-96.
Blanton, R.E., S.A. Kowalewski, G. Feinman & J. Appel. 1981. *Ancient Mesoamerica: A Comparison of Change in Three Regions.* Cambridge: Cambridge University Press.
Bloch, M. 1983. *Marxism and Anthropology: The History of a Relationship.* Oxford: Oxford University Press.
Blumenschine, R.J. 1987. Characteristics of an Early Hominid Scavenging Niche. *Current Anthropology* 28: 383-407.
Boas, F. 1887. Museums of Ethnology and their Classification. *Science* 9: 587-89.
Boucher, D. & P. Kelly (eds.). 1994. *The Social Contract from Hobbes to Rawls.* London : Routledge.
Boule, M. 1921. *Les hommes fossiles.* Paris: Masson.
Bourdieu, P. 1977. *Outline of a Theory of Practice.* Cambridge : Cambridge University Press.
Boyd, R. & P.J. Richerson. 1985. *Culture and the Evolutionary Process.* Chicago: University of Chicago Press.
Brain, C.K. 1981. *The Hunters or the Hunted?: An Introduction to African Cave Taphonomy.* Chicago: University of Chicago Press.
Brace, C.L. 1964. The Fate of the "Classic" Neanderthals : A Consideration of Hominid Catastrophism. *Current Anthropology* 5: 3-43.
Brace, C.L. & M.F.A. Montagu. 1965. *Man's Evolution : An Introduction to Physical Anthropology.* New York: Macmillan.
Bradley, R. 1993. Archaeology : The Loss of Nerve. In N. Yoffee & A. Sherratt (eds.). *Archaeological Theory: Who Sets the Agenda?* Cambridge: Cambridge University Press, 131-33.
Bradley, R. & I. Hodder. 1979. British Prehistory: An Integrated View. *Man* 14: 93-104.
Braidwood, R.J. 1974. The Iraq Jarmo Project. In G.R. Willey (ed.). *Archaeological Researches in Retrospect.* Cambridge, MA: Winthrop, 59-83.
Brasser, T.J.C. 1971. Group Identification along a Moving Frontier. Munich: *Verhandlungen des XXXVIII Internationalen Amerikanistenkongresses* II: 261-65.
Brenner, R. 1994. *Labyrinths of Prosperity: Economic Follies, Democratic Remedies.* Ann Arbor: University of Michigan Press.
Bronowski, J. 1971. Symposium on Technology and Social Criticism: Introduction - Technology and Culture in Evolution. *Philosophy of the Social Sciences* 1: 195-206.
Brown, D.E. 1991. *Human Universals.* Philadelphia: Temple University Press.
Brown, J.A. (ed.). 1971. *Approaches to the Social Dimensions of Mortuary Practices.* Washington, DC: Society for American Archaeology, Memoir, 25.
Brown, J. A. & S. Struever. 1973. The Organization of Archaeological Research: An Illinois Example. In C.L. Redman (ed.). *Research and Theory in Current Archeology.* New York: Wiley, 261-80.
Bray, W. 1982. Review of J.A. Sabloff (ed.), Handbook of Middle American Indians, Supplement 1, Archaeology. *Man* 17: 781.
Brumfiel, E.M. 1983. Aztec State Making: Ecology, Structure, and the Origin of the State. *American Anthropologist* 85: 261-84.

Budd, P. & T. Taylor. 1995. The Faerie Smith Meets the Bronze Industry: Magic versus Science in the Interpretation of Prehistoric Metal-Making. *World Archaeology* 27: 133-43.

Bulkin, V.A., L.S. Klejn & G.S. Lebedev. 1982. Attainments and Problems of Soviet Archaeology. *World Archaeology* 13: 272-95.

Bunge, M.A. 1996. *Finding Philosophy in Social Science*. New Haven, CT: Yale University Press.

Butterworth, B. 1999. *What Counts: How Every Brain is Hardwired for Math*. New York: Free Press.

Caldwell, J.R. 1958. *Trend and Tradition in the Prehistory of the Eastern United States*. Menasha: American Anthropological Association, Memoir, 88.

—. 1959. The New American Archeology. *Science* 129: 303-07.

—. 1964. Interaction Spheres in Prehistory. In J.R. Caldwell & R.L. Hall (eds.). *Hopewellian Studies*. Springfield, IL: State Museum Science Papers, 12, 133-43.

Campbell, H. 1913. Man's Mental Evolution, Past and Future. *Lancet* vol. I for 1913 : 1260-62, 1333-35, 1408-10, 1473-76.

Campeau, L. 1977. Review of B. Trigger, The Children of Aataentsic. *Revue d'histoire de l'Amérique française* 31: 437-40.

Cannon, A. 1989. The Historical Dimension in Mortuary Expressions of Status and Sentiment. *Current Anthropology* 30: 437-58.

Carneiro, R.L. 1970. Scale Analysis, Evolutionary Sequences, and the Rating of Cultures. In R. Naroll & R. Cohen (eds.). *A Handbook of Method in Cultural Anthropology*. New York: Columbia University Press, 834-71.

Carr, E.H. 1967. *What is History?* New York: Vintage.

Carrithers, M. 1992. *Why Humans Have Cultures: Explaining Anthropology and Social Diversity*. Oxford: Oxford University Press.

Cartmill, M., D. Pilbeam & G. Isaac. 1986. One Hundred Years of Paleoanthropology. *American Scientist* 74: 410-20.

Chakrabarti, D.K. 1982. The Development of Archaeology in the Indian Subcontinent. *World Archaeology* 13: 326-44.

Chamberlin, T.C. 1944. The Method of Multiple Working Hypotheses. *Scientific Monthly* 59: 357-62.

Chang, K.C. 1962. China. In R.J. Braidwood & G.R. Willey (eds.). *Courses Toward Urban Life*. Chicago: Aldine, 177-92.

—. 1963. *The Archaeology of Ancient China*. New Haven, CT: Yale University Press.

—. 1981. Archaeology and Chinese Historiography. *World Archaeology* 13: 156-69.

Chapman, R., I. Kinnes & K. Randsborg (eds.). 1981. *The Archaeology of Death*. Cambridge: Cambridge University Press.

Charlton, T. H. 1981. Archaeology, Ethnohistory, and Ethnology: Interpretive Interfaces. *Advances in Archaeological Method and Theory* 4: 129-76.

Cheek, A.L. & B.C. Keel. 1984. Value Conflicts in Osteo-archaeology. In E.L. Green (ed.). *Ethics and Values in Archaeology*. New York: Free Press, 194-207.

Childe, V.G. 1925. *The Dawn of European Civilization*. London: Kegan Paul.

—. 1932. Chronology of Prehistoric Europe: A Review. *Antiquity* 6: 206-12.

—. 1934. *New Light on the Most Ancient East*. London: Kegan Paul.

—. 1936. *Man Makes Himself*. London: Watts.

—. 1942. Prehistory in the U.S.S.R. *Man* 42: 98-100, 100-103, 130-36.

—. 1946a. *Scotland Before the Scots*. London: Methuen.

—. 1946b. Archaeology and Anthropology. *Southwestern Journal of Anthropology* 2: 243-51.

—. 1947. *History*. London: Cobbett.

—. 1949. *Social Worlds of Knowledge.* London: Oxford University Press.
—. 1950. *Magic, Craftsmanship and Science.* Liverpool: Liverpool University Press.
—. 1951. *Social Evolution.* New York: Schuman.
—. 1956a. *Society and Knowledge: The Growth of Human Traditions.* New York: Harper.
—. 1956b. *Piecing Together the Past: The Interpretation of Archaeological Data.* London: Routledge & Kegan Paul.
—. 1958. *The Prehistory of European Society.* Harmondsworth: Penguin.
Chippindale, C. 1993. Ambition, Deference, Discrepancy, Consumption: The Intellectual Background to a Post-Processual Archaeology. In N. Yoffee & A. Sherratt (eds.). *Archaeological Theory: Who Sets the Agenda?* Cambridge: Cambridge University Press, 27-36.
Chisholm, R.M. 1966. *Theory of Knowledge.* Englewood Cliffs, NJ: Prentice-Hall.
Chomsky, N. 1988. *Language and Problems of Knowledge: The Managua Lectures.* Cambridge, MA: MIT Press.
Clark, G.A. 1982. Quantifying Archaeological Research. *Advances in Archaeological Method and Theory* 5: 217-73.
Clark, J.G.D. 1939. *Archaeology and Society.* London: Methuen.
—. 1952. *Prehistoric Europe: The Economic Basis.* London: Methuen.
—. 1954. *Excavations at Star Carr.* Cambridge: Cambridge University Press.
—. 1957. *Archaeology and Society* (3rd ed.). London: Methuen.
—. 1969. *World Prehistory: A New Outline.* Cambridge: Cambridge University Press.
—. 1989. *Economic Prehistory.* Cambridge: Cambridge University Press.
Clarke, D.L. 1968. *Analytical Archaeology.* London: Methuen.
—. 1973. Archaeology: The Loss of Innocence. *Antiquity* 47: 6-18.
—. 1979. *Analytical Archaeologist.* London: Academic Press.
Coe, M.D. 1992. *Breaking the Maya Code.* London: Thames & Hudson.
Cohen, M.N. 1977. *The Food Crisis in Prehistory.* New Haven, CT: Yale University Press.
Cohen, S. 1986. *Historical Culture.* Berkeley: University of California Press.
Cole, J.R. 1980. Cult Archaeology and Unscientific Method and Theory. *Advances in Archaeological Method and Theory* 3: 1-33.
Collingwood, R.G. 1930. *The Archaeology of Roman Britain.* London: Methuen.
—. 1939. *An Autobiography.* Oxford: Oxford University Press.
—. 1946. *The Idea of History.* Oxford: Oxford University Press.
Conkey, M.W. & J.D. Spector. 1984. Archaeology and the Study of Gender. *Advances in Archaeological Method and Theory* 7: 1-38.
Conkey, M.W. & R.E. Tringham. 1995. Archaeology and the Goddess: Exploring the Contours of Feminist Archaeology. In D.C. Stanton & A.J. Stewart (eds.). *Feminisms in the Academy.* Ann Arbor: University of Michigan Press, 199-247.
Conrad, G.W. 1981. Cultural Materialism, Split Inheritance, and the Expansion of Ancient Peruvian Empires. *American Antiquity* 46: 3-26.
Conrad, G.W. & A.A. Demarest. 1984. *Religion and Empire: The Dynamics of Aztec and Inca Expansionism.* Cambridge: Cambridge University Press.
Conroy, G.C. 1990. *Primate Evolution.* New York: W. W. Norton.
Copleston, F.C. 1953-1974. *A History of Philosophy* (9 vols). London: Burns & Oates.
Cordell, L. S. & F. Plog. 1979. Escaping the Confines of Normative Thought: A Reevaluation of Puebloan Prehistory. *American Antiquity* 44: 405-29.
Cordy, R.H. 1981. *A Study of Prehistoric Social Change.* New York: Academic Press.
Courbin, P. 1988. *What is Archaeology? An Essay on the Nature of Archaeological Research.* Chicago: University of Chicago Press.
Crone, P. 1989. *Pre-industrial Societies.* Oxford: Blackwell Publishers.

Culbert, T.P. (ed.). 1973. *The Classic Maya Collapse*. Albuquerque: University of New Mexico Press.
Cushing, F. H. 1886. A Study of Pueblo Pottery as Illustrative of Zuñi Culture Growth. Washington, DC: *Bureau of American Ethnology, 4th Annual Report*, 467-521.
Dall, W.H. 1877. On Succession in the Shell-Heaps of the Aleutian Islands. Washington, DC: *United States Department of the Interior, Contributions to North American Ethnology*, 1: 41-91.
Dalton, G. 1981. Anthropological Models in Archaeological Perspective. In I. Hodder, G. Isaac & N. Hammond (eds*.*). *Pattern of the Past: Studies in Honour of David Clarke*. Cambridge: Cambridge University Press, 17-48.
Damerow, P. 1996. *Abstraction and Representation: Essays on the Cultural Evolution of Thinking*. Dordrecht: Kluwer.
Daniel, G. 1950. *A Hundred Years of Archaeology*. London: Duckworth.
—. 1975. *A Hundred and Fifty Years of Archaeology*. London: Duckworth.
—. (ed.). 1981. *Towards a History of Archaeology*. London: Thames & Hudson.
Darnell, R. 1971. The Professionalization of American Anthropology: A Case Study in the Sociology of Knowledge. *Social Science Information* 10: 83-103.
Dart, R.A. 1949. The Predatory Implemental Technique of Australopithecus. *American Journal of Physical Anthropology* 7: 1-38.
Day, M. 1990. Archaeological Ethics and the Treatment of the Dead. *Anthropology Today* 6(1): 15-16.
Deagan, K. 1982. Avenues of Inquiry in Historical Archaeology. *Advances in Archaeological Method and Theory* 5: 151-77.
Debetz, G.F. 1961. The Social Life of Early Paleolithic Man as Seen Through the Work of the Soviet Anthropologists. In S.L. Washburn (ed.). *Social Life of Early Man*. Chicago: Aldine, 137-49.
Deetz, J.J.F. 1977. *In Small Things Forgotten*. Garden City, NY: Anchor.
—. 1996. *In Small Things Forgotten : An Archaeology of Early American Life*. (rev. ed.). New York : Anchor Books.
Devore, I. (ed.). 1965. *Primate Behavior*. New York: Holt, Rinehart & Winston.
Dilthey, W. 1883. *Einleitung in die Geisteswissenschaften: Versuch einer Grundlegung für das Studien der Gesellschaft und der Geschichte*. Leipzig: Duncker und Humblot.
Dixon, R. B. 1913. Some Aspects of North American Archaeology. *American Anthropologist* 15: 549-77.
Donnan, C.B. 1976. *Moche Art and Iconography*. Los Angeles: UCLA Latin American Center Publications.
Doxtator, D. 1988. The Home of Indian Culture and Other Stories in the Museum. *Muse* 6(3): 26-8.
Dray, W.H. 1957. *Laws and Explanation in History*. Oxford: Oxford University Press.
Driver, H.E. & W.C. Massey. 1957. Comparative Studies of North American Indians. *Transactions of the American Philosophical Society* 47: 165-456.
Dumond, D.E. 1977. Science in Archaeology: The Saints Go Marching In. *American Antiquity* 42: 330-49.
Dunnell, R.C. 1971. *Systematics in Prehistory*. New York: Free Press.
—. 1979. Trends in Current Americanist Archaeology. *American Journal of Archaeology* 83: 437-49.
—. 1980a. Americanist Archaeology: The 1979 Contribution. *American Journal of Archaeology* 84: 463-78.
—. 1980b. Evolutionary Theory and Archaeology. *Advances in Archaeological Method and Theory* 3: 35-99.

—. 1981. Americanist Archaeology: The 1980 Literature. *American Journal of Archaeology* 85: 429-45.
—. 1982. Americanist Archaeological Literature: 1981. *American Journal of Archaeology* 86: 509-29.
Earle, T.K. 1977. A Reappraisal of Redistribution: Complex Hawaiian Chiefdoms. In T.K. Earle & J.E. Ericson (eds.). *Exchange Systems in Prehistory.* New York: Academic Press, 213-29.
—. 1978. *Economic and Social Organization of a Complex Chiefdom: The Halelea District, Kauai, Hawaii.* Ann Arbor: University of Michigan, Museum of Anthropology, Anthropological Papers, 63.
Eggan, F.R. 1966. *The American Indian.* London: Weidenfeld & Nicolson.
Eiseley, L.C. 1958. *Darwin's Century: Evolution and the Men who Discovered It.* Garden City, NY: Doubleday.
Eisenstadt, S.N. (ed.). 1986. *The Origins and Diversity of Axial Age Civilizations.* Albany, NY: State University of New York Press.
Ekholm, G.F. & G.R. Willey. (eds.). 1966. *Handbook of Middle American Indians,* Vol. IV, *Archaeological Frontiers and External Connections.* Austin: University of Texas Press.
Ekholm, K. & J. Friedman. 1979. "Capital", Imperialism and Exploitation in Ancient World Systems. In M.T. Larsen (ed.). *Power and Propaganda: A Symposium on Ancient Empires.* Copenhagen: Akademisk Forlag, 41-58.
Embree, L. 1987. Archaeology: The Most Basic Science of All. *Antiquity* 61: 75-78.
—. 1992. The Future and Past of Metaarchaeology. In L. Embree (ed.). *Metaarchaeology: Reflections by Archaeologists and Philosophers.* Dordrecht: Kluwer, 3-50.
Emerson, J.N. 1961. Problems of Huron Origins. *Anthropologica* 3: 181-201.
Engels, F. 1962. The Part Played by Labour in the Transition from Ape to Man. In K. Marx & F. Engels, *Selected Works in Two Volumes.* Moscow: Foreign Languages Publishing House, II: 80-92.
Evans-Pritchard, E.E. 1949. *The Sanusi of Cyrenaica.* Oxford: Oxford University Press.
—. 1962. Anthropology and History. In E.E. Evans-Pritchard, *Essays in Social Anthropology.* London: Methuen, 45-65.
Eve, R.A. & F.B. Harrold. 1986. Creationism, Cult Archaeology, and Other Pseudoscientific Beliefs. *Youth and Society* 17: 396-412.
Ewing, A.C. 1934. *Idealism: A Critical Survey.* London: Methuen.
Eyerman, R. 1981. *False Consciousness and Ideology in Marxist Theory.* Atlantic Highlands, NJ: Humanities Press.
Fagan, B.M. 1981. Two Hundred and Four Years of African Archaeology. In J.D. Evans, B. Cunliffe & C. Renfrew (eds.). *Antiquity and Man.* London: Thames & Hudson, 42-51.
—. 1998. *From Black Land to Fifth Sun: The Science of Sacred Sites.* Reading, MA: Addison-Wesley.
Fagette, P. 1996. *Digging for Dollars: American Archaeology and the New Deal.* Albuquerque: University of New Mexico Press.
Feder, K.L. 1984. Irrationality and Popular Archaeology. *American Antiquity* 49: 525-41.
Fedigan, L.M. The Changing Role of Women in Models of Human Evolution. *Annual Review of Anthropology* 15: 25-66.
Feeley-Harnik, G. 1985. Issues in Divine Kingship. *Annual Review of Anthropology* 14: 273-313.
Feit, H.A. 1978. *Waswanipi Realities and Adaptations: Resource Management & Cognitive Structure.* Montreal: Unpublished Ph.D dissertation, McGill University.

Ferguson, T.J. 1984. Archaeological Ethics and Values in a Tribal Cultural Resource Management Program at the Pueblo of Zuñi. In E.L. Green (ed.). *Ethics and Values in Archaeology*. New York: Free Press, 224-35.

Fewkes, J.W. 1896. The Prehistoric Culture of Tusayan. *American Anthropologist* 9: 151-173.

Feyerabend, P.K. 1975. *Against Method: Outline of an Anarchistic Theory of Knowledge*. London: NLB.

—. 1987. *Farewell to Reason*. London: Verso.

Fischer, D.H. 1971. *Historians' Fallacies: Toward a Logic of Historical Thought*. London: Routledge & Kegan Paul.

Fischer, J.L. 1961. Art Styles as Cultural Cognitive Maps. *American Anthropologist* 63: 79-93.

Fitting, J. E. 1973. Plumbing, Philosophy, and Poetry. In J.E. Fitting (ed.). *The Development of North American Archaeology*. New York: Anchor Press, 286-91.

Flannery, K.V. 1972. The Cultural Evolution of Civilizations. *Annual Review of Ecology and Systematics* 3: 399-426.

Flannery, K.V. & J. Marcus. 1976. Formative Oaxaca and the Zapotec Cosmos. *American Scientist* 64: 374-383.

—. (eds.). 1983. *The Cloud People: Divergent Evolution of the Zapotec and Mixtec Civilizations*. New York: Academic Press.

Ford, C.S. (ed.). 1967. *Cross-Cultural Approaches: Readings in Comparative Research*. New Haven, CT: HRAF Press.

Ford, J. A. & G. R. Willey. 1941. An Interpretation of the Prehistory of the Eastern United States. *American Anthropologist* 43: 325-63.

Fowler, D.D. 1987. Uses of the Past: Archaeology in the Service of the State. *American Antiquity* 52: 229-48.

Fox, W.A. 1989. Native Archaeology in Ontario: A Status Report. *Arch Notes* 89(6): 30-31.

Francis, D. & T. Morantz. 1983. *Partners in Furs: A History of the Fur Trade in Eastern James Bay, 1600-1870*. Montreal: McGill-Queen's University Press.

Frankfort, H. 1948. *Kingship and the Gods: A Study of Near Eastern Religion as the Integration of Society and Nature*. Chicago: University of Chicago Press.

—. 1956. *The Birth of Civilization in the Near East*. New York: Doubleday.

Fried, M.H. 1967. *The Evolution of Political Society: An Essay in Political Anthropology*. New York: Random House.

—. 1975. *The Notion of Tribe*. Menlo Park, CA: Cummings.

Friedman, J. & M.J. Rowlands. 1978. Notes Towards an Epigenetic Model of the Evolution of "Civilisation." In J. Friedman & M.J. Rowlands (eds.). *The Evolution of Social Systems*. Pittsburgh: University of Pittsburgh Press, 201-76.

Fuller, P. 1980. *Beyond the Crisis in Art*. London: Writers & Readers.

Furst, P.T. 1977. The Roots and Continuities of Shamanism. In A.T. Brodzky, R. Danesewich & N. Johnson (eds.). *Stones, Bones and Skin: Ritual and Shamanistic Art*. Toronto: Society for Art Publications, 1-28.

Gallay, A. 1986. *L'Archéologie demain*. Paris: Belfond.

Gardin, J.-C. 1980. *Archaeological Constructs*. Cambridge: Cambridge University Press.

Garlake, P.S. 1973. *Great Zimbabwe*. London: Thames & Hudson.

Garnsey, P. 1988. *Famine and Food Supply in the Greco-Roman World*. Cambridge: Cambridge University Press.

Gathercole, P. 1981. New Zealand Prehistory before 1950. In G. Daniel (ed.). *Towards a History of Archaeology*. London: Thames & Hudson, 159-68.

—. 1984. A Consideration of Ideology. In M. Spriggs (ed.). *Marxist Perspectives in Archaeology*. Cambridge: Cambridge University Press, 149-54.
Gathercole, P. & D. Lowenthal (eds.). 1990. *The Politics of the Past*. London: Unwin Hyman.
Gazzaniga, M.S. 1992. *Nature's Mind: The Biological Roots of Thinking, Emotions, Sexuality, Language, and Intelligence*. New York: Basic Books.
—. 1998. *The Mind's Past*. Berkeley: University of California Press.
Gellner, E. 1982. What is Structuralisme? In A.C. Renfrew, M.J. Rowlands & B.A. Segraves (eds.). *Theory and Explanation in Archaeology: The Southampton Conference*. New York: Academic Press, 97-123.
Gibbon, G. 1984. *Anthropological Archaeology*. New York: Columbia University Press.
—. 1989. *Explanation in Archaeology*. Oxford: Blackwell Publishers.
Giddens, A. 1984. *The Constitution of Society: Outline of the Theory of Structuration*. Berkeley: University of California Press.
Gillespie, S.D. 1989. *The Aztec Kings: The Construction of Rulership in Mexican History*. Tucson: University of Arizona Press.
Gimbutas, M. 1982. *The Goddesses and Gods of Old Europe: Myths and Cult Images*. London: Thames & Hudson.
Gladwin, W. & H. S. Gladwin. 1934. *A Method for Designation of Cultures and their Variations*. Globe: Medallion Papers, 15.
Glassie, H.H. 1975. *Folk Housing in Middle Virginia: A Structural Analysis of Historical Artifacts*. Knoxville: University of Tennessee Press.
Godelier, M. 1986. *The Mental and the Material*. London: Verso.
Goff, B.L. 1963. *Symbols of Prehistoric Mesopotamia*. New Haven, CT: Yale University Press.
Goldenweiser, A.A. 1913. The Principle of Limited Possibilities in the Development of Culture. *Journal of American Folk-Lore* 26: 259-90.
Goldie, T. 1989. *Fear and Temptation: The Image of the Indigene in Canadian, Australian, and New Zealand Literatures*. Montreal: McGill-Queen's University Press.
Golson, J. 1977. *The Ladder of Social Evolution: Archaeology and the Bottom Rungs*. Canberra: Australian Academy of the Humanities.
Goodenough, E.R. 1953-1968. *Jewish Symbols in the Greco-Roman Period* (13 vols.). New York: Pantheon Books.
Gosden, C. 1994. *Social Time and Being*. Oxford: Blackwell Publishers.
Gough, J.W. 1957. *The Social Contract: A Critical Study of its Development* (2nd ed.). Oxford: Oxford University Press.
Gould, R.A. (ed.). 1978a. *Explorations in Ethnoarchaeology*. Albuquerque: University of New Mexico Press.
—. 1978b. Beyond Analogy in Ethnoarchaeology. In R.A. Gould, (ed.). *Explorations in Ethnoarchaeology*. Albuquerque: University of New Mexico Press, 249-93.
—. 1980. *Living Archaeology*. Cambridge: Cambridge University Press.
Gramsci, A. 1992. *Prison Notebooks*. New York: Columbia University Press.
Gräslund, B. 1974. *Relativ Datering: Om Kronologisk Metod i Nordisk Arkeologi*. Uppsala: Almqvist & Wiksell.
Grayson, D.K. 1983. *The Establishment of Human Antiquity*. New York: Academic Press.
—. 1986. Eoliths, Archaeological Ambiguity, and the Generation of "Middle-Range" Research. In D.J. Meltzer, D.D. Fowler & J.A. Sabloff (eds.). *American Archaeology Past and Future*. Washington, DC: Smithsonian Institution Press, 77-103.
Green, E.L. (ed.). 1984. *Ethics and Values in Archaeology*. New York: Free Press.
Griffin, J. B. 1943. *The Fort Ancient Aspect*. Ann Arbor: University of Michigan Press.

Haas, J. 1982. *The Evolution of the Prehistoric State.* New York: Columbia University Press.
Habermas, J. 1971. *Knowledge and Human Interests.* Boston: Beacon Press.
—. 1975. *Legitimation Crisis.* Boston: Beacon Press.
Hall, J.A. 1985. *Powers and Liberties: The Causes and Consequences of the Rise of the West.* Oxford: Blackwell Publishers.
Hall, R.L. 1979. In Search of the Ideology of the Adena-Hopewell Climax. In D.S. Brose & N. Greber (eds.). *Hopewell Archaeology: The Chillicothe Conference.* Kent: Kent State University Press, 258-65.
Hallpike, C.R. 1979. *The Foundations of Primitive Thought.* Oxford: Oxford University Press.
—. 1986. *The Principles of Social Evolution.* Oxford: Oxford University Press.
Hamell, G.R. 1980. *Sun Serpents, Tawiskaron and Quartz Crystals.* Rochester: Rochester Museum Science Center (Mimeo.).
—. 1987. Strawberries, Floating Islands, and Rabbit Captains: Mythical Realities and European Contact in the Northeast during the Sixteenth and Seventeenth Centuries. *Journal of Canadian Studies* 21 (4): 72-94.
Hamill, J.F. 1990. *Ethno-Logic: The Anthropology of Human Reasoning.* Urbana: University of Illinois Press.
Hamilton, N. et al. 1996. Can We Interpret Figurines? *Cambridge Archaeological Journal* 6: 281-307.
Hanen, M. & J. Kelley. 1992. Gender and Archaeological Knowledge. In L. Embree (ed.). *Metaarchaeology.* Dordrecht: Kluwer, 195-225.
Harré, R. 1970. *The Principles of Scientific Thinking.* Chicago: University of Chicago Press.
—. 1972. *The Philosophies of Science: An Introductory Survey.* Oxford: Oxford University Press.
Harré, R. & E.H. Madden. 1975. *Causal Powers: A Theory of Natural Necessity.* Totowa, NJ: Rowman & Littlefield.
Harris, M. 1968. *The Rise of Anthropological Theory: A History of Theories of Culture.* New York: Crowell.
—. 1979. *Cultural Materialism: The Struggle for a Science of Culture.* New York: Random House.
Harrold, F.B. & R.A. Eve (eds.). 1987. *Cult Archaeology and Creationism.* Iowa City: University of Iowa Press.
Hassan, F.A. 1981. *Demographic Archaeology.* New York: Academic Press.
Haven, S.F. 1856. *Archaeology of the United States.* Smithsonian Contributions to Knowledge, 8.
Hawkes, C.F. 1954. Archeological Theory and Method: Some Suggestions from the Old World. *American Anthropologist* 56: 155-68.
Hays, K.A. 1993. When is a Symbol Archaeologically Meaningful?: Meaning, Function, and Prehistoric Visual Arts. In N. Yoffee & A. Sherratt (eds.). *Archaeological Theory: Who Sets the Agenda?* Cambridge: Cambridge University Press, 81-92.
Held, D. 1980. *Introduction to Critical Theory: Horkheimer to Habermas.* Berkeley: University of California Press.
Hempel, C.G. 1965. *Aspects of Scientific Explanation, and Other Essays in the Philosophy of Science.* New York: Free Press.
Hempel, C.G. & P. Oppenheim. 1948. Studies in the Logic of Explanation. *Philosophy of Science* 15: 135-75.
Hertzberg, H.W. 1971. *The Search for an American Indian Identity.* Syracuse, NY: Syracuse University Press.

Hill, J.E.C. 1972. *The World Turned Upside Down: Radical Ideas During the English Revolution.* Harmondsworth: Penguin.
Hill, R. 1988. Sacred Trust: Cultural Obligation of Museums to Native People. *Muse* 6(3): 32-3.
Hindess, B. & P.Q. Hirst. 1975. *Pre-Capitalist Modes of Production.* London: Routledge and Kegan Paul.
Hinsley, C.M., Jr. 1981. *Savages and Scientists: The Smithsonian Institution and the Development of American Anthropology 1846-1910.* Washington, DC: Smithsonian Institution Press.
Hodder, I. (ed.). 1978. *Simulation Studies in Archaeology.* Cambridge: Cambridge University Press.
—. 1979. Economic and Social Stress and Material Culture Patterning. *American Antiquity* 44: 446-54.
—. 1981. Society, Economy and Culture: An Ethnographic Case Study Amongst the Lozi. In I. Hodder, G. Isaac and N. Hammond (eds.). *Pattern of the Past.* Cambridge: Cambridge University Press, 67-95.
—. (ed.). 1982a. *Symbolic and Structural Archaeology.* Cambridge: Cambridge University Press.
—. 1982b. *Symbols in Action: Ethnoarchaeological Studies of Material Culture.* Cambridge: Cambridge University Press.
—. 1982c. *The Present Past: An Introduction to Anthropology for Archaeologists.* London: Batsford.
—. 1983. Archaeology, Ideology and Contemporary Society. *Royal Anthropological Institute News* 56: 6-7.
—. 1984. Archaeology in 1984. *Antiquity* 58: 25-32.
—. 1986. *Reading the Past: Current Approaches to Interpretation in Archaeology.* Cambridge: Cambridge University Press.
—. (ed.). 1987a. *Archaeology as Long-Term History.* Cambridge: Cambridge University Press.
—. (ed.). 1987b. *The Archaeology of Contextual Meanings.* Cambridge: Cambridge University Press.
—. 1988. Material Culture Texts and Social Change: A Theoretical Discussion and Some Archaeological Examples. *Proceedings of the Prehistoric Society* 54: 67-75.
—. 1990. *The Domestication of Europe: Structure and Contingency in Neolithic Societies.* Oxford: Blackwell Publishers.
—. 1991. *Reading the Past: Current Approaches to Interpretation in Archaeology* (2nd ed.). Cambridge: Cambridge University Press.
—. 1999. *The Archaeological Process: An Introduction.* Oxford: Blackwell Publishers.
Hoebel, E.A. 1949. *Man in the Primitive World.* New York: McGraw-Hill.
Hoernle, R.F. 1924. *Idealism as a Philosophical Doctrine.* London: Hodder and Stoughton.
Hollis, M. & S. Lukes (eds.). 1982. *Rationality and Relativism.* Cambridge, MA: MIT Press.
Holloway, R.L., Jr. 1967. Tools and Teeth: Some Speculations Regarding Canine Reduction. *American Anthropologist* 69: 63-67.
Holmes, W.H. 1903. Aboriginal Pottery of the Eastern United States. Washington, DC: *Bureau of American Ethnology, 20th Annual Report,* pp. 1-237.
—. 1914. Areas of American Culture Characterization Tentatively Outlined as an Aid in the Study of the Antiquities. *American Anthropologist* 16: 413-46.
Hooton, E.A. 1938. *Apes, Men, and Morons.* London: Allen and Unwin.
Hosler, D. 1995a. Sound, Color and Meaning in the Metallurgy of Ancient West Mexico. *World Archaeology* 27: 100-15.

—. 1995b. *The Sounds and Colors of Power: The Sacred Metallurgical Technology of Ancient West Mexico*. Cambridge, MA: MIT Press.
Hudson, K. 1981. *A Social History of Archaeology: The British Experience*. London: Macmillan.
Hunt, G.T. 1940. *The Wars of the Iroquois*. Madison: University of Wisconsin Press.
Huntington, R. & P. Metcalf. 1979. *Celebrations of Death: The Anthropology of Mortuary Ritual*. Cambridge: Cambridge University Press.
Iggers, G.G. & J.M. Powell (eds.). 1990. *Leopold von Ranke and the Shaping of the Historical Discipline*. Syracuse, NY: Syracuse University Press.
Ikawa-Smith, F. 1982. Co-Traditions in Japanese Archaeology. *World Archaeology* 13: 296-309.
Ingold, T. 1996. Hunting and Gathering as Ways of Perceiving the Environment. In R. Ellen & K. Fukui (eds.). *Redefining Nature: Ecology, Culture, and Domestication*. Washington, DC: Berg Publishers, 117-55.
Irvine, W. 1955. *Apes, Angels, and Victorians: The Study of Darwin, Huxley, and Evolution*. New York: McGraw-Hill.
Isaac, G.L. 1971. The Diet of Early Man: Aspects of Archaeological Evidence from Lower and Middle Pleistocene Sites in Africa. *World Archaeology* 2: 278-99.
Isaac, R. 1982. *The Transformation of Virginia, 1740-1790*. Chapel Hill, NC: University of North Carolina Press.
Jasanoff, J.H. & A. Nussbaum. 1996. Word Games: The Linguistic Evidence in Black Athena. In M.R. Lefkowitz & G.M. Rogers (eds.). *Black Athena Revisited*. Chapel Hill: University of North Carolina Press, 177-205.
Jenness, D. 1932. Fifty Years of Archaeology in Canada. *Anniversary Volume, 1882-1932*. Toronto: Royal Society of Canada, 71-76.
Jennings, F. 1975. *The Invasion of America*. Chapel Hill: University of North Carolina Press.
Johnson, F. 1944. Review of The Pre-Iroquoian Occupations of New York State, by W. A. Ritchie. *American Anthropologist* 46: 530-35.
—. (ed.). 1946. *Man in Northeastern North America*. Andover, MA: Papers of the Robert S. Peabody Foundation for Archaeology, 3.
Johnson, G.A. 1978. Information Sources and the Development of Decision-Making Organizations. In C.L. Redman et al. (eds.). *Social Archaeology*. New York: Academic Press, 87-112.
—. 1981. Monitoring Complex System Integration and Boundary Phenomena with Settlement Size Data. In S.E. Van der Leeuw (ed.). *Archaeological Approaches to the Study of Complexity*. Amsterdam: Van Giffen Institute, 143-88.
Johnson, M. 1996. *An Archaeology of Capitalism*. Oxford: Blackwell Publishers.
—. 1999. *Archaeological Theory: An Introduction*. Oxford: Blackwell Publishers.
Johnston, B. 1976. The Cultural and Ethical Aspects of Archaeology in Canada: An Indian Point of View. In A.G. McKay (ed.). *New Perspectives in Canadian Archaeology*. Ottawa: Royal Society of Canada, 173-75.
Jones, W.T. 1969. *A History of Western Philosophy* (2nd ed.) (4 vols.). New York: Harcourt, Brace & World.
Karlsson, Håkan. 1998. *Re-Thinking Archaeology*. Göteborg: Novum Grafiska.
Kelley, J.H. & M.P. Hanen. 1988. *Archaeology and the Methodology of Science*. Albuquerque: University of New Mexico Press.
Kemp, B.J. 1989. *Ancient Egypt: Anatomy of a Civilization*. London: Routledge.
Kidder, A.V. 1924. *An Introduction to the Study of Southwestern Archaeology*. New Haven, CT: Papers of the Southwestern Expedition, Phillips Academy, 1.

—. 1935. *Year Book*, No. 34. Washington, DC: Carnegie Foundation.
—. 1973. The Development of Maya Research. In R.B. Woodbury, *Alfred V. Kidder*. New York: Columbia University Press, 137-41.
Kinzey, W.G. (ed.). 1987. *The Evolution of Human Behavior: Primate Models*. Albany: State University of New York Press.
Ki-Zerbo, J. (ed.). 1981. *General History of Africa, I, Methodology and African Prehistory*. Berkeley: University of California Press.
Klejn, L.S. 1974. Kossinna in Abstand von vierzig Jahren. *Jahresschrift für Mitteldeutsche Vorgeschichte* 58: 7-55.
—. 1977. A Panorama of Theoretical Archaeology. *Current Anthropology* 18: 1-42.
Klindt-Jensen, O. 1975. *A History of Scandinavian Archaeology*. London: Thames & Hudson.
Kluckhohn, C. 1940. The Conceptual Structure in Middle American Studies. In C.L. Hay et al. (eds.). *The Maya and their Neighbors*. New York: Appleton-Century, 41-51.
Knapp, A.B. 1996. Archaeology without Gravity: Postmodernism and the Past. *Journal of Archaeological Method and Theory* 3: 127-58.
Kohl, P.L. 1978. The Balance of Trade in Southwestern Asia in the Mid-Third Millennium B.C. *Current Anthropology* 19: 463-92.
—. 1979. The "World Economy" of West Asia in the Third Millennium B.C. In M. Taddei (ed.). *South Asian Archaeology 1977*. Naples: Istituto Universitario Orientale, Seminario di Studi Asiatici, 55-85.
—. 1981. Materialist Approaches in Prehistory. *Annual Review of Anthropology* 10: 89-118.
—. 1987. The Ancient Economy, Transferable Technologies, and the Bronze Age World-System: A View from the Northeastern Frontier of the Ancient Near East. In M. Rowlands, M.T. Larsen & K. Kristiansen (eds.). *Centre and Periphery in the Ancient World*. Cambridge: Cambridge University Press, 13-24.
Kohl, P.L. & C. Fawcett (eds.). 1995. *Nationalism, Politics, and the Practice of Archaeology*. Cambridge: Cambridge University Press.
Kolakowski, L. 1968. *The Alienation of Reason: A History of Positivist Thought*. Garden City, NY: Anchor.
—. 1972. *Positivist Philosophy from Hume to the Vienna Circle*. Harmondsworth: Penguin.
—. 1976. *La Philosophie positiviste*. Paris: Denoël.
—. 1978. *Main Currents of Marxism, III, The Breakdown*. Oxford: Oxford University Press.
Kopytoff, I. 1981. Aghem Ethnogenesis and the Grasslands Ecumene. In C. Tardits (ed.). *Contribution de la recherche ethnologique à l'histoire des civilisations du Cameroun*. Paris: Editions du CNRS, 371-81.
Kossinna, G. 1911. *Die Herkunft der Germanen: Zur Methode der Siedlungsarchäologie*. Leipzig: Kabitzsch.
—. 1912. *Die deutsche Vorgeschichte: Eine hervorragend nationale Wissenschaft*. Würzburg: Kabitzsch.
Kramer, C. (ed.). 1979. *Ethnoarchaeology: Implications of Ethnography for Archaeology*. New York: Columbia University Press.
Kristiansen, K. 1981. A Social History of Danish Archaeology (1805-1975). In G. Daniel (ed.). *Towards a History of Archaeology*. London: Thames & Hudson, 20-44.
—. 1988. The Black and the Red: Shanks and Tilley's Programme for a Radical Archaeology. *Antiquity* 62: 473-82.
Kroeber, A.L. 1909. The Archaeology of California. In F. Boas et al. (eds.). *Putnam Anniversary Volume: Anthropological Essays*. New York: Stechert, 1-42.

—. 1948. *Anthropology: Race, Language, Culture, Psychology, Prehistory.* New York: Harcourt, Brace.
—. 1952. *The Nature of Culture.* Chicago: University of Chicago Press.
Kroker, A. 1984. *Technology and the Canadian Mind: Innis/McLuhan/Grant.* Montreal: New World Perspectives.
Kruglov, A.P. & G.V. Podgayetskiy. 1935. *Rodovoe Obshchestvo Stepey Vostochnoy Yevropy.* Leningrad: Isvestiya GAIMK, 119.
Kuhn, T.S. 1962. *The Structure of Scientific Revolutions.* Chicago: University of Chicago Press.
Kuklick, H. 1991. Contested Monuments: The Politics of Archaeology in Southern Africa. In G.W. Stocking, Jr. (ed.). *Colonial Situations: Essays on the Contextualization of Ethnographic Knowledge.* Madison: University of Wisconsin Press, 135-69.
Lakoff, G. 1987. *Women, Fire, and Dangerous Things: What Categories Reveal about the Mind.* Chicago: University of Chicago Press.
Lakoff, G. & M. Johnson. 1980. *Metaphors We Live By.* Chicago: University of Chicago Press.
Lamberg-Karlovsky, C.C. 1975. Third Millennium Modes of Exchange and Modes of Production. In J.A. Sabloff & C.C. Lamberg-Karlovsky (eds.). *Ancient Civilization and Trade.* Albuquerque: University of New Mexico Press, 341-68.
Langford, R.F. 1983. Our Heritage — Your Playground. *Australian Archaeology* 16: 1-6.
Laudan, L. 1990. *Science and Relativism: Some Key Controversies in the Philosophy of Science.* Chicago: University of Chicago Press.
Laufer, B. 1913. Remarks. *American Anthropologist* 15: 573-77.
Leach, E.R. 1954. *Political Systems of Highland Burma: A Study of Kachin Social Structure.* Cambridge, MA: Harvard University Press.
Leacock, E.B. (ed.). 1972. *The Origin of the Family, Private Property and the State, in the Light of the Researches of Lewis H. Morgan,* by F. Engels. New York: International Publishers.
Leakey, M.D. 1971. *Olduvai Gorge, III: Excavations in Beds I and II, 1960-1963.* Cambridge: Cambridge University Press.
Lechtman, H. 1977. Style in Technology- Some Early Thoughts. In H. Lechtman & R. Merill (eds.). *Material Culture: Style, Organization and Dynamics of Technology.* St. Paul, MN: West, 3-20.
LeGros Clark, W.E. 1955. *The Fossil Evidence for Human Evolution.* Chicago: University of Chicago Press.
Lenoble, P. 1991. Plateaux de gobelets dans les sépultures de Méroé: Un équipement liturgique de la libation Isiaque 'éthiopienne'. In W.V. Davies (ed.). *Egypt and Africa: Nubia from Prehistory to Islam.* London: British Museum Press, 246-52.
Leone, M.P. 1975. Views of Traditional Archaeology. *Reviews in Anthropology* 2: 191-99.
—. 1982. Some Opinions about Recovering Mind. *American Antiquity* 47: 742-60.
—. 1984. Interpreting Ideology in Historical Archaeology: Using the Rules of Perspective in the William Paca Garden in Annapolis, Maryland. In D. Miller & C. Tilley (eds.). *Ideology, Power and Prehistory.* Cambridge: Cambridge University Press, 25-35.
—. 1986. Symbolic, Structural, and Critical Archaeology. In D.J. Meltzer, D.D. Fowler & J.A. Sabloff (eds.). *American Archaeology Past and Future.* Washington, DC: Smithsonian Institution Press, 415-38.
Leone, M.P. & P.B. Potter, Jr. (eds.). 1988. *The Recovery of Meaning: Historical Archaeology in the Eastern United States.* Washington, DC: Smithsonian Institution Press.
Lévi-Strauss, C. 1963. *Structural Anthropology.* New York: Basic Books.
—. 1966. *The Savage Mind.* London: Weidenfeld & Nicolson.

Lewis, T.M.N. & M. Kneberg. 1946. *Hiwasee Island*. Knoxville: University of Tennessee Press.
Lewis-Williams, J.D. & T.A. Dowson. 1988. The Signs of All Times: Entoptic Phenomena in Upper Palaeolithic Art. *Current Anthropology* 29: 201-45.
Linton, R. (ed.). 1940. *Acculturation in Seven American Indian Tribes*. New York: Appleton-Century.
Lissarrague, F. 1990. *The Aesthetics of the Greek Banquet: Images of Wine and Ritual*. Princeton, NJ: Princeton University Press.
Lloyd, G.E.R. 1990. *Demystifying Mentalities*. Cambridge: Cambridge University Press.
Lord, B. 1974. *The History of Painting in Canada*. Toronto: NC Press.
Lorenzo, J.L. 1981. Archaeology South of the Rio Grande. *World Archaeology* 13: 190-208.
Low, B.S. 1999. *Why Sex Matters: A Darwinian Look at Human Behavior*. Princeton, NJ: Princeton University Press.
Lowenthal, D. 1985. *The Past is a Foreign Country*. Cambridge: Cambridge University Press.
Lowther, G.R. 1962. Epistemology and Archaeological Theory. *Current Anthropology* 3: 495-509.
Lubbock, J. 1870. *The Origin of Civilisation and the Primitive Condition of Man*. London: Longmans, Green.
—. 1913. *Prehistoric Times* (7th ed.). New York: Holt.
Lunn, E. 1982. *Marxism and Modernism*. Berkeley: University of California Press.
Lustig, J. 1993. *Ideologies of Social Relations in Middle Kingdom Egypt: Gender, Kinship, Ancestors*. Philadelphia: Unpublished Ph.D. dissertation, University of Pennsylvania.
Lyell, C. 1872. *Principles of Geology, or, The Modern Changes of the Earth and its Inhabitants Considered as Illustrative of Geology* (11th ed.). London: Murray.
Lyon, E.A. 1996. *A New Deal for Southeastern Archaeology*. Tuscaloosa: University of Alabama Press.
Lyotard, J.F. 1984. *The Postmodern Condition: A Report on Knowledge*. Manchester: Manchester University Press.
MacCormack, C.P. & M. Strathern (eds.). 1980. *Nature, Culture and Gender*. Cambridge: Cambridge University Press.
Macfarlane, A. 1970. *Witchcraft in Tudor and Stuart England*. London: Routledge and Kegan Paul.
MacGaffey, W. 1966. Concepts of Race in the Historiography of Northeast Africa. *Journal of African History* 7: 1-17.
MacNeish, R.S. 1952. *Iroquois Pottery Types: A Technique for the Study of Iroquois Prehistory*. Ottawa: National Museum of Canada, Bulletin 124.
—. 1978. *The Science of Archaeology?* North Scituate, MA: Duxbury Press.
McCullagh, C.B. 1984. *Justifying Historical Descriptions*. Cambridge: Cambridge University Press.
McGhee, R. 1989. Who Owns Prehistory? The Bering Land Bridge Dilemma. *Canadian Journal of Archaeology* 13: 13-20.
McGuire, J.D. 1897. Pipes and Smoking Customs of the American Aborigines. Washington, DC: *Report of the United States National Museum, 1897*, part I: 361-645.
McGuire, R.H. 1983. Breaking Down Cultural Complexity: Inequality and Heterogeneity. *Advances in Archaeological Method and Theory* 6: 91-142.
—. 1992. *A Marxist Archaeology*. San Diego: Academic Press.
McGuire, R.H. & R. Paynter (eds.). 1991. *The Archaeology of Inequality*. Oxford: Blackwell Publishers.

McKern, W.C. 1939. The Midwestern Taxonomic Method as an Aid to Archaeological Culture Study. *American Antiquity* 4: 301-13.

McLennan, G. 1981. *Marxism and the Methodologies of History*. London: Verso.

McNeill, W.H. 1986. *Mythistory and Other Essays*. Chicago: University of Chicago Press.

Mandelbaum, M.H. 1977. *The Anatomy of Historical Knowledge*. Baltimore, MD: Johns Hopkins University Press.

Marcuse, H. 1964. *One Dimensional Man: Studies in the Ideology of Advanced Industrial Society*. Boston: Beacon Press.

Marinatos, N. 1993. *Minoan Religion: Ritual, Image, & Symbol*. Columbia, SC: University of South Carolina Press.

Martin, P.S. & F. Plog. 1973. *The Archaeology of Arizona*. Garden City, NY: Natural History Press.

Martin, P.S., G.I. Quimby & D. Collier. 1947. *Indians Before Columbus*. Chicago: University of Chicago Press.

Marvin, U.B. 1973. *Continental Drift: The Evolution of a Concept*. Washington, DC: Smithsonian Institution Press.

Marx, K. & F. Engels. 1962. *Selected Works in Two Volumes*. Moscow: Foreign Languages Publishing House.

Maschner, H.D. (ed.). 1996. *Darwinian Archaeologies*. New York: Plenum.

Mason, O.T. 1895. *The Origins of Invention*. London: Walter Scott.

—. 1896. Influence of Environment upon Human Industries or Arts. Washington, DC: *Annual Report of the Smithsonian Institution for 1895*, 639-65.

Meggers, B.J. 1955. The Coming of Age of American Archeology. In M.T. Newman (ed.). *New Interpretations of Aboriginal American Culture History*. Washington, DC: Anthropological Society of Washington, 116-29.

—. 1960. The Law of Cultural Evolution as a Practical Research Tool. In G.E. Dole & R.L. Carneiro (eds.). *Essays in the Science of Culture*. New York: Crowell, 302-16.

Meighan, C.W. 1984. Archaeology: Science or Sacrilege? In E.L. Green (ed.). *Ethics and Values in Archaeology*. New York: Free Press, 208-23.

Meinander, C.F. 1981. The Concept of Culture in European Archaeological Literature. In G. Daniel (ed.). *Towards a History of Archaeology*. London: Thames & Hudson, 100-111.

Mellars, P. 1996. *The Neanderthal Legacy: An Archaeological Perspective from Western Europe*. Princeton, NJ: Princeton University Press.

Meltzer, D.J. 1983. The Antiquity of Man and the Development of American Archaeology. *Advances in Archaeological Method and Theory* 6: 1-51.

Meltzer, D.J., D.D. Fowler & J.A. Sabloff (eds.). 1986. *American Archaeology Past and Future: A Celebration of the Society for American Archaeology 1935-1985*. Washington, DC: Smithsonian Institution Press.

Meskell, L.M. (ed.). 1998. *Archaeology under Fire: Nationalism, Politics and Heritage in the Eastern Mediterranean and Middle East*. London: Routledge.

—. 1999. *Archaeologies of Social Life: Age, Sex, Class et cetera in Ancient Egypt*. Oxford: Blackwell Publishers.

Miller, D. 1980. Archaeology and Development. *Current Anthropology* 21: 709-26.

—. 1984. Modernism and Suburbia as Material Ideology. In D. Miller & C.Y. Tilley (eds.). *Ideology, Power and Prehistory*. Cambridge: Cambridge University Press, 37-49.

—. 1987. *Material Culture and Mass Consumption*. Oxford: Blackwell Publishers.

Miller, D. & C.Y. Tilley (eds.). 1984a. *Ideology, Power and Prehistory*. Cambridge: Cambridge University Press.

—. 1984b. Ideology, Power and Long-Term Social Change. In D. Miller & C.Y. Tilley (eds.). *Ideology, Power and Prehistory*. Cambridge: Cambridge University Press, 147-52.
Miller, M. 1956. *Archaeology in the U.S.S.R*. London: Atlantic Press.
Mills, W.C. 1902. Excavations of the Adena Mound. *Ohio Archaeological and Historical Quarterly* 10: 452-79.
Mithen, S.J. 1990. *Thoughtful Foragers: A Study of Prehistoric Decision Making*. Cambridge: Cambridge University Press.
—. 1996. *The Prehistory of the Mind: A Search for the Origins of Art, Religion and Science*. London: Thames & Hudson.
Moberg, C.-A. 1981. From Artefacts to Timetables to Maps (to Mankind?): Regional Traditions in Archaeological Research in Scandinavia. *World Archaeology* 13: 209-21.
Mongait, A.L. 1959. *Archaeology in the U.S.S.R*. Moscow: Foreign Languages Publishing House.
Monks, G.G. 1981. Seasonality Studies. *Advances in Archaeological Method and Theory* 4: 177-240.
Montané, J.C. 1980. *Marxismo y Arqueología*. Mexico: Ediciones de Cultura Popular.
Moore, C.B. 1892. Certain Shell Heaps of the St. John's River, Florida, Hitherto Unexplored. *American Naturalist* 26: 912-22.
Moore, F.W. (ed.). 1961. *Readings in Cross-Cultural Methodology*. New Haven, CT: HRAF Press.
Moore, J.A. & A.S. Keene (eds.). 1983. *Archaeological Hammers and Theories*. New York: Academic Press.
Moorehead, W.K. 1909. A Study of Primitive Culture in Ohio. In F. Boas et al. (eds.). *Putnam Anniversary Volume: Anthropological Essays*. New York: Stechert, 137-50.
—. 1910. *The Stone Age in North America* (2 vols). London: Constable.
Morgan, C.G. 1973. Archaeology and Explanation. *World Archaeology* 4: 259-76.
—. 1974. Explanation and Scientific Archaeology. *World Archaeology* 6: 133-37.
Morgan, L.H. 1877. *Ancient Society*. New York: Holt.
—. 1881. *Houses and House-life of the American Aborigines*. Washington, DC: Contributions to North American Ethnology, 4.
Morlot, A. 1861. General Views on Archaeology. Washington, DC: *Annual Report of the Smithsonian Institution for 1860*, 284-343.
Morris, I. 1987. *Burial and Ancient Society: The Rise of the Greek City-State*. Cambridge: Cambridge University Press.
—. 2000. *Archaeology as Cultural History: Words and Things in Iron Age Greece*. Oxford: Blackwell Publishers.
Mulvaney, D.J. 1981. Gum Leaves on the Golden Bough: Australia's Palaeolithic Survivals Discovered. In J.D. Evans, B. Cunliffe & C. Renfrew (eds.). *Antiquity and Man*. London: Thames & Hudson, 52-64.
Murdock, G.P. 1949. *Social Structure*. New York: Macmillan.
—. 1981. *Atlas of World Cultures*. Pittsburgh: University of Pittsburgh Press.
Murray, T. & J.P. White. 1981. Cambridge in the Bush? Archaeology in Australia and New Guinea. *World Archaeology* 13: 255-63.
Myres, J.L. 1911. *The Dawn of History*. London: Williams & Norgate.
Nagel, E. 1961. *The Structure of Science*. New York: Harcourt, Brace & World.
Noble, W. & I. Davidson. 1996. *Human Evolution, Language, and Mind: A Psychological and Archaeological Inquiry*. Cambridge: Cambridge University Press.
Nicholson, H.B. (ed.). 1976. *Origins of Religious Art and Iconography in Preclassic Mesoamerica*. Los Angeles: UCLA Latin American Center Publications.

Oakley, K.P. 1957. Tools Makyth Man. *Antiquity* 31: 199-209.
O'Brien, M.J. (ed.). 1996. *Evolutionary Archaeology: Theory and Application.* Salt Lake City: University of Utah Press.
O'Brien, M.J. & R.L. Lyman. 2000. *Applying Evolutionary Archaeology: A Systematic Approach.* New York: Plenum.
Olsen, B. 1990. Roland Barthes: From Sign to Text. In C.Y. Tilley (ed.). *Reading Material Culture: Structuralism, Hermeneutics and Post-Structuralism.* Oxford: Blackwell Publishers, 163-205.
Ortiz, A. 1972. *New Perspectives on the Pueblos.* Albuquerque: University of New Mexico Press.
O'Shea, J.M. 1984. *Mortuary Variability: An Archaeological Investigation.* New York: Academic Press.
Panofsky, E. 1939. *Studies in Iconology: Humanistic Themes in the Art of the Renaissance.* Oxford: Oxford University Press.
—. 1960. *Renaissance and Renascences in Western Art.* Stockholm: Almqvist & Wiksell.
Parker, A.C. 1907. *Excavations in an Erie Village and Burial Site at Ripley, Chautauqua County, New York.* Albany: New York State Museum, Bulletin, 117.
Parsons, J.R., E. Brumfiel, M.H. Parsons & D.J. Wilson. 1982. *Prehispanic Settlement Patterns in the Southern Valley of Mexico: The Chalco-Xochimilco Region.* Ann Arbor: University of Michigan, Museum of Anthropology, Memoirs, 14.
Patrik, L.E. 1985. Is There an Archaeological Record? *Advances in Archaeological Method and Theory* 8: 27-62.
Patterson, T.C. 1986a. The Last Sixty Years: Toward a Social History of Americanist Archeology in the United States. *American Anthropologist* 88: 7-26.
—. 1986b. Some Postwar Theoretical Trends in U.S. Archaeology. *Culture* 6(2): 43-54.
—. 1989. History and the Post-Processual Archaeologies. *Man* 24: 555-66.
Peace, W.J. 1993. Leslie White and Evolutionary Theory. *Dialectical Anthropology* 18: 123-51.
Pearson, M.P. 1984. Social Change, Ideology and the Archaeological Record. In M. Spriggs (ed.). *Marxist Perspectives in Archaeology.* Cambridge: Cambridge University Press, 59-71.
Peebles, C. & S. Kus. 1977. Some Archaeological Correlates of Ranked Societies. *American Antiquity* 42: 421-48.
Petrie, W.M.F. 1899. Sequences in Prehistoric Remains. *Journal of the Royal Anthropological Institute* 29: 295-301.
Piggott, S. 1950. *William Stukeley: An Eighteenth-Century Antiquary.* Oxford: Oxford University Press.
—. 1958. Vere Gordon Childe, 1892-1957. *Proceedings of the British Academy* 44: 305-12.
—. 1959. *Approach to Archaeology.* Cambridge, MA: Harvard University Press.
—. 1965. *Ancient Europe from the Beginnings of Agriculture to Classical Antiquity.* Chicago: Aldine.
Plog, F. 1973. Diachronic Anthropology. In C.L. Redman (ed.). *Research and Theory in Current Archeology.* New York: Wiley, 181-98.
—. 1974. *The Study of Prehistoric Change.* New York: Academic Press.
Popper, K.R. 1957. *The Poverty of Historicism.* Boston: Beacon Press.
Posnansky, M. 1982. African Archaeology Comes of Age. *World Archaeology* 13: 345-58.
Preucel, R.W. 1991. The Philosophy of Archaeology. In R.W. Preucel (ed.). *Processual and Postprocessual Archaeologies: Multiple Ways of Knowing the Past.* Carbondale: Center for Archaeological Investigations, Southern Illinois University at Carbondale, 17-29.

Price, B. 1977. Shifts in Production and Organization: A Cluster-Interaction Model. *Current Anthropology* 18: 209-33.
Price, T.D. & J.A. Brown (eds.). 1985. *Prehistoric Hunter-Gatherers: The Emergence of Cultural Complexity*. New York: Academic Press.
Pritchard, J.S. 1987. L'Amérindien victime de l'incompétence des historiens. *Revue d'histoire de l'Amérique française* 41: 63-70.
Ramsden, P.G. 1977. *A Refinement of Some Aspects of Huron Ceramic Analysis*. Ottawa: Archaeological Survey of Canada, Mercury Series, 63.
Rappaport, R.A. 1968. *Pigs for the Ancestors: Ritual in the Ecology of a New Guinea People*. New Haven, CT: Yale University Press.
Ratzel, F. 1882-91. *Anthropogeographie*. Stuttgart: Engelhorn.
—. 1896-98. *The History of Mankind* (3 vols.). London: Macmillan.
Redfield, R., R. Linton & M. J. Herskovits. 1936. Outline for the Study of Acculturation. *American Anthropologist* 38: 149-52.
Redman, C.L. et al. (eds.). 1978. *Social Archeology*. New York: Academic Press.
Renfrew, A.C. 1972. *The Emergence of Civilisation*. London: Methuen.
—. 1973a. *Before Civilization: The Radiocarbon Revolution and Prehistoric Europe*. London: Cape.
—. 1973b. *Social Archaeology*. Southampton: The University.
—. 1978a. Space, Time and Polity. In J. Friedman & M.J. Rowlands (eds.). *The Evolution of Social Systems*. Pittsburgh: University of Pittsburgh Press, 89-92.
—. 1978b. Trajectory Discontinuity and Morphogenesis. *American Antiquity* 43: 203-22.
—. 1982a. Polity and Power: Interaction, Intensification and Exploitation. In A.C. Renfrew & M. Wagstaff (eds.). *An Island Polity: The Archaeology of Exploitation in Melos*. Cambridge: Cambridge University Press, 264-90.
—. 1982b. Socio-Economic Change in Ranked Societies. In A.C. Renfrew & S. Shennan (eds.). *Ranking, Resource and Exchange: Aspects of the Archaeology of Early European Society*. Cambridge: Cambridge University Press, 1-8.
—. 1983. Divided We Stand: Aspects of Archaeology and Information. *American Antiquity* 48: 3-16.
—. 1989. Comments on Archaeology into the 1990s. *Norwegian Archaeological Review* 22: 33-41.
—. 1990. Review of A History of Archaeological Thought, by B. Trigger. *Nature* 345: 777.
Renfrew, A.C. & K.L. Cooke (eds.). 1979. *Transformations: Mathematical Approaches to Culture Change*. New York: Academic Press.
Renfrew, A.C., M.J. Rowlands & B.A. Segraves (eds.). 1982. *Theory and Explanation in Archaeology: The Southampton Conference*. New York: Academic Press.
Renfrew, A.C. & S. Shennan (eds.). 1982. *Ranking, Resource and Exchange: Aspects of the Archaeology of Early European Society*. Cambridge: Cambridge University Press.
Renfrew, A.C. & E.B.W. Zubrow (eds.). 1994. *The Ancient Mind: Elements of Cognitive Archaeology*. Cambridge: Cambridge University Press.
Richardson, B. 1987. The Indian Ordeal: A Century of Decline. *Beaver* (Feb.-Mar.): 16-41.
—. 1990. *Time to Change: Canada's Place in a World in Crisis*. Toronto: Summerhill Press.
Ridley, F. 1952a. The Huron and Lalonde Occupations of Ontario. *American Antiquity* 17: 197-210.
—. 1952b. The Fallis Site, Ontario. *American Antiquity* 18: 7-14.
Riley, P. 1982. *Will and Political Legitimacy: A Critical Exposition of Social Contract Theory in Hobbes, Locke, Rousseau, Kant, & Hegel*. Cambridge, MA: Harvard University Press.

Roberts, C. 1996. *The Logic of Historical Explanation.* University Park, PA: Pennsylvania State University Press.
Robertshaw, P.T. (ed.). 1990. *History of African Archaeology.* London: James Currey.
Rodin, M., K. Michaelson & G.M. Britan. 1978. Systems Theory in Anthropology. *Current Anthropology* 19: 747-62.
Rose, M.A. 1991. *The Post-Modern and the Post-Industrial: A Critical Analysis.* Cambridge: Cambridge University Press.
Rosen, L. 1980. The Excavation of American Indian Burial Sites: A Problem of Law and Professional Responsibility. *American Anthropologist* 82: 5-27.
Rouse, I.B. 1972. *Introduction to Prehistory: A Systematic Approach.* New York: McGraw-Hill.
Rowe, J.H. 1962. Alfred Louis Kroeber, 1876-1960. *American Antiquity* 27: 395-415.
Rowlands, M.J. 1982. Processual Archaeology as Historical Social Science. In A.C. Renfrew, M.J. Rowlands & B.A. Segraves (eds.). *Theory and Explanation in Archaeology: The Southampton Conference.* New York: Academic Press, 155-74.
Rudner, R.S. 1966. *Philosophy of Social Science.* Englewood Cliffs, NJ: Prentice-Hall.
Rudwick, M.J.S. 1985. *The Great Devonian Controversy.* Chicago: University of Chicago Press.
Sabloff, J.A. (ed.). 1981. *Simulations in Archaeology.* Albuquerque: University of New Mexico Press.
—. 1990. *The New Archaeology and the Ancient Maya.* New York: Scientific American Library.
Sahlins, M.D. 1958. *Social Stratification in Polynesia.* Seattle: University of Washington Press.
—. 1968. *Tribesmen.* Englewood Cliffs, NJ: Prentice-Hall.
—. 1976. *Culture and Practical Reason.* Chicago: University of Chicago Press.
Sahlins, M.D. & E. Service. 1960. *Evolution and Culture.* Ann Arbor: University of Michigan Press.
Saitta, D.J. 1983. The Poverty of Philosophy in Archaeology. In J.A. Moore & A.S. Keene (eds.). *Archaeological Hammers and Theories.* New York: Academic Press, 299-304.
Salmon, M.H. 1982. *Philosophy and Archaeology.* New York: Academic Press.
Salmon, W.C. 1967. *The Foundations of Scientific Inference.* Pittsburgh: University of Pittsburgh Press.
—. 1982. Causality in Archaeological Explanation. In A.C. Renfrew, M.J. Rowlands & B.A. Segraves (eds.). *Theory and Explanation in Archaeology: The Southampton Conference.* New York: Academic Press, 45-55.
—. 1984. *Scientific Explanation and the Causal Structure of the World.* Princeton, NJ: Princeton University Press.
—. 1992. Explanation in Archaeology: An Update. In L. Embree (ed.). *Metaarchaeology.* Dordrecht: Kluwer, 243-53.
Sanders, W.T., J.R. Parsons & R.S. Santley. 1979. *The Basin of Mexico: Ecological Processes in the Evolution of a Civilization.* New York: Academic Press.
Sapir, E. 1916. *Time Perspective in Aboriginal American Culture.* Ottawa: Canada, Department of Mines, Memoir, 90.
Sayers, S. 1996. Engels and Materialism. In C.J. Arthur (ed.). *Engels Today: A Centenary Appreciation.* New York: St. Martin's Press, 153-72.
Schaedel, R.P. & I. Shimada. 1982. Peruvian Archaeology, 1946-80: An Analytic Overview. *World Archaeology* 13: 359-71.
Schick, K.D. & N. Toth. 1993. *Making Silent Stones Speak: Human Evolution and the Dawn of Technology.* New York: Simon & Schuster.

Schiffer, M.B. 1975. Archaeology as Behavioral Science. *American Anthropologist* 77: 836-48.
—. 1976. *Behavioral Archeology*. New York: Academic Press.
—. 1995. *Behavioral Archaeology: First Principles*. Salt Lake City: University of Utah Press.
Schrire, C. 1980. An Inquiry into the Evolutionary Status and Apparent Identity of San Hunter-Gatherers. *Human Ecology* 8: 9-32.
—. (ed.). 1984. *Past and Present in Hunter Gatherer Studies*. New York: Academic Press.
Schwartz, D.W. 1967. *Conceptions of Kentucky Prehistory: A Case Study in the History of Archeology*. Lexington: University of Kentucky Press.
Seaman, G. & J.S. Day (eds.). 1994. *Ancient Traditions: Shamanism in Central Asia and the Americas*. Niwot: University Press of Colorado.
Service, E.R. 1962. *Primitive Social Organization*. New York: Random House.
—. 1971. *Primitive Social Organization: An Evolutionary Perspective* (2nd ed.). New York: Random House.
—. 1975. *Origins of the State and Civilization: The Process of Cultural Evolution*. New York: W. W. Norton.
Shanks, M. 1992. *Experiencing the Past: On the Character of Archaeology*. London: Routledge.
—. 1996. *Classical Archaeology of Greece: Experiences of the Discipline*. London: Routledge.
Shanks, M. & C.Y. Tilley. 1987a. *Re-Constructing Archaeology: Theory and Practice*. Cambridge: Cambridge University Press.
—. 1987b. *Social Theory and Archaeology*. Cambridge: Polity Press.
—. 1989a. Archaeology into the 1990s. *Norwegian Archaeological Review* 22: 1-54.
—. 1989b. Questions Rather than Answers: Reply to Comments on Archaeology into the 1990s. *Norwegian Archaeological Review* 22: 42-54.
Shennan, S.J. 1978. Archaeological "Cultures": An Empirical Investigation. In I. Hodder (ed.). *The Spatial Organisation of Culture*. London: Duckworth, 113-39.
Shetrone, H.C. 1920. The Culture Problem in Ohio Archaeology. *American Anthropologist* 22:144-72.
Silberman, N.A. 1982. *Digging for God and Country*. New York: Alfred A. Knopf.
—. 1989. *Between Past and Present: Archaeology, Ideology, and Nationalism in the Modern Middle East*. New York: Henry Holt.
Silverberg, R. 1968. *Mound Builders of Ancient America*. Greenwich, CT: New York Graphic Society.
Sioui, G.E. 1989. *Pour une autohistoire amérindienne*. Quebec: Les Presses de l'Université Laval.
Sklenar, K. 1981. The History of Archaeology in Czechoslovakia. In G. Daniel (ed.). *Towards a History of Archaeology*. London: Thames & Hudson, 150-58.
—. 1983. *Archaeology in Central Europe: The First 500 Years*. Leicester: University Press.
Smith, H.I. 1910. *The Prehistoric Ethnology of a Kentucky Site*. New York: Anthropological Papers of the American Museum of Natural History, 6(2).
Smith, P.E.L. 1976. *Food Production and Its Consequences*. Menlo Park, CA: Cummings.
Snodgrass, A.M. 1987. *An Archaeology of Greece: The Present State and Future Scope of a Discipline*. Berkeley: University of California Press.
Spaulding, A.C. 1968. Explanation in Archeology. In S.R. Binford & L.R. Binford (eds.). *New Perspectives in Archeology*. Chicago: Aldine, 33-39.
—. 1988. Archaeology and Anthropology. *American Anthropologist* 90: 263-71.

Spinden, H.J. 1928. *Ancient Civilizations of Mexico and Central America.* New York: American Museum of Natural History, Handbook Series, 3.
Spriggs, M. (ed.). 1984. *Marxist Perspectives in Archaeology.* Cambridge: Cambridge University Press.
Squier, E.G. & E.H. Davis. 1848. *Ancient Monuments of the Mississippi Valley.* Washington, DC: Smithsonian Contributions to Knowledge, 1.
Stein, G.J. 1988. Biological Science and the Roots of Nazism. *American Scientist* 76: 50-58.
Sterud, E.L. 1973. A Paradigmatic View of Prehistory. In A.C. Renfrew (ed.). *The Explanation of Culture Change: Models in Prehistory.* London: Duckworth, 3-17.
Steward, J.H. 1949. Cultural Causality and Law: A Trial Formulation of the Development of Early Civilizations. *American Anthropologist* 51: 1-27.
—. 1953. Evolution and Process. In A.L. Kroeber (ed.). *Anthropology Today: An Encyclopedic Inventory.* Chicago: University of Chicago Press, 313-26.
—. 1955. *Theory of Culture Change.* Urbana: University of Illinois Press.
Steward, J.H. & F.M. Setzler. 1938. Function and Configuration in Archaeology. *American Antiquity* 4: 4-10.
Struever, S. 1968. Problems, Methods and Organization: A Disparity in the Growth of Archeology. In B.J. Meggers (ed.). *Anthropological Archeology in the Americas.* Washington, DC: Anthropology Society of Washington, 131-51.
Swinton, G. 1976. Archaeology as a Concern of the Inuit Community. In A.G. McKay (ed.). New *Perspectives in Canadian Archaeology.* Ottawa: Royal Society of Canada, 163-71.
Tainter, J.A. 1988. *The Collapse of Complex Societies.* Cambridge: Cambridge University Press.
Tallgren, A.M. 1936. Archaeological Studies in Soviet Russia. *Eurasia Septentrionalis Antiqua* 10: 129-70.
—. 1937. The Method of Prehistoric Archaeology. *Antiquity* 11: 152-61.
Tanner, A. 1979. *Bringing Home Animals: Religious Ideology and Mode of Production of the Mistassini Cree Hunters.* St John's: Memorial University of Newfoundland, Institute of Social and Economic Research, Social and Economic Studies, 23.
Taylor, C. 1975. *Hegel.* Cambridge: Cambridge University Press.
Taylor, W.W. 1948. *A Study of Archeology.* Menasha, WI: Memoir Series of the American Anthropological Association, 69.
Teltser, P.A. (ed.). 1995. *Evolutionary Archaeology: Methodological Issues.* Tucson: University of Arizona Press.
Textor, R.B. 1967. *A Cross-Cultural Summary.* New Haven, CT: HRAF Press.
Thomas, C. 1894. Report on the Mound Explorations of the Bureau of Ethnology. Washington, DC: *Bureau of American Ethnology, Twelfth Annual Report,* 3-742.
—. 1898. *Introduction to the Study of North American Archaeology.* Cincinnati, OH: Robert Clarke.
Thomas, D.H. 1974. An Archaeological Perspective on Shoshonean Bands. *American Anthropologist* 76: 11-23.
Thomas, J. 1996. *Time, Culture and Identity: An Interpretative Archaeology.* London: Routledge.
Thruston, G.P. 1890. *The Antiquities of Tennessee.* Cincinnati: Robert Clarke.
Tilley, C.Y. 1982. Social Formation, Social Structures and Social Change. In I. Hodder (ed.). *Symbolic and Structural Archaeology.* Cambridge: Cambridge University Press, 26-38.
—. 1984. Ideology and the Legitimation of Power in the Middle Neolithic of Southern Sweden. In D. Miller & C. Tilley (eds.). *Ideology, Power and Prehistory.* Cambridge: Cambridge University Press, 111-46.

—. 1990. Michel Foucault: Towards an Archaeology of Archaeology. In C.Y. Tilley (ed.). *Reading Material Culture*. Oxford: Blackwell Publishers, 281-347.
—. 1991. *Material Culture and Text: The Art of Ambiguity*. London: Routledge.
—. (ed.). 1993. *Interpretative Archaeology*. Oxford: Berg.
—. 1994. *A Phenomenology of Landscape: Places, Paths, and Monuments*. Oxford: Berg.
—. 1995. Clowns and Circus Acts. *Critique of Anthropology* 15: 337-41.
—. 1996. Structuralism. In B.M. Fagan (ed.). *The Oxford Companion to Archaeology*. Oxford: Oxford University Press, 699-700.
—. 1999. *Metaphor and Material Culture*. Oxford: Blackwell Publishers.
Toulmin, S.E. & J. Goodfield. 1966. *The Discovery of Time*. New York: Harper & Row.
Trevelyan, G.M. 1952. *Illustrated English Social History*, IV. London: Longmans, Green.
Trigger, B.G. 1962. The Historic Location of the Hurons. *Ontario History* 54: 137-48.
—. 1963. Settlement as an Aspect of Iroquoian Adaptation at the Time of Contact. *American Anthropologist* 65: 86-101.
—. 1965. *History and Settlement in Lower Nubia*. New Haven, CT: Yale University Publications in Anthropology, 69.
—. 1968a. *Beyond History: The Methods of Prehistory*. New York: Holt, Rinehart & Winston.
—. 1968b. Major Concepts of Archaeology in Historical Perspective. *Man* 3: 527-41.
—. 1968c. The Determinants of Settlement Patterns. In K.C. Chang (ed.). *Settlement Archaeology*. Palo Alto, CA: National Press Books, 53-78.
—. 1970a. Aims in Prehistoric Archaeology. *Antiquity* 44: 26-37.
—. 1970b. The Strategy of Iroquoian Prehistory. *Ontario Archaeology* 14: 3-48.
—. 1971. Archaeology and Ecology. *World Archaeology* 2: 321-36.
—. 1973. The Future of Archeology is the Past. In C.L. Redman (ed.). *Research and Theory in Current Archeology*. New York: Wiley, 95-111.
—. 1976. *The Children of Aataentsic* (2 vols.). Montreal: McGill-Queen's University Press.
—. 1978a. *Time and Traditions: Essays in Archaeological Interpretation*. New York: Columbia University Press.
—. 1978b. Ethnohistory and Archaeology. *Ontario Archaeology* 30: 17-24.
—. 1979. Egypt and the Comparative Study of Early Civilizations. In K. Weeks (ed.). *Egyptology and the Social Sciences*. Cairo: American University in Cairo Press, 23-56.
—. 1980. Archaeology and the Image of the American Indian. *American Antiquity* 45: 662-76.
—. 1981a. Anglo-American Archaeology. *World Archaeology* 13: 138-55.
—. 1981b. Prehistoric Social and Political Organization: An Iroquoian Case Study. In D.R. Snow (ed.). *Foundations of Northeast Archaeology*. New York: Academic Press, 1-50.
—. 1981c. Archaeology and the Ethnographic Present. *Anthropologica* 23: 3-17.
—. 1981d. La arqueología como ciencia histórica. *Boletín de Antropología Americana* 4: 55-89.
—. 1982. Archaeological Analysis and Concepts of Causality. *Culture* 2(2): 31-42.
—. 1983. American Archaeology as Native History: A Review Essay. *William & Mary Quarterly* 40: 413-52.
—. 1984a. Alternative Archaeologies: Nationalist, Colonialist, Imperialist. *Man* 19: 355-70.
—. 1984b. Archaeology at the Cross-Roads: What's New? *Annual Review of Anthropology* 13: 275-300.
—. 1985a. *Natives and Newcomers: Canada's "Heroic Age" Reconsidered*. Montreal: McGill-Queen's University Press.
—. 1985b. Writing the History of Archaeology: A Survey of Trends. In G.W. Stocking, Jr.

(ed.). *Objects and Others: Essays on Museums and Material Culture*. Madison: University of Wisconsin Press, 218-35.
—. 1985c. Marxism in Archaeology: Real or Spurious? *Reviews in Anthropology* 12: 114-23.
—. 1986a. *Archaeology and the Future*. Montreal: McGill University, Faculty of Arts, Distinguished Lecture.
—. 1986b. Prospects for a World Archaeology. *World Archaeology* 18: 1-20.
—. 1987. Preface to the 1987 Reprinting. In B.G. Trigger, *The Children of Aataentsic*. Montreal: McGill-Queen's University Press, xix-xxxvii.
—. 1988. A Present of their Past? Anthropologists, Native People and their Heritage. *Culture* 8(1): 71-79.
—. 1989a. *A History of Archaeological Thought*. Cambridge: Cambridge University Press.
—. 1989b. Hyperrelativism, Responsibility, and the Social Sciences. *Canadian Review of Sociology and Anthropology* 26: 776-97.
—. 1993. *Early Civilizations: Ancient Egypt in Context*. Cairo: American University in Cairo Press.
—. 1998a. *Sociocultural Evolution: Calculation and Contingency*. Oxford: Blackwell Publishers.
—. 1998b. Archaeology and Epistemology: Dialoguing across the Darwinian Chasm. *American Journal of Archaeology* 102: 1-34.
—. 2003. *Understanding Early Civilizations*. Cambridge: Cambridge University Press.
Trigger, B.G. & I. Glover (eds.). 1981a; 1982. Regional Traditions of Archaeological Research I, II. *World Archaeology* 13(2), 13(3).
Trigger, B.G. & I. Glover. 1981b. Editorial. *World Archaeology* 13: 133-37.
Ucko, P.J. 1968. *Anthropomorphic Figurines of Predynastic Egypt and Neolithic Crete*. London: Royal Anthropological Institute, Occasional Papers, 24.
—. 1983. Australian Academic Archaeology: Aboriginal Transformation of its Aims and Practices. *Australian Archaeology* 16: 11-26.
—. 1990. Foreward. In P. Gathercole & D. Lowenthal (eds.). *The Politics of the Past*. London: Unwin Hyman, ix-xxi.
Uhle, M. 1907. The Emeryville Shellmound. Berkeley, CA: *University of California Publications in American Archaeology and Ethnology*, 7(1): 1-107.
Vallois, H.-V. 1962. The Origin of *Homo sapiens*. In W. Howells (ed.). *Ideas on Human Evolution: Selected Essays, 1949-1961*. Cambridge, MA: Harvard University Press, 473-99.
Van der Leeuw, S.E. (ed.). 1981a. *Archaeological Approaches to the Study of Complexity*. Amsterdam: Van Giffen Institute.
—.1981b. Information Flows, Flow Structures and the Explanation of Change in Human Institutions. In S.E. Van der Leeuw (ed.). *Archaeological Approaches to the Study of Complexity*. Amsterdam: Van Giffen Institute, 229-329.
Van Trong. 1979. New Knowledge on Dong-s'on Culture from Archaeological Discoveries these Twenty Years Ago. In *Recent Discoveries and New Views on Some Archaeological Problems in Vietnam*. Hanoi: Institute of Archaeology, 1-8.
Vaughan, A.T. 1982. From White Man to Red Skin: Changing Anglo-American Perceptions of the American Indian. *American Historical Review* 87: 917-53.
Vecsey, C. 1980. American Indian Environmental Religions. In C. Vecsey & R.W. Venables (eds.). *American Indian Environments: Ecological Issues in Native American History*. Syracuse, NY: Syracuse University Press, 1-37.
von Gernet, A.D. & P. Timmins. 1987. Pipes and Parakeets: Constructing Meaning in an Early Iroquoian Context. In I. Hodder (ed.). *Archaeology as Long-Term History*. Cambridge: Cambridge University Press, 31-42.

von Mises, R. 1951. *Positivism: A Study in Human Understanding.* Cambridge, MA: Harvard University Press.
Walker, J.W.S. 1971. The Indian in Canadian Historical Writing. *Canadian Historical Association, Historical Papers, 1971*: 21-47.
Walker, S.T. 1883. The Aborigines of Florida. Washington, DC: *Annual Report of the Smithsonian Institution for 1881*, 677-80.
Walker, W.H. 1995. Ceremonial Trash? In J.M. Skibo, W.H. Walker & A.E. Nielson (eds.). *Expanding Archaeology.* Salt Lake City: University of Utah Press, 67-79.
Wallace, A.R. 1864. The Origin of Human Races and the Antiquity of Man Deduced from the "Theory of Natural Selection." *Anthropological Review* and *Journal of the Anthropological Society of London* 2: clviii-clxxxvii.
Wallerstein, I. 1974. *The Modern World-System,* I. New York: Academic Press.
Warren, C. N. 1973. California. In J.E. Fitting (ed.). *The Development of North American Archaeology.* Garden City, NY: Anchor Books, 213-49.
Washburn, S.L. 1953. The Strategy of Physical Anthropology. In A.L. Kroeber (ed.). *Anthropology Today: An Encyclopedic Inventory.* Chicago: University of Chicago Press, 714-27.
—. 1960. Tools and Human Evolution. *Scientific American* 203(3): 62-75.
Washburn, S.L. & F.C. Howell. 1960. Human Evolution and Culture. In S. Tax (ed.). *Evolution after Darwin,* II, *The Evolution of Man.* Chicago: University of Chicago Press, 33-56.
Washburn, S.L. & C.S. Lancaster. 1968. The Evolution of Hunting. In R.B. Lee & I. DeVore (eds.). *Man the Hunter.* Chicago: Aldine, 293-303.
Watson, J.B. 1929. *Psychology, from the Standpoint of a Behaviorist* (3rd ed.). Philadelphia: Lippincott.
Watson, P.J., S.A. LeBlanc & C.L. Redman. 1971. *Explanation in Archeology: An Explicitly Scientific Approach.* New York: Columbia University Press.
Watson, R.A. 1972. The "New Archaeology" of the 1960s. *Antiquity* 46: 210-15.
—. 1990. Ozymandias, King of Kings: Postprocessual Radical Archaeology as Critique. *American Antiquity* 55: 673-89.
—. 1991. What the New Archaeology has Accomplished. *Current Anthropology* 32: 275-91.
Watson, W. 1981. The Progress of Archaeology in China. In J.D. Evans, B. Cunliffe & C. Renfrew (eds.). *Antiquity and Man.* London: Thames & Hudson, 65-70.
Wax, M.L. 1997. On Negating Positivism: An Anthropological Dialectic. *American Anthropologist* 99: 17-23.
Webster, G.C. 1988. The "R" Word: Repatriation. *Muse* 6(3): 43-44.
Wedel, W.R. 1938. *The Direct-Historical Approach in Pawnee Archeology.* Washington, DC: Smithsonian Miscellaneous Collections, 97 (7).
Wegener, A. 1915. *Die Entstehung der Kontinente und Ozeane.* Brunswick: Vieweg.
Weiner, J.S. 1955. *The Piltdown Forgery.* London: Oxford University Press.
Wenke, R.J. 1981. Explaining the Evolution of Cultural Complexity: A Review. *Advances in Archaeological Method and Theory* 4: 79-127.
Whallon, R. 1982. Comments on "Explanation." In A.C. Renfrew & S. Shennan (eds.). *Ranking, Resource and Exchange: Aspects of the Archaeology of Early European Society.* Cambridge: Cambridge University Press, 155-58.
White, L.A. 1945. "Diffusion vs. Evolution": An Anti-Evolutionist Fallacy. *American Anthropologist* 47: 339-56.
—. 1949. *The Science of Culture.* New York: Farrar, Straus.
—. 1959. *The Evolution of Culture: The Development of Civilization to the Fall of Rome.* New York: McGraw-Hill.

White, R. 1982. Rethinking the Middle/Upper Paleolithic Transition. *Current Anthropology* 23: 169-92.
Wilcox, D.R. & W.B. Masse (eds.). 1981. *The Protohistoric Period in the North American Southwest, AD 1450-1700*. Tempe: Arizona State University, Anthropological Research Paper, 24.
Wildesen, L.E. 1982. The Study of Impacts on Archaeological Sites. *Advances in Archaeological Method and Theory* 5: 51-96.
Wilk, R.R. 1985. The Ancient Maya and the Political Present. *Journal of Anthropological Research* 41: 307-26.
Willey, G.R. 1953. *Prehistoric Settlement Patterns in the Virú Valley, Peru*. Washington, DC: Bureau of American Ethnology, Bulletin, 155.
—. (ed.). 1956. *Prehistoric Settlement Patterns in the New World*. New York: Viking Fund Publications in Anthropology, 23.
Willey, G.R. & P. Phillips. 1958. *Method and Theory in American Archaeology*. Chicago: University of Chicago Press.
Willey, G.R. & J.A. Sabloff. 1974. *A History of American Archaeology*. London: Thames & Hudson.
—. 1980. *A History of American Archaeology* (2nd ed.). San Francisco: Freeman.
—. 1993. *A History of American Archaeology* (3rd ed.). New York: Freeman.
Wilson, D. 1876. *Prehistoric Man* (2 vols.) (3rd ed.). London: Macmillan.
Wilson, J.A. 1964. *Signs and Wonders upon Pharaoh*. Chicago: University of Chicago Press.
Wintemberg, W.J. 1935. Archaeological Evidences of Algonkian Influences on Iroquoian Culture. Ottawa: *Transactions of the Royal Society of Canada, 3rd series,* 29(ii): 231-42.
Wiseman, F.M. 1983. Subsistence and Complex Societies: The Case of the Maya. *Advances in Archaeological Method and Theory* 6: 143-89.
Wiseman, J. 1983. Conflicts in Archaeology: Education and Practice. *Journal of Field Archaeology* 10: 1-9.
Wissler, C. 1914. Material Cultures of the North American Indians. *American Anthropologist* 16: 447-505.
Wobst, H.M. 1977. Stylistic Behavior and Information Exchange. In C.E. Cleland (ed.). *For the Director: Research Essays in Honor of James B. Griffin*. Ann Arbor: University of Michigan, Museum of Anthropology, Papers, 61.
—. 1978. The Archaeo-Ethnology of Hunter-Gatherers or the Tyranny of the Ethnographic Record in Archaeology. *American Antiquity* 43: 303-9.
Wolf, E.R. 1982. *Europe and the People without History*. Berkeley: University of California Press.
Woolfson, C. 1982. *The Labour Theory of Culture*. London: Routledge & Kegan Paul.
Woozley, A.D. 1949. *Theory of Knowledge: An Introduction*. London: Hutchinson.
Wright, H.T. 1969. *The Administration of Rural Production in an Early Mesopotamian Town*. Ann Arbor: University of Michigan, Museum of Anthropology, Papers, 38.
Wylie, M.A. 1982. Epistemological Issues Raised by a Structuralist Archaeology. In I. Hodder (ed.). *Symbolic and Structural Archaeology*. Cambridge: Cambridge University Press, 39-46.
—. 1985. Facts of the Record and Facts of the Past: Mandelbaum on the Anatomy of History "Proper." *International Studies in Philosophy* 17: 71-85.
—. 1989. Archaeological Cables and Tacking: The Implications of Practice for Bernstein's "Options beyond Objectivism and Relativism." *Philosophy of the Social Sciences* 19: 1-18.

—. 1992. The Interplay of Evidential Constraints and Political Interests: Recent Archaeological Research on Gender. *American Antiquity* 57: 15-35.

—. 1997. The Engendering of Archaeology: Refiguring Feminist Science Studies. *Osiris* 12: 80-99.

Wyman, J. 1875. Fresh-Water Shell Mounds of the St. John's River, Florida. Salem, MA: *Memoirs of the Peabody Academy of Science* 1(4): 3-94.

Yellen, J.E. 1977. *Archaeological Approaches to the Present: Models for Reconstructing the Past*. New York: Academic Press.

Yoffee, N. & G.L. Cowgill (eds.). 1988. *The Collapse of Ancient States and Civilizations*. Tucson: University of Arizona Press.

Zipf, G.K. 1949. *Human Behavior and the Principle of Least Effort*. Cambridge, MA: Addison-Wesley.

Index

Abbott, C.C., 52, 180
Aborigines (Australia), 76
abstract expressionism, 83
acculturation, 62-63, 102-104, 153-154
Achaemenid Persia, 72
Adams, R.McC., 93, 100
adaptation, ecological, 9, 28
　　see also behavior, symbols
Adena culture, 107
Adorno, T., 124-125
aesthetics, 107, 152
agency, 21, 160
agriculture, origins of, 7, 129, 184
Alexander, J., 104
Algonkians, 50
Anglo-Saxon England, 101
anthropology, *see* social anthropology; sociocultural anthropology; archaeology and anthropology
antiquarianism, 68-70
apes, *see* primates
Arcelin, A., 179
archaeology
　　abuse of, 27, 47, 70, 73, 77, 125-126, 128-129, 171-172, 203-205
　　and anthropology, 45, 60, 87-89, 95, 103, 105-106, 120
　　and history, 63-65, 77-78, 105, 111, 136, 188-189
　　and philosophy, 133-154, 160
　　and social science, 1, 104, 131, 154
　　funding of, 10, 111, 118, 157, 163, 196
　　limitations of, 1, 18, 30, 88-89, 117-118, 133, 148-149
　　national traditions, 17-18, 67-86
　　relations with indigenous peoples, 16-17, 27, 45-66, 195, 197-198, 200-203, 207
　　social and political functions, 10, 22, 61, 111, 131, 157, 196, 200, 203-207
　　see also classical archaeology; colonial archaeology; contextual archaeology; ecological-cultural archaeology; evolutionary (Darwinian) archaeology; historical archaeology; imperialistic archaeology; landscape archaeology; nationalistic archaeology; Palaeolithic archaeology; postprocessual archaeology; processual archaeology
Archaic pattern, 58, 107, 167-168
Ardrey, R., 182
Aswan, 8
Australia, 75-76
Australopithecus, 182
Aztecs, 47

Bacon, R., 147
Bantu, 77, 102, 129
Barnes, A.S., 179-180
Barnes, B., 125-126
behavior
　　and beliefs, 28, 149-150, 164
　　cultural mediation, 24-25, 149-151
　　instinctive, 24-26, 29, 145-146
　　learned, 145-146
　　maladaptive, 146-147
　　material expression, 1, 29-30, 57, 88-89, 110, 156
behaviorism, 10, 156-157
beliefs
　　adaptive, 25, 150-151
　　archaeological inference, 30, 96, 149, 156-157, 159, 164-169
　　effect on behavior, 150, 154, 159
　　seen as epiphenomenal, 106
　　see also culture; symbols; religion
Benedict, R., 95
bias, 108, 114, 127-128, 161-163, 171, 198, 199, 206
Binford, L.R., 2, 8-11, 13, 18, 20, 87-88, 97, 102-103, 111, 119, 156-157, 167-168, 182-183, 189
biological evolution, 25-26, 31-43, 139-140, 144-146, 153-154, 191

237

see also polyphyletism; hominids, early; human origins
Blanton, R.E., 100
Boas, F., 4, 49, 53-54, 118
Boasian anthropology, 12, 21, 54, 95, 112
Bontch-Osmolovski, G.A., 38
Boserup, E., 92, 109
Boule, M., 40, 42
boundaries between cultures, 19, 99-102
Bourdieu, P., 24
Bourgeois, Abbé L., 179
Boyd, R., 150-151
Brace, C.L., 41
Bradley, R., 177, 183
Braidwood, R.J., 6-7
Bunge, M.A., 133, 143, 188
Bure, J., 70
burials, 107-108, 121, 159, 166-168

Caesar, J., 116
Caldwell, J.R., 7-8, 90
California, 48
Campbell, H., 179
Canaanites, 46
Canada, 75-76
Carneiro, R.L. 189
Carr, E.H., 116-117
cataclysmic evolution, 83-84
Caton Thompson, G., 77, 129, 172
Chamberlin, T.C., 190
Chang, K.C., 93
change, *see* cultural change
chiefdoms, 96
Childe, V.G., 6-7, 14-16, 24, 48, 53, 59, 82, 90, 97, 105-106, 146, 163-164, 173
China, 72-73
Chippindale, C., 133
Chomsky, N., 140
civilizations, *see* early civilizations
Clark, J.G.D., 6, 90, 204
Clarke, D.L., 67, 87, 97
class conflict, 4, 81, 94
classical archaeology, 135-137
classificatory-historical period, 53-59
coherence, logical, 170
Collingwood, R.G., 14, 23, 135-138, 141, 164, 188
colonial archaeology, 17, 70, 74-78, 79, 84-86

colonialism, 27, 46-47, 51, 76-77
comparative studies, *see* cross-cultural research
competition, 104, 181
contextual archaeology, 30, 121, 166
continental drift, 178
cooperation, 181
correlations, 108
correspondence, factual, 170
Courbin, P., 158
covering laws, 9, 142
creationism, 47, 70, 130, 204
creativity, *see* imagination
Cree, 30
critical theory, 161-162
cross-cultural research, 11, 103, 108, 120, 165, 189
Crowshoe, J. Sr., 201
cultural change, 45-66, 75-76, 95, 99, 103-104, 110, 112, 172, 199
see also explanation, interaction spheres
cultural chronologies, 48, 54-56, 58-59, 61, 89
cultural ecology, 6, 15, 90-92
cultural evolution, 9, 47-48, 79, 91-92, 94-97, 104, 111, 114, 118-119, 138-139, 155, 157-158, 189, 191-193
see also human origins, multilinear evolution, neoevolutionism, unilinear evolution
Cultural Revolution (China), 72-73
cultural traditions, 12, 19, 150-151, 167, 185, 195
culture areas, 49
culture, as means of adaptation, 146, 150-154, 156
culture-historical anthropology, *see* Boasian anthropology, historical particularism
culture-historical archaeology, 3-4, 10, 53-59, 75, 89
cultures, archaeological, 54-56, 93
systemic view, 91-94, 97-99
Cushing, F.H., 50
cybernetics, 92
Cyprus, 129
Czechs, 71

Dall, W.H. 48
Daniel, G., 137, 173
Dart, R.A. 182

Index   239

Darwin, C., 31, 34, 36, 178
Davis, E.H., 49
de Mortillet, G., 79, 179
Debetz, G.F., 38
deduction, 13, 31, 64, 92
determinism, 96, 105
    cultural, 151, 190
    demographic, 92
    ecological, 15, 92, 94, 118-119, 190
    economic, 92, 119
    technological, 15, 92, 96
diffusion, 17, 58-59, 75, 80, 93, 100-101, 103, 172-173
direct historical approach, 51, 57, 167-168, 200
disciplines, historical, 138, 190-191
Dixon, R.B., 50
Driver, H.E., 103
Dubois, E., 31
Dunnell, R.C., 106
Durkheim, E., 91-92, 97-98

Earle, T.K., 96
early civilizations, 23-26, 29, 165-166
ecological-cultural archaeology, 21-22, 27
ecology, *see* adaptation, cultural ecology, determinism, environmental degradation
economics, 107
Egypt (ancient), 167-168
Egypt (modern), 72
Emerson, J.N., 5
empiricism, 128
Engels, F., 13-15, 31-43
Enlightenment, 138-139, 178
environmental degradation, 83-84, 109, 205-206
eoliths, 179-180
epistemology, 1-3, 113, 133-154, 173-175
equifinality, 108
ethnicity, ethnic groups, 49-50, 53, 56, 58-59, 71-74
ethnoarchaeology, 60, 89, 156, 159
ethnography, *see* sociocultural anthropology
ethnohistory, 20, 63
European archaeology, 62
Evans-Pritchard, E.E., 7
evidence, constraint of, 15, 17-18, 22-23, 42, 67, 115-116, 127-130, 172-173, 198-199, 206
evolution, *see* biological evolution, cataclysmic evolution, cultural evolution, human origins
evolutionary (Darwinian) archaeology, 2
explanation, 25, 106-112, 117, 142, 190
    historical, 54, 63-64, 105, 192-193
    see also cultural change, functionalism, multiple working hypotheses, nomothetic generalizations, interpretation
feminism, 14, 162, 181
Feyerabend, P.K., 125
focus, *see* cultures, archaeological
Fontéchevade (early hominid), 41
Ford, J.A., 59
Fort Ancient culture, 55
Foucault, M., 198
Fox Farm (site), 50-51
Frankfurt School, 161
Fried, M.H., 96, 118, 155
functionalism, 7, 91-92

Garlake, P.S., 77
Gellner, E., 24, 151
generalizations, *see* explanation; nomothetic generalizations
Germany, 4, 54, 73, 84
Gibbon, G., 143
Giddens, A., 24
Glacial Kame culture, 55
Gladwin system, 58
Gladwin, H.S. and W., 55-56
Glover, I., 17
Golson, J., 104
Goodall, J., 182
Gould, R.A., 97, 164
Gramsci, A., 161
Grayson, D.K., 179, 199
Griffin, J.B., 8

Habermas, J., 125
Hall, R.L., 107-108
Hamell, G.R., 107-108
Hamitic hypothesis, 76-77
Hanen, M.P., 190
Harris, M., 22, 92, 118-119
Harrison, W.H., 55
Hawaii, 96
Hawkes, C.F., 96, 137
Hegel, G.F.W., 124, 139

240   Artifacts and Ideas

Heichelheim, F., 7
Hempel, C.G., 9, 135, 142, 157
Herder, J., 4
hermeneutics, 25, 30, 148
historical archaeology, 30, 107, 166
historical particularism, 95, 120, 195
history, 20, 115-117
Hobbes, T., 139
Hodder, I., 2, 20, 29-30, 94, 98-99, 120, 151, 159, 166, 184-186
Holmes, W.H., 49, 52, 180
hominids, early, 13, 31-43, 145, 179-183
homologies, 19
Hopewell culture, 55
Horkheimer, M., 124-125
Hottentot, 102
Howell, F.C., 42
Howells, W.W., 40
Hrdlièka, A., 41, 52, 180
human nature, 25-29
human origins, 129, 139, 179, 204
Human Relations Area Files, 189
Hume, D., 140
Hunt, G.T., 50
hunter-gatherers, 102-103, 181, 186
hyperrelativism, *see* relativism, extreme

idealism, 20-21, 24, 28, 32, 134-137, 141, 143, 147-148, 151, 163-164, 169, 174, 187
    ontological, 150, 173-174
ideas, 106, 136, 150-151, 154, 160
imagination, 177-178, 183-184, 187-189
imperialism, 17, 78
imperialist archaeology, 70, 78-86
India, 85
Indians (indigenous peoples of North America)
    as archaeologists, 65, 197, 200-203, 207
    stereotypes, 16-17, 45-66, 74-75, 114, 128, 161-162, 172-173
    see also archaeology, myth of the 'unchanging savage', pan-Indianism, Mound Builders
Indo-Europeans, 73
induction, 13, 31
Industrial Revolution, 69, 78
integration of cultures, 92, 191-192
    see also functionalism

interaction spheres, 99-102
interpretation, 110, 137, 187
    see also explanation
Inuit, 60
Iran, 72
Ireland, 85
Iroquoians, Iroquoian archaeology, 5, 12, 47, 50, 56
Israel, 72, 84

Japan, 70, 101
Jarmo (site), 6-7
Java, 32

Kanjera (early hominid), 41
Kant, I., 141
Kelley, J.H., 190
Kidder, A.V., 55, 61, 90
Kiik-Koba (site), 38
Kluckhohn, C., 59-61
Kohl, P.L., 101
Kolakowski, L., 125, 147
Kossinna, G., 53, 73, 80, 84, 126, 203
Kroeber, A.L., 33, 48, 55, 190-191
Kuhn, T.S., 10, 122, 126

labor, 33-37
Lamarckian evolution, 35-36, 39
Lamberg-Karlovsky, C.C., 99
landscape archaeology, 23, 186
language, 43, 139-140, 151-152
Laufer, B., 53
Leach, E.R., 7
Leakey, L.S.B., 40, 182
Leakey, M.D., 182
learning, *see* behavior
Lévi-Strauss, C., 185
Locke, J., 139
logic, 170
Lowie, R., 118
Lubbock, J., 79
Lyell, C., 179
Lysenko, T., 39-40

MacNeish, R.S., 7
McCarthyism, 13
McGuire, J.D., 49
McIlwraith, T.F., 5
McKern system, 58
McKern, W.C., 56
McNeill, W.H., 204
Mandelbaum, M.H., 116

Maori, 76
Marcuse, H., 124-125, 147
Marinatos, N., 168-169
Marr, N., 81
Martin, P.S., 59-60, 64, 196
Marx, K., 19, 24, 34-37, 40, 97, 105, 121, 124, 131, 193
Marxism, 5, 13-16, 18-19, 34-35, 40, 43, 73, 81-82, 92, 160
Masada (site), 72
Mason, O.T., 49
Massey, W.C., 103
material culture, 29, 88-89
materialism, 29, 119, 150, 152, 156, 164, 174
Maya, 105
Mayer-Oakes, W.J., 7
Meggers, B.J., 94
Mesoamerica, 47, 99-100
Mesopotamia, 99-100
metaarchaeology (theoretical archaeology), 134
Mexico, 72, 84
middle-range theory, 18-19, 29, 88-89, 108, 111, 158, 165
Midwestern Taxonomic Method, 4-5, 8, 11, 56-57
migration, 50, 58-59
Mills, W.C., 55
Minoans (Crete), 168-169
Mississippian pattern, 56, 58
Moa-hunters, 76
Mohammed, A., 104
Mont Auxois (site), 71
Mont Réa (site), 71
Montelius, O., 49, 80
Moore, C.B., 48
Moorehead, W.K., 51, 55, 57
Morgan, L.H., 37, 47, 114
Mound Builders, 51-53, 55, 75, 161, 171-172
multilinear evolution, 91, 97
multiple working hypotheses, 123, 190
myth of the 'unchanging savage', 17, 45-53, 61, 74-75, 110-111, 114, 128, 162, 172, 199, 203
mythistory, 204

Napoleon III, 71
National Science Foundation, 10, 118
National Socialism (Nazis), 73, 84-85, 126

nationalism, 4, 27, 69, 71, 83
nationalistic archaeology, 17, 70-74, 78, 84-86
natural selection, *see* biological evolution
nature-culture dichotomy, 97-98, 185-186
Neanderthals, 31-32, 38, 40-41
Nelson, N.C., 55
neocolonialism, 111
neoevolutionism, 9, 11-12, 15-16, 83, 91, 95-97, 118-120, 155, 157-158
  see also cultural evolution, unilinear evolution, multilinear evolution
neo-Marxism, 124, 161
New Archaeology, *see* processual archaeology
New Guinea, 96
New Zealand, 75-76
Nietzsche, F., 124
nomothetic generalizations, 24-25, 61, 82, 90, 106-110, 112, 120, 170
Nubia, 8
Nunamiut, 156

Oakley, K.P., 33, 41-42
objectivity, 109, 113-117, 131, 137
  see also value-free science
Oceania, 11
ontology, 29, 150, 153, 174
  see also materialism, idealism
Ortiz, A., 64

Palaeolithic archaeology, 13, 31-43, 52, 179-180, 182-183
Palestine, 129
Pangaea, 178
pan-Indianism, 197, 201-202
paradigm, 10, 122
Parker, A.C., 197
Parsons, J.R., 94
Pecos classification, 55
perception, 28-29, 140-142, 144-145, 152, 174
  see also positivism, idealism
Petrie, W.M.F., 55
phase, *see* cultures, archaeological
Phillips, P., 61, 90
philosophy, 133-154
Phoenicians, 77
Piggott, S., 137, 173
Piltdown hoax, 33
Plato, 124
Plog, F., 64, 196

political correctness, 183-184
polygenesis, 52
polyphyletism, 33, 38, 41
Pontiac, 114
Popper, K.R., 188
positivism, 9-10, 24, 28, 118-119, 125, 134, 140-143, 147-148, 157, 170
Posnansky, M., 77
possibilism, 12, 19
postprocessual archaeology, 2, 20-23, 159-163
Powell, J.W., 52, 114
pragmatism, 143
prediction, 92, 105
Prescott, W.H., 47
primates, 144-145, 180-182
process, study of, *see* functionalism, processual archaeology
processual archaeology, 2, 8-12, 19-20, 24, 30, 59-64, 82-83, 90, 92-97, 104, 106, 111-112, 118-122, 142, 155-159, 189-191, 196
progress, 78-79
progress, scientific, 177-178
psychology, 28
Pueblo Indians, 50, 65
Putnam, F.W., 52, 55, 180

racism, 46, 122
radiocarbon dating, 62, 69
Randall-MacIver, D., 77
Rappaport, R.A., 19
Ratzel, F., 4, 54
realism, 24, 19, 128, 134, 141-143, 147, 173-175
reductionism, 140-141
relativism, 18, 21-23, 113-117, 122-131, 160-161, 163
  extreme, 115, 123-126, 169-171, 198
  moderate, 109, 127-128, 171-173, 198-199
religion, 25, 101, 106-107, 130, 149, 154, 159, 164-168
  see also beliefs, symbols
Renaissance (Italian), 68
Renfrew, A.C., 97
Rhodes, C., 77, 128
Richerson, P.J., 150-151
Ritchie, W.A., 57
Roberts, C., 193
Roginskii, Ia., 38

Roman Britain, 135
Roman Empire, 105
romanticism, 4
Rousseau, J.-J., 139
Russia, 80

Sabaeans, 77
Sabloff, J.A., 16, 53
Sahlins, M.D., 24, 91, 118, 155
San, 102
Sanders, W.T., 11, 94, 100
Santayana, G., 3
Santley, R.S., 94
Saudi Arabia, 166
Sayers, S., 139
Scandinavia, 69-71
scavenging, 182-183
science
  political control, 125-126, 131
  social influences, 109, 113-117, 122-124, 128, 131, 160-163
  status of, 21, 126-127
  see also objectivity, physical sciences
sciences, physical, 126-127
Service, E.R., 91, 118, 155
settlement patterns (archaeological study of), 6, 8, 11, 90
Setzler, F.M., 6, 59-60
shamanism, 168
Shanks, M., 22-23, 170, 187
Shetrone, H.C., 55-56
Silverberg, R., 16, 161
Smith, H.I., 50
social anthropology, 7
social contract, 139
social systems, 5, 81, 97-99
sociocultural anthropology, 62-63, 157-158
Song Dynasty (China), 68
Soviet Union, 5, 14-15, 38-40, 43, 80-82
Spaulding, A.C., 63-64
Speck, F., 118
Spencer, W.B., 76
Spier, L., 55
Squier, E.G., 49
Stalinism, 39-40
Star Carr (site), 6
statistical-relevance (as basis for explanation), 142-143
Steinheim (early hominid), 41
Stephens, J.L., 47

stereotypes, 16, 45, 59
Steward, J.H., 6, 9, 15, 59-60, 90-94, 97, 118, 155-156, 192, 195
Stiles, E., 46
stratigraphy, 48, 55
Strong, W.D., 59-60
structuralism, 98, 184-185
Struever, S., 94
subjectivism, 14, 122-125, 163, 187, 196
Sub-Saharan Africa, 76-78
subsistence patterns, 6
Sudan, 104
Sumerians, 130
Swanscombe (early hominid), 41
symbols, 20, 98-99, 106, 146, 151, 163-169, 185-186
see also beliefs, ideas
systems theory, 92, 97

Tallgren, A.M., 6, 82, 90
Taylor, W.W., 6, 57, 60, 61, 90
Tecumseh, 114
Tehuacan Valley, 7
Teilhard de Chardin, P., 40
Teotihuacan, 100
testing, verification 25, 108, 111, 119, 122-123, 127, 142, 158, 165, 187-188
see also coherence, correspondence
textual sources (use by archaeologists), 19-20, 121, 136-137, 166-167, 188-189
Thenay (site), 179
Thomas, C., 49-52, 172
Thruston, G.P., 55
Tilley, C.Y., 22-23, 170, 187
Tokugawa period (Japan), 68
tool-making, 33-36, 38, 40-42
Tret'yakov, P.N., 5
tribal societies, 95-96, 102

Ucko, P.J., 170
Uhle, M., 48

uniformitarianism, geological, 178
unilinear evolution, 9, 91, 94-97, 143, 155-156
United Kingdom, 78-80, 83
United States (archaeological tradition), 45-66, 74-75, 82-84
universals, 26, 144, 170

Valley of Mexico, 100
Vallois, H.-V., 40
value-free science, 114-116, 170
verstehen, *see* hermeneutics
Vietnam, 73
Vikings, 71
Viru Valley, 6, 90, 100
von Däniken, E., 70, 130
von Ranke, L., 116-117, 137-138

Walker, S.T., 48
Wallace, A.R., 32, 34, 36
Wallerstein, I., 100-101
Washburn, S.L., 42
Webb, W.S., 57
Wegener, A., 178
Weidenreich, F., 41
Weinert, H., 41
White, L.A., 8-9, 15, 90-92, 94, 96, 118, 150, 155-156
Willey, G.R., 6-7, 16, 20, 53, 59-61, 90, 93
Wilson, D., 74
Wissler, C., 49
Wolf, E.R., 153
Woodland pattern, 56, 58, 107
world-systems analysis, 68-69, 85-86, 100-101
Worm, O., 70
Wylie, M.A., 22, 171, 199
Wyman, J., 48

Zimbabwe, 77, 128-129, 171-172
Zipf, G.K., 26
Zuni Indians, 65